# ACCOUNTING FOR INCOME TAXES

## A Survey of Practice

James E. Wheeler
Professor of Accounting
University of Michigan

Edmund Outslay
Associate Professor of Accounting
Michigan State University

A Publication of Financial Executives Research Foundation

Accounting for Income Taxes:
A Survey of Practice



Financial Executives Research Foundation
10 Madison Avenue, P. O. Box 1938
Morristown, New Jersey 07960

International Standard Book Number 0-910586-59-4
Library of Congress Catalog Card Number 85-81107
Printed in the United States of America

First Printing

Cover design by Malcolm Grear Designers

Financial Executives Research Foundation is the research arm of Financial Executives Institute. The Foundation's basic purpose is to conduct fundamental research and publish authoritative material in the field of business management, with particular emphasis on the principles and practices of financial management and its evolving role in the management of business.

Publication of a research study should not be interpreted as constituting endorsement by the Board as a whole, or by individual Trustees.

# Project Advisory Committee

Bernard R. Doyle
Manager, Corporate Accounting Services
General Electric Company

Roland L. Laing
Director of Research
Financial Executives Research Foundation

Gaylen N. Larson
Group Vice President & Controller
Household International Inc.

Frederick H. Ober
Senior Research Associate
Financial Executives Research Foundation

Robert A. Orben (FERF President)
Vice President-Controller
Cummins Engine Company, Inc.

Joseph P. Paquette, Jr.
Vice President
Philadelphia Electric Company

John F. Ruffle (Committee Chairman)
Executive Vice President
Morgan Guaranty Trust Company

Robert B. Scharlotte
Assistant Controller
Goodyear Tire & Rubber Company

---

Denise M. Pontillo
Publications Associate
Financial Executives Research Foundation

# Table of Contents

# Executive Summary

This is the third work sponsored by Financial Executives Research Foundation (FERF) concerning interperiod income tax allocation.[1] While this study is a reexamination and extension of the study done by Wheeler and Galliart ten years previously, it is much more ambitious in scope and in data collection than was the predecessor study.[2] Its primary objectives, however, remain the same--to analyze the experiences and opinions of a wide range of preparers and users of financial statements on the subject of interperiod income tax allocation.

The impetus for this study was the decision by the Financial Accounting Standards Board in January 1982 to place a reevaluation of accounting for income taxes on its official agenda. Primary reasons for this decision were increasing criticisms about the complexities of the current rules (especially as they might affect smaller companies) and a growing concern about the meaningfulness of the results reported in light of an accelerating growth in deferred tax

---

[1]The first two were John W. Buckley, Income Tax Allocation: An Inquiry into Problems of Methodology and Estimation (New York: Financial Executives Research Foundation, 1972) and James E. Wheeler and Willard H. Galliart, An Appraisal of Interperiod Income Tax Allocation (New York: Financial Executives Research Foundation, 1974).

[2]The earlier study, An Appraisal of Interperiod Income Tax Allocation, utilized financial data from only 14 corporations, but also obtained opinions from users.

accounts on balance sheets. The enactment of accelerated cost recovery (ACRS) and liberalized investment credit provisions in recent tax legislation (in particular, the Economic Recovery Tax Act of 1981) has the potential to heighten the concern over growing deferred tax accounts even further. In addition, the FASB has reopened the question as to whether a deferred tax account meets the definition of a liability in the course of developing a conceptual framework of accounting.

Because of this renewed interest in interperiod tax allocation, the FERF Board of Trustees authorized a research study to examine the experiences and attitudes of both preparers of financial statements and users of financial statement information concerning accounting for income taxes. This study, along with the extensive literature review conducted for the FASB by Ernst and Whinney,[3] provides a comprehensive foundation for meaningful discussion of accounting for income taxes alternatives.

## Objectives of the Study

The objectives of this study were as follows:

1. To gather and analyze historical data on timing differences from statement preparers and to obtain their expectations for future changes in these amounts using the existing comprehensive allocation concept and the deferred method approach;

2. To obtain the opinions of both financial statement preparers and users on accounting for income taxes; and

3. To examine the concerns of specific industries such as oil and gas and the rate-regulated public utilities.

---

[3]Dennis R. Beresford, Lawrence C. Best, Paul W. Craig, and Joseph V. Weber, Accounting for Income Taxes: A Review of Alternatives (Stamford: Financial Accounting Standards Board of the Financial Accounting Foundation, 1983).

## Scope of the Study

To obtain the information needed to satisfy the analytical objectives of the study, data were gathered from the following sources.

1. An extensive questionnaire was mailed to 2,204 corporations in which their experiences with the current accounting for income taxes rules and their opinions about the current and proposed rules were solicited. Two hundred fifty-eight usable responses were received (12 percent), of which fifty-nine were from rate-regulated companies.

2. An extensive questionnaire was mailed to all fifteen members of the Financial Accounting Policies Committee of the Financial Analysts Federation and to a random sample of 500 members of the Financial Analysts Federation. Opinions were solicited from this group about the current and proposed accounting for income taxes rules, experiences with using the financial information generated from such rules, and an appraisal of financial statement disclosures. Usable responses were received from eight of the policy committee members (53 percent) and nine of the random sample (2 percent).

## Summary of Findings: Preparer (Corporate) Questionnaire

Analysis of the Financial Data Provided for the Years 1977 and 1982

1. The average balance in the net deferred tax credit accounts of the responding corporations increased from $109.5 million in 1977 to $263 million in 1982, an increase of 140 percent.

2. The increase for nonregulated companies was from $65.1 million to $174.3 million (168 percent) and for regulated companies was from $244.2 million to $535.1 million (119 percent). The average balance in the

deferred investment credit accounts of the responding corporations increased from $83 million in 1977 to $193.3 million in 1982, an increase of 133 percent. The increase for nonregulated companies was from $27.4 million to $54.7 million (100 percent) and for regulated companies was from $114 million to $260 million (128 percent).

3. The most frequently mentioned items included in a respondent's list of the five largest sources of deferred charges were deferred compensation and inventory valuations.

4. The most frequently mentioned items included in a respondent's list of the five largest sources of deferred credits were depreciation and intangible drilling costs. Depreciation was mentioned more than five times as often in this category as was the second most frequently mentioned item.

5. The deferred credit balances that increased in size by the greatest percentage for regulated companies between 1977 and 1982 were plant shutdowns (638 percent). This timing difference produces a deferred charge for nonregulated companies. Other large deferred credit balances among the responding corporations were long-term contracts (515 percent), state tax deferrals (411 percent), and purchased gas adjustment (334 percent). The deferred credit depreciation timing difference increased 118 percent, while the investment tax credit increased 133 percent.

6. Deferred tax credits as a percentage of total assets increased steadily from 4.7 percent in 1977 to 6.2 percent in 1982. Similarly, deferred tax credits as a percentage of owners' equity rose from 12 percent to 16.8 percent during this same period.

## Analysis of Current Interperiod Income Tax Allocation Practices

- Of the respondents, 86.3 percent reported using the comprehensive method exclusively to allocate interperiod income taxes.

- The net change method was the preferred allocation method among respondents (57.1 percent). More than 90 percent of the respondents are using the deferred method of accounting for the tax effects of changes in timing differences.

- The predominant balance sheet classification of deferred tax credit accounts by nonregulated companies was as a liability (68 percent), whereas for regulated companies it was as a separate classification (53.4 percent).

## Preparer Opinions on the Current and Proposed Interperiod Income Tax Allocation Rules

1. Seventy-two percent of the nonregulated companies and 98 percent of the regulated companies were at least "generally satisfied" with the current rules for accounting for income taxes. Twenty-six percent of the nonregulated companies and 66 percent of the regulated companies felt that no changes were necessary at the current time. More than 90 percent of each group was at least "generally satisfied" with the investment credit rules, but both groups were less satisfied with the absence of formal rules in the foreign tax credit area.

2. The area cited most often as needing changes, according to both nonregulated and regulated respondents, was the issue of responding to tax rate changes (36 percent). Accounting for the tax benefits of NOLs was second (22 percent) and the deferred method was third (20 percent). The least cited area was discounting (12 percent). Thirteen percent of the nonregulated respondents and 42 percent of the regulated respondents felt that none of the FASB's issues needed reconsideration.

3. In each group, a significant majority of preparers (83 percent of the nonregulated and 98 percent of the regulated) favors the retention of interperiod tax allocation. Three-fourths of the nonregulated group and 100 percent of the regulated group prefer comprehensive allocation over partial allocation,

although almost 40 percent of the nonregulated group believe that partial allocation should be allowable as an alternative.

4. The majority of respondents in each group continued to support the deferred method, but there was considerable support for allowing the liability and net-of-tax methods as alternatives. This acknowledgement of the credibility of the liability method is further evidenced by the fact that more than one-half of the nonregulated companies agreed that prior deferred tax charges and credits should be adjusted to the current period tax rate whenever the rates change.

5. There was little support for the discounting of long-term deferred tax amounts.

6. Less than one-half of each group (44 percent and 34 percent, respectively) was in favor of relaxing the NOL recognition rules. It was most frequently suggested that "probable" or "reasonably assured" be substituted for the current "beyond any reasonable doubt" standard.

7. A sizeable majority of each group (77 percent and 84 percent) felt that there existed a need for more formal guidance on accounting for tax credits other than the investment credit. Guidelines were preferred over definitive rules. Two-thirds of the nonregulated companies, but only one-half of the regulated companies favored continuing alternative accounting methods for the investment credit.

8. In a series of questions directed to regulated companies only, 89 percent of the respondents reported that they anticipate no net turnaround in their deferred credit account within the next five years.[4] This survey was conducted before the Tax Reform Act of 1984 was passed and before any of the Administration's tax reform proposals were published. Eighty-one percent of these companies projected that the adoption

---

[4] This survey was conducted before the Tax Reform Act of 1984 was passed and before any of the Administration's tax reform proposals were published.

of partial allocation would lower rates in the short run, but that rates would increase in the longer run. Similarly, eighty-eight percent of these companies felt that an exception should be made for regulated companies should the flow-through method of accounting for the investment credit be mandated. Please note that this survey was conducted before the recent Treasury proposals to revise the tax code.

## User (Financial Analysts) Questionnaire

The response rate from users of financial statement data was too small to fairly evaluate the opinions of users as a group. Those who did respond provided insightful perspectives on their individual experiences with interpreting information provided by interperiod income tax allocation. These comments are discussed in more detail in Chapter 3. It was apparent from reading the user responses that the information relating to interperiod income tax allocation is interpreted and used in dichotomous ways by the analysts. While the few users who responded were reasonably satisfied with the current allocation rules, there was strong sentiment for the liability method and improved disclosure practices. There was also strong opposition to changes that would impair the comparability of financial statements.

# 1 Accounting for Income Taxes and the Impact on Public Utilities

## Measurement of the Income Tax Provision

In order to understand the complexity of accounting for income taxes, it is important to have a thorough knowledge of the official accounting pronouncements. This section presents some of the effects of these pronouncements, in the form of a formula for computing the federal income tax provision and liability. In addition, four examples utilizing the investment tax credit (ITC) are employed to demonstrate the complexity of accounting for carryforward tax attributes.

Pretax book income and taxable income are the starting points in computing the federal income tax provision and liability, respectively. These two starting points are reflected in the following diagram showing timing and permanent differences.

TABLE 1.1 *Types of Transactions Included in Income for Financial Reporting and Tax Reporting*

---

Transactions Included in Both Pretax Book Income and Taxable Income

Items of revenue (gross income) or expense (deductions) impacting both pretax book income and taxable income in the same periods.

| Transactions Included in Pretax Book Income | Transactions Included in Taxable Income |
|---|---|
| • Permanent Differences (Type A)<br>Items of revenue or expense impacting pretax book income but never impacting taxable income | • Permanent Differences (Type B)<br>Items of gross income, deductions or exclusions impacting taxable income but never pretax book income |
| • Timing Differences (Type A)<br>Items of revenue or expense impacting pretax book income in a period(s) before they impact taxable income-- as reversals of these timing differences | • Timing Differences (Type B)<br>Items of gross income or deductions impacting taxable income in a period(s) before impacting pretax book income--as reversals of these timing differences |

Other Items Included in Neither Income Measure But Affect Final Tax Expense or Taxes Due

Items that impact net income (after Tax) and the tax liability (often in different periods) without impacting either pretax book income or taxable income (e.g., the tax provision itself and all of the various income tax credits).

It should also be noted that some items, such as the "unremitted earnings of a subsidiary," can be either timing or permanent differences. This is determined by whether management has the subsidiary distribute prior unremitted earnings or leaves these funds permanently invested in the subsidiary, retaining the same level of ownership interest of the subsidiary.

---

# Explanation of Terms in Table 1.1

## Differences Between Pretax Financial Reporting Income and Taxable Income

Permanent differences These items impact either pretax income for financial reporting or taxable income for tax reporting but are not reflected on any other set of books.

Timing differences These items (taken individually or as a group) impact in different periods both pretax income for financial reporting and taxable income for tax reporting. These timing differences usually result from different accounting methods being used for financial reporting and income tax purposes. The excess shown in one reporting medium in an early period(s) is offset by an equal excess in the other medium in a later period(s). Timing differences can also result from the use of different depreciable lives and different accounting bases, e.g., accrual basis for financial reporting and the cash basis for tax purposes.

## Other Items Similar to Permanent Differences or Timing Differences

Some items have the same effect on recorded income tax provision or income tax liability as permanent differences or timing differences.

- All tax credits, including the foreign tax credit and the investment tax credit, have the same effect. Because these tax credits impact the tax liability (but not pretax financial income or taxable income) sometimes in different periods for financial report and tax purposes, they can have effects similar to timing differences.

- Carryforward deduction for capital loss and contributions are generally timing differences which are usually recognized for financial reporting prior to their recognition (if ever) for tax. For financial reporting the tax effect of these items is either: (1) recorded as a reduction (draw-down) of a timing difference, (2) recorded as an asset (in very limited situations), or (3) reported only as a footnote to the financial statements. If these carryforwards expire unused, they become permanent differences.

- <u>Carryforward deductions for net operating losses</u> (foreign or domestic) are permanent differences in that these losses are not deductible for financial reporting. In fact NOLs can be viewed as second deductions for tax purposes. NOLs result or arise from expenses, losses, and special statutory deduc- tion items (e.g., dividends received or paid deductions) for tax purposes in a loss year. The excess of these deductions over tax revenues (negative taxable incomes or NOLs) is then deducted, if ever, a "second" time for tax purposes in a carryback or carry- forward year. There is no second deduction of a net loss for book purposes; thus an NOL deduction is a permanent difference.

- <u>Excess expenses or deductions because of "different initially-recorded bases" of assets</u> can also be viewed as a permanent difference. Quasi-permanent differences arise whenever the initial book basis of an asset differs from its initial tax basis. This "basis" difference is reflected in pretax book income or taxable income when or as the asset is depreciated, written off, or sold. It should be noted that realization of a permanent basis difference affects the medium (pretax financial reporting income or taxable income) that had the higher basis.

As an example, basis differences arise frequently in asset acquisitions. When the cost in excess of the underlying book value of a newly-acquired subsidiary is allocated to that subsidiary's assets in consolidation, without a corresponding adjustment for tax purposes (under Internal Revenue Code Section 338), there is a basis difference. As this basis difference is depreciated, it produces a permanent difference. Permanent differences are also prevalent in public utility accounting. The increase in both book income and the basis of a plant under construction, for the imputed interest on shareholder equity in the plant, is a permanent difference that reverses as the increased basis is depreciated. The reversal of this permanent difference is achieved by affecting the same medium (pretax book income) rather than the opposite medium (taxable income) as is the case for timing differences. If there is a difference between the book and the tax bases of a depreciable asset and when different depreciation methods or useful lives are used, there will be a commingling of timing and permanent differences.

## Interactions Between Available, Applied, and Recognized

Explained below is the process of relating a tax deduction or credit that is available with the amounts that may be recognized for financial reporting or applied for reporting taxes.

1. The available tax deduction or tax credit will always exceed or equal the applied and also may exceed or equal the recognized tax deduction or tax credit.

2. The recognized deduction or tax credit can be more or less than the applied deduction or tax credit.

3. Only the excess of the available over the applied is eligible for tax purposes to be carried back or forward according to the provisions in the tax law.

4. When the applied and the recognized amounts differ, the carryback and carryforward amounts will also differ for both book and tax reporting purposes.

5. The federal income tax provision is recorded using the recognized deductions and recognized tax credits.

6. To the extent of carryforwards for the excess of the available over the recognized tax deductions or tax credits, further recognition (affecting the federal income tax provision) may be achieved as follows:

(a) By drawing down deferred tax credits for net timing differences that would turn around in the carryforward period, or

(b) By recording the carryforward (excess of available over the recognized amounts) as an asset (losses only), but only where there is no reasonable doubt concerning future use of the carryforwards.

7. Where there are no timing differences to draw-down within the carryforward period and where future use of a carryforward is in doubt, the carryforward amount is disclosed only in a footnote (i.e., it is not currently recognized in the federal income tax provision).

## Income Tax Allocation Model

The following tax allocation model and especially the subsequent four examples are meant for those who have a particular interest in the complexity of the measurement and recording aspect. Other readers may wish to go directly to the discussion in this chapter of the public utility aspect.

TABLE 1.2 *Model of the Income Tax Allocation Process*

| | Financial Reporting | | Tax Reporting | |
|---|---|---|---|---|
| Notes | Symbol | Description | Symbol | Description |
| | Start | Pretax income | | |
| | -/+ | Permanent Differences: Type A and B (Table 1, p.000) | | |
| (1) | = | Book equivalent of taxable income | Start | Taxable income |
| | x | Corporate tax rates | x | Corporate tax rates |
| | = | Income tax provision before credits and other items | = | Gross tax liability |
| (2) | - | Recognized tax credits (Table 3) | - | Applied tax credits (Table 3) |
| | +/- | Draw-downs and reinstatements of timing differences to recognize carryforward deductions or tax credits (Table 4) | | |
| (3) | = | Income tax provision before other tax additions | = | Income tax liability before other tax additions |
| | + | Minimum tax on preference income | + | Minimum tax on preference income |
| | + | ITC recapture | + | ITC recapture |
| | +/- | Adjustment to "cushion for possible tax deficiencies" | | |
| (3) | = | Recorded income tax provision | = | Income tax liability before prepayments |

Notes for Table 1.2

(1) Amount of taxable income and its book equivalent will differ. The various reconciling differences are called "timing differences". In Table 1, two types of timing differences are defined.

(2) Amount of a particular tax credit recognized for financial reporting may be more or less than the amount applied in reporting taxes. Neither the recognized nor the applied amount may exceed the amount of the credit available.

(3) Amounts for financial reporting and tax reporting will differ.

TABLE 1.3 *Tax Credits: Recognized for Financial Reporting and Applied in Reporting Taxes**

| Description | IR Code Section |
|---|---|
| Foreign Tax Credit | §27 |
| Clinical testing expenses of certain drugs | §28 |
| Credit for fuel from unconventional sources | §29 |
| Credit for increasing research activities | §30 |
| General business credit (includes investment credit and targeted jobs credit) | §38 |
| Credit for alcohol used as fuel | §40 |
| Employee stock option credit | §41 |
| Fuel credit for certain uses | §39 |

* Tax credits are listed in order of application for tax reporting

TABLE 1.4 *Draw-Downs and Reinstatement of Timing Differences*

| Description | Limitation |
|---|---|
| Type I Draw-downs: Amount recognized for book exceeds amount applied for taxes: | |
| (1) Draw-downs of timing differences for the tax effect of a carry-forward deduction or tax credit, | Tax effect of timing differences which reverse in carryforward period. |
| - or - | |
| (2) the tax effect of recording the carryforward deduction as an asset. | Tax benefit assured to be utilized in future years. |
| Type II Draw-downs: Amount available exceeds amount recognized for book which exceeds amount applied for taxes: | |
| (1) Draw-downs of timing differences for the tax effect of a carry-forward deductions or tax credit, | Tax effect of timing differences which reverse in carryforward period. |
| - or - | |
| (2) the tax effect of recording the carryforward deduction or tax credit as an asset. | Tax benefit assured to be utilized in future years. |
| Reinstatements of prior draw-downs: Amount applied on current tax return relates to draw-downs (Type I and Type II above). | Tax benefit of a carryforward applied on the tax return less the tax effect of timing differences which have reversed. |

## Further Explanation of Terms Used in Table 1.2 to 1.4

Available = The total amount of a tax deduction or tax credit that would have been utilized (in a given year) had there been no limiting tax rules or circumstances (e.g., not enough income or tax).

Applied = The total amount of a deduction or tax credit that has been applied (in a given year) in the tax return computation recognizing all limiting rules and circumstances.

Recognized = The total amount of a deduction or tax credit that has been recognized in the measurement of financial (book) income (in a given year). Limitations here (under the with and without method) are often the result of the application of tax rules to different financial reporting base amounts (i.e., book income or the book tax provision before a certain credit).

## Four Examples of Carryforward Tax Attributes

Examples of Recording the Effects of the Investment Tax Credit (ITC) *

| Separate Cases | I | II | III | IV |
|---|---|---|---|---|
| Available ITC | 40 | 40 | 40 | 40 |
| Recognized ITC (book) | 30 | 30 | 25 | 25 |
| Applied ITC (tax) | 25 | 25 | 30 | 30 |
| Reversible timing differences (net) | 25 | 13 | 15 | 8 |

*The available ITC is assumed to be the amount earned each year through the purchase of qualified assets.

For the recognized ITC, (30, 30, 25 and 25) it is assumed that these amounts were measured based on the current year federal income tax provision before the ITC. For the applied ITC (25, 25, 30 and 30) it is assumed that these amounts were measured based on the federal income tax liability before the ITC. It is also assumed that excess amounts available can only be carried forward (i.e., the ITC in prior years equalled the maximum that could be applied in those years and it is also assumed that there are no ITC carryforwards from those prior years). Reversible timing differences are those net timing differences (deferred credits) which will reverse in the 15-year carryforward period of the ITC.

The four examples were created using the flow-through method to demonstrate the recording of Type I and Type II draw-downs of deferred tax credits from timing differences. To simplify the resulting journal entries only the impact of the investment tax credit (ITC) on the federal income tax provision (FIT provision) is examined assuming no NOLs or other potential carryforward items.

## Journal Entires for Financial Reporting of Only the Tax Effects of the ITC

### Case I

| | | |
|---|---|---|
| FIT Payable (ITC applied) | 25 | |
| Deferred tax credit (draw-down of timing differences)* | 5 | |
| FIT provision (ITC recognized) | | 30 |

This draw-down (Type I) is for the excess of recognized (under the with and without method) over the applied ITC (30-25). It is assumed that the flow through method is being used for book purposes.

| | | |
|---|---|---|
| Deferred tax credit (draw-down)* | 10 | |
| FIT provision | | 10 |

The draw-down (Type II) is for the excess of the available over the recognized ITC (40-30). This records the book ITC carryforward of 10 and leaves the tax ITC carryforward of 15 (40-25) to be disclosed in a footnote. Thus for Case I, reversible timing differences (deferred credits from timing differences) are now shown as 10 in the balance sheet (25-5-10).

* The tax benefit(s) will be realized in future years. Where recorded as a draw-down of timing differences, the amount(s) cannot exceed the net deferred tax credits (net of deferred charges) that would reverse within the carryforward period.

## Case II

| | | |
|---|---|---|
| FIT payable (ITC applied) | 25 | |
| Deferred tax credit (draw-down)* | 5 | |
| FIT provision (ITC recognized) | | 30 |

The draw-down (Type I) is for the excess of recognized over applied ITC (30-25).

| | | |
|---|---|---|
| Deferred tax credit (draw-down)* | 8 | |
| FIT provision | | 8 |

The draw-down (Type II) is for the excess of the available over the recognized ITC (40-30) which is the ITC carryforward for book, but not to exceed the reversible timing differences 8 (13 reversible net deferred tax credits less 5 drawn down in the first entry). The 2 (40-30-8) available but unrecorded ITC for book would be disclosed in a footnote as would the 15 (40-25) ITC carryforward for tax. Note that this results in a different unrecorded book and tax credit carryforward for the same item (ITC). These two entries also remove the reversible timing differences from the balance sheet.

* Where recorded as a draw-down of timing differences the amount(s) cannot exceed the net deferred tax credits (net of deferred charges) that would reverse within the carryforward period.

## Case III

| | | |
|---|---|---|
| FIT payable (ITC applied) | 30 | |
| FIT provision (ITC recognized) | | 25 |
| Unrecognized ITC (applied in excess of recognized) | | 5 |

Because the applied ITC (30) exceeds the recognized ITC (25) there is no (Type I) draw-down of deferred tax credits (from timing differences) but this excess creates an unrecognized ITC "liability." Note that this is not a timing difference (although it has similar effects) as the ITC is neither a timing nor a permanent difference (i.e., it never reduces pretax book income or taxable income). It should also be noted that, even though the flow through method is being used, this journal entry results in recording an ITC yet to be recognized.

| | | |
|---|---|---|
| Deferred tax credit (draw-down)* | 10 | |
| FIT provision | | 10 |

The draw-down (Type II) is for the excess of the available (40) ITC over the greater of the recognized (25) or the applied (30) ITC. The book ITC carryforward is 15 (40-25) of which this entry recognizes 10, while the tax ITC carryforward is 10 (40-30) which is to be disclosed in a footnote.

* Where recorded as a draw-down of timing differences the amount(s) cannot exceed the net deferred tax credits (net of deferred charges) that would reverse within the carryforward period.

## Case IV

| | | |
|---|---|---|
| FIT payable (ITC applied) | 30 | |
| FIT provision (ITC recognized) | | 25 |
| Unrecognized ITC (Excess of applied over recognized) | | 5 |

Because the applied ITC (30) exceeds the recognized ITC (25) there is no (Type I) draw-down of deferred tax credits (from timing differences). Note that the 5 increase in ITC "liability" is not a timing difference. Since the ITC is neither a timing nor a permanent difference, it cannot result in a timing difference. This journal entry results in the recording of a deferred ITC, even though the flow-through method of recording the ITC is being used. Presumably we could have drawn-down net deferred charges (if they had existed) instead of recording the deferred ITC of 5.

| | | |
|---|---|---|
| Deferred tax credit (draw-down)* | 8 | |
| FIT provision | | 8 |

The draw-down (Type II) is for the excess of the available ITC (40) over the greater of the recognized ITC (25) or the applied ITC (30) but not in excess of the reversible net credit timing differences (8). The 7 (40-25-8) available but unrecognized ITC for book should be disclosed in a footnote as would the 10 (40-30) ITC carryforward for tax purposes. The 7 carryforward for book is the 15 (40-25) less the 8 draw-down of deferred tax credits. Note that the 5 of ITC "liability" (unrecognized ITC) established in the balance sheet has not yet affected net income.

* Where recorded as a draw-down of timing differences the amount(s) cannot exceed the net deferred tax credits (net of deferred charges) that would reverse within the carryforward period.

## Public Utility Aspects

It is almost impossible to overstate the potential significance a change in accounting for income taxes could have on regulated public utilities. How a particular transaction is recorded may affect net income, but seldom does it impact directly on cash flows. However, this is not the case with public utilities and income taxes.

As a general rule, regulated public utility rates are set at amounts that will recover a utility's "cost of service," which includes all allowable operating expenses (including allowable losses and taxes) and a return on capital. Interest is not allowed as an item of expense to be recovered, but debt is a component in the computation of the weighted average cost of capital rate. The return on capital is determined by multiplying the rate base (which generally equals the creditor and shareholder equities) by the weighted average cost of capital rate. This rate, if it is properly determined, compensates utilities by allowing a fair rate of return on those assets comprising the rate base. The following, in an overly simplified fashion, indicates the items included in the cost of service:

All allowable operating expenses

\+ Return on capital (rate base X an established weighted average cost of capital rate)

Cost of Service = Regulated revenues

Thus, revenues (regulated rates) to a regulated public utility are determined by the allowable expenses (including income taxes and losses), the size of the rate base, and the weighted average cost of capital rate that is applied to the rate base.

Increased cash inflows, through regulated revenues, can be obtained whenever an allowable expense (such as taxes) is increased without there being a corresponding cash outflow for that item. There is a cash flow incentive, therefore, to have deferred tax credits for timing differences and to amortize the ITC over the book life of the asset. Each of these items results in an increased federal income tax provision, without a corresponding cash outflow, as shown in partial journal entries below:

| | | |
|---|---|---|
| Federal income tax provision | XX | |
| Deferred tax credits | | XX |
| Federal income tax provision | XX | |
| Unamortized ITC | | XX |

These entries increase the income tax provision and this provision is an allowable expense in the determination of public utility rates. It should be noted that a deferred tax charge would have the opposite effect:

| | | |
|---|---|---|
| Deferred tax charge | XX | |
| Federal income tax provision | | XX |

Thus, rate-regulated corporations have a cash flow incentive to avoid deferred charge items.

***Investment Tax Credit*** Internal Revenue Code Section 46(f)--previously 46(e)--permits public utilities to use one of two forms of deferral (normalization) for the ITC. The first of these, frequently termed "rate base normalization," allows a reduction in the rate base for the ITC, but the reduction is restored to the rate base as the ITC is amortized. The federal income tax provision for rate regulation purposes is determined as though there were no ITC. Thus, neither the ITC nor its amortization affects the allowable expenses to be charged to customers, but the return on the capital portion of the cost of service is reduced because of the unrestored reduction in the rate base.

The second form of normalization, frequently termed "cost of service normalization," allows for a ratable reduction in the federal income tax provision for the ITC over the book life of the asset. This is a decrease in the allowable expense portion of the cost of service over the life of the asset. The unamortized portions of the ITC however, earn a rate of return equal to the rate for common shareholders' equity (or a composite cost of capital rate in some jurisdictions) in the cost of capital portion of the cost of service computation. Of the two forms of normalization for the ITC, the second is reportedly the most commonly used method.

*Depreciation* In the computation of the federal income tax portion of the "cost of service" for public utilities (except for a few utilities which have continuously elected to use flow through), Internal Revenue Code Sections 167(1) and 168(e)(3) require deferral of the tax effects of depreciation for pre-1981 asset acquisitions. For post-1980 asset acquisitions (after a transition period expires) flow through will not be permitted. Therefore, in computing the allowable expense portion of the cost of service, the federal income tax provision is (with some adjustments) the same amount as it would have been had book rather than tax depreciation been used to determine the tax provision. (One of the adjustments would be for the excess book depreciation caused by capitalizing prior year imputed interest costs in the allowance for funds used in construction and currently depreciating this excess book basis.) The return on capital portion of the cost of service is not increased because of the resulting deferred tax credits. These credit balances are usually used to reduce the rate base, but alternatively may be assigned a zero cost in the weighted average cost of capital computation (assuming rate commissions will follow the FASB standard).

As will be seen in the analysis of timing differences and other data, interperiod income tax allocation provides a large and growing source of investment capital to public utilities.

# 2 Survey Design

The primary objective of this research study was to survey both the preparers of financial statements and users of financial statement information. These two groups were questioned on their experiences with the current accounting for income taxes rules, and their opinions about the current and proposed rules. The primary target was the preparers of financial statements and, therefore, the number of preparers surveyed was much larger than the number of users.

In both cases, the method of survey was a written questionnaire mailed to a random and non-random sample of each target group. The questionnaires are reproduced in Appendices C and D. Each questionnaire is divided into two sections. The first section focuses on the respondent's experience with the accounting rules for recording and measuring income taxes. In section two, the users and preparers were asked to express levels of agreement or disagreement with respect to various accounting statements made. Because many of the accounting for income taxes topics are encountered by only a small group of companies, each statement contained a "no opinion" option as one of the responses.

Each questionnaire was reviewed by the FERF Project Steering Committee and was field-tested before being mailed to the selected samples of corporations or financial analysts. More detailed information on the composition of the preparer group sample and the user group sample is provided in the following pages. It must be pointed out, however, that the number of responses received from the user sample was insufficient to support any statements about the general opinions of the user population as a group. This will be discussed in the user section of this chapter.

## Composition of the Preparer Group Sample

The primary population from which the sample of corporations was drawn was the membership list of the Financial Executives Institute (FEI). From this membership list of approximately 6,000 firms, 2,009 firms were randomly selected to receive the preparer questionnaire.

A second, non-random sample was subsequently chosen from information gathered from the compustat tapes.[1] Due to the fact that some of the most difficult and complex problem areas in the accounting for income taxes are not universally encountered, it was felt that the questionnaire should be sent to an additional group of corporations that would have a greater likelihood of experiencing these complexities. The criteria used for selecting this group of corporations were that the financial statement had to report one of the following:

1. A net operating loss carryforward of $5 million or more.

2. A ratio of deferred tax credits to shareholders' equity of 20 percent or more and a deferred tax credit account balance of at least $100 million.

3. Either a negative deferred tax or a negative federal income tax provision in the income statement.

---

[1]Compustat is a collection of selected financial statement information on several thousand corporations, compiled by Standard and Poor's Compustat Services, Inc.

Through this procedure, a total of 249 corporations were selected. One hundred twenty-two corporations were selected under criterion one, 109 under criterion two, and 18 under criterion three. The 249 originally selected were subsequently reduced to 169 as follows:

| | |
|---|---|
| 249 | Corporations initially selected |
| - 6 | Corporations that qualified under more than one criterion |
| - 57 | Corporations that were already included in the random sample of FEI firms |
| - 17 | Corporations for which no address could be readily located (primarily foreign corporations) |
| 169 | Corporations mailed questionnaires |

The response rate for each of the three groups of corporations surveyed is summarized below.

| Sample Group | Mailed | Returned | Percentage | Unusable | Usable |
|---|---|---|---|---|---|
| Random | 2,009 | 220 | 11% | 12 | 208 |
| Bias | 169 | 36 | 21% | 1 | 35 |
| Field test only[2] | 26 | 15 | 58% | 0 | 15 |
| Totals | 2,204 | 271 | 12% | 13 | 258 |

On six of the unusable responses in the random sample (from FEI members) the respondents indicated that they are partnerships or Subchapter S corporations, which are primarily nontaxable entities at the federal level. Six respondents indicated that they are subsidiaries and thus could not supply the data requested.

The response rate for the entire group was 12 percent, but was substantially higher for the bias group. From the entire bias group of 226 (169 + 57 that were also in the random group) there were 54 responses for a 24 percent response rate. The response rate for the 57 firms included in both the random and the original bias group selections was 37 percent (21/57) even though they received only one questionnaire.

---

[2]Eight of the field test corporations initially selected were also in another group--two in the random sample and six in the bias sample. Their responses are included in this group rather than with the field test group.

While an overall response rate of 12 percent may be considered low, the length and degree of difficulty in supplying data would preclude a large response rate. Among the field test corporations, the time required to complete and review this questionnaire ranged from 3 to 30 hours, and this information was supplied in the questionnaire. Few corporations could complete and review this questionnaire in less than a one person-day of effort.

One concern that arose in light of the response rate and the population from which the sample was drawn was the need for a broad representation. A limitation of using a written, self-reporting questionnaire to solicit opinions is that those groups with a vested interest in either retaining the status quo or changing the current rules, tend to respond in higher numbers than those groups that are relatively neutral. One indication that such an interest was a motivating factor in this study involved two gas pipeline public utility trade associations. These associations sent letters to their members encouraging them to respond to the study and to show support for the existing policy. While the impact of their attempted suasion is not known, it does underscore the economic motivation that certain industry groups have in the accounting for income taxes discussion.[3]

In addition, the length and complexity of the questionnaire likely had a more negative effect on the response rate of small corporations than it did on the response rate of large corporations. As a result, the responses summarized in this survey tend to reflect the opinions of larger corporations.

The respondents to the questionnaire were initially divided into three measurement classifications: (1) by basic SIC group, (2) by asset size, and (3) by regulatory and nonregulatory status (SIC codes 48 and 49). Table 2.1 summarizes the number of usable responses received by each measurement classification.

---

[3]The effect of the trade associations' encouragements probably increased the response rates of certain utility groups, but had negligible effect on the attitudinal scores. The public utility groups that were not part of these trade associations responded in a manner almost identical to those utilities belonging to the trade associations.

The responses by SIC classification were concentrated in groups as follows: manufacturing 46.5 percent; transportation, communication, and other public utilities 26.4 percent; and finance, insurance, and real estate 10.9 percent. The fewest responses were received from corporations in the construction industry and the agriculture, forest, and fishing industry. Because FEI does not record the SIC classification of its members, it was not possible to determine if the ratio of responses is a reflection of the make-up of the FEI membership list or a reflection of the industries most interested in the accounting for income taxes discussion.

TABLE 2.1 *Profile of Responding Corporations*

| SIC Number | | Number of Responding Corporations | Corporations with Total Assets under 250 M | Corporations with Total Assets over 250 M | Corporations that are Non-Regulated | Corporations that are Regulated |
|---|---|---|---|---|---|---|
| 1 | Agriculture, forest, and fishing | 4 | 0 | 4 | 4 | 0 |
| 2 | Mining | 12 | 2 | 10 | 12 | 0 |
| 3 | Construction | 1 | 1 | 0 | 1 | 0 |
| 4 | Manufacturing | 120 | 38* | 81* | 120 | 0 |
| 5 | Transportation, communication, and other public utilities | 68 | 6 | 62 | 8 | 60** |
| 6 | Wholesale trade | 7 | 6 | 1 | 7 | 0 |
| 7 | Retail trade | 7 | 1 | 6 | 7 | 0 |
| 8 | Finance, insurance, and real estate | 28 | 3 | 25 | 28 | 0 |
| 9 | Service | 11 | 5 | 6 | 11 | 0 |
| | Total number of corporations responding to the questionnaire | 258 | 62* | 195* | 198 | 60 |

* Asset data missing for one corporation.

** Four corporations in this category have assets of less than $250 million.

In an effort to determine significant differences in the responses for corporations of various size, the sample was split between "large" and "small" corporations based on net assets of greater than or less than $250 million. The size of demarcation was chosen because it approximates the cutoff point to be listed in the "Fortune 500." This proved to be a nondiscriminating factor in all of the attitudinal analysis. Many observers would argue that a "small" corporation should be restricted to an asset size of between $1 million and $4 million. Unfortunately, the FEI membership list contains few, if any, corporations of this size. As it was, corporations with assets below $250 million comprised 24.1 percent of the response group.

Finally, the respondents were divided into a regulatory and nonregulatory group. The regulatory category contained corporations with SIC codes 48 and 49. This permitted some media corporations to be included in the regulatory group, but this was necessary to capture telephone corporations in this category. The regulated group accounted for 23.3 percent of the respondents, which is a much higher ratio than generally exists in industry. Much of the analysis is presented with these two groups shown separately.

A further test was conducted to determine the response rates of each classification of corporations by sample group (random, bias, and field test). This information is contained in Table 2.2. This table shows that there is some diversity in responding firms between the random sample and the bias sample by SIC category. There is a higher proportion of large corporations in the bias groups (95.9 percent to 71.2 percent, respectively). This is due largely to the field test corporations, all of which were large corporations. As to regulatory status, there appear to be slightly more regulated corporations in the bias group than in the random group (28.0 percent to 22.1 percent, respectively). This is due to the initial selection of 109 bias corporations on a deferred tax credit to shareholder equity ratio of more than 20 percent, which captured a substantial number of public utilities. Overall, however, it does not appear that including the bias groups has greatly distorted the returns of any of the three divisions of responding firms.

TABLE 2.2 *A Comparison of Questionnaires*

| SIC Category | Responding Corporations Number | Responding Corporations Percent | From the Random Test Group Number | From the Random Test Group Percent | From the Bias and Field Test Group Number | From the Bias and Field Test Group Percent |
|---|---|---|---|---|---|---|
| 1 | 4 | 1.6% | 1 | .5% | 3 | 6.0% |
| 2 | 12 | 4.7 | 9 | 4.3 | 3 | 6.0 |
| 3 | 1 | .4 | 1 | .5 | 0 | .0 |
| 4 | 120 | 46.5 | 100 | 48.0 | 20 | 40.0 |
| 5 | 68 | 26.4 | 52 | 25.0 | 16 | 32.0 |
| 6 | 7 | 2.7 | 6 | 2.9 | 1 | 2.0 |
| 7 | 7 | 2.7 | 7 | 3.4 | 0 | .0 |
| 8 | 28 | 10.8 | 22 | 10.6 | 6 | 12.0 |
| 9 | 11 | 4.2 | 10 | 4.8 | 1 | 2.0 |
| Totals | 258 | 100.0% | 208 | 100.0% | 50 | 100.0% |
| Asset Size: | | | | | | |
| Small | 62 | 24.1% | 60 | 28.8% | 2 | 4.1% |
| Large | 195 | 75.9 | 148 | 71.2 | 47 | 95.9 |
| Totals | 257* | 100.0% | 208 | 100.0% | 49* | 100.0% |
| Regulatory Status: | | | | | | |
| Nonregulated | 198 | 76.7% | 162 | 77.9% | 36 | 72.0 |
| Regulated | 60 | 23.3 | 46 | 22.1 | 14 | 28.0 |
| Totals | 258 | 100.0% | 208 | 100.0% | 50 | 100.0% |

*One company did not furnish data on asset size.

## Composition of the User Group Sample

The user questionnaire was initially sent to a random sample of 500 financial analysts who were members of the Financial Analysts Federation. This approach proved to be very unsuccessful, as only nine persons responded within the determined time period. Although this low response rate was disappointing, it was expected in light of the length of the questionnaire and the past reluctance of users of financial information to participate in accounting pronouncement related surveys. It was suggested that rather than continue to pursue responses from financial analysts at large, it would be more productive and informative to solicit the opinions of a small group of experienced users such as members of the Financial Accounting Policies Committee of the Financial Analysts Federation. Each of the fifteen members of this committee was personally contacted about his willingness to participate in this project. Eight of the fifteen members returned completed questionnaires. A profile of this group as well as a profile of the random sample of respondents follows. It must be emphasized that the responses of this group of users are not represented to be reflective of the attitudes of users as a group toward accounting for income taxes.

The respondents to the user questionnaire were diverse in their occupations and industry specializations. The occupations and number of persons involved in each are listed below.

Occupations of User Sample

|  |  |
|---|---|
| Investment analyst | 5 |
| Financial analyst | 4 |
| Investment counselor | 2 |
| University professor | 2 |
| Portfolio manager | 1 |
| Investment banker | 1 |
| Corporate finance | 1 |
| Chief executive | 1 |
| Total | 17 |

Industry Specializations of User Sample*

| | |
|---|---|
| Generalist | 7 |
| Banking | 3 |
| Retailing | 2 |
| Electronics | 2 |
| Insurance | 1 |
| Energy | 1 |
| Chemicals | 1 |
| Automotive | 1 |
| Manufacturing | 1 |
| Aerospace | 1 |
| Consumer | 1 |
| Utilities | 1 |
| Computers | 1 |
| Total | 23 |

* In some cases, users indicated more than one industry specialization.

The average asset size of the companies analyzed by these respondents was $2.25 billion, with the range of asset size varying from $20 million to $100 billion. The majority of respondents (ten of the seventeen) indicated that they are in personal contact with the companies they evaluate.

The experience level of those surveyed as users in their stated occupations was quite high. The average number of years of experience in their field was 19.4 years. The range of years of experience extended from 5.5 years to 48 years. Approximately one-half of the group had 20 or more years of experience (8 of 17), and all but one had 10 or more years of experience.

On the question that related to the respondents' experience in the deferred tax area, thirteen members of the group are involved in a detailed analysis of a company's deferred tax accounts on at least an occasional basis. Five members of the group characterized their level of involvement with deferred taxes as frequent, eight as occasional, and four as infrequent.

The combination of the experience level of the users in this survey and their exposure to deferred tax accounting is reflected in the users' self-assessments of their knowledge on the issues involving accounting for income taxes. Users were asked if they considered themselves technically and conceptually proficient in this area, conceptually proficient only, or neither conceptually nor technically proficient (see Question 3). The breakdown of responses is as follows:

| | |
|---|---|
| Technically and conceptually proficient | 8 |
| Conceptually proficient only | 6 |
| Neither technically nor conceptually proficient | 3 |

Finally, the users were asked to rate their level of interest in the FASB's reconsideration of accounting for income taxes. A ten-point scale was used, with one being no interest and ten being high interest. The number of responses at each scale point is summarized below.

| NO INTEREST | 1 | 2 | 3 | 4 | 5 | 6 | 7 | 8 | 9 | 10 | HIGH INTEREST |
|---|---|---|---|---|---|---|---|---|---|---|---|
| | 1 | 0 | 1 | 1 | 2 | 2 | 3 | 2 | 1 | 4 | |

It is evident from the scale that the interest level of the user sample is concentrated in the upper half of the scale (the average score is 6.8). The interest level of the FAF policy committee is 7.3.

In summary, while the number of users that comprise the sample in this survey is too small to subject to any statistical analysis, these people are experienced, knowledgeable, and interested in the FASB project. Their comments and opinions, which are summarized in Chapter 3, provide some valuable individual insights on the topic of interperiod tax allocation.

# 3 User Opinions on Interperiod Income Tax Allocation

As discussed in Chapter 2, the number of responses from the user group was inadequate to support any generalized statements about the attitudes of the users of financial information as a group toward current and proposed rules of accounting for income taxes. The seventeen user responses to the questionnaire will be summarized in this chapter, but no statistical analyses will be presented.

## Overall Satisfaction with Existing Rules

The users and the preparers were asked the same overall satisfaction questions regarding existing rules for income taxes, the investment credit, and foreign tax credits. (Questions 7-9 of the user questionnaire correspond to Questions 20-22 of the preparer questionnaire.)

The users and the nonregulated preparers expressed satisfaction with the existing rules for allocating the effects of timing differences between periods. Eleven of sixteen user respondents were at least generally satisfied with the existing rules. However, all users responding to this question expressed a desire to see some degree of change. The high level of satisfaction that was voiced by the preparers with the existing investment credit rules, was also reflected in the responses of the users to Question 8. On the other hand, the users were more dissatisfied with the lack of formal rules to guide accounting for the foreign tax credit (Question 9) than were the preparers. Ten of fifteen user respondents were dissatisfied with the absence of formal rules.

The user group was asked one additional overall satisfaction question not asked the preparers. In Question 10, the users were asked to describe their current level of satisfaction with the presentation of the deferred tax analysis in the footnotes accompanying companies' financial statements. The responses reflected a level of general satisfaction with existing practice (fourteen of sixteen respondents), although a majority did want to see at least minor changes made. (Only three of the fourteen were totally satisfied with current practices.)

## Issues Identified as Needing Reconsideration

The user group and the preparer group were presented the same list of accounting for income taxes issues and asked to identify those issues they felt were in need of immediate reconsideration. (Question 11 of the user questionnaire corresponds to Question 23 of the preparer questionnaire.) An analysis of the responses is presented in Table 3.1.

The issue identified most frequently by the user group as needing immediate reconsideration was the deferred method requirement for tax allocation. The issue of accounting for the future tax benefits of NOL carryforwards received the second highest frequency of votes. Comprehensive allocation and accounting for tax credits received recognition from four members of the user group. A disparity between the responses of the user group and the preparer group existed on the tax rates issue. This issue received the most votes from the preparer group, but received the least votes from the user group. Finally, six members of the user group felt that no changes in the current rules are required at this time.

TABLE 3.1 *Number of Respondents Indentifying Issues as Needing Reconsideration (Question 11)*

| Issue | Total |
|---|---|
| Allocation requirement | 3 |
| Comprehensive allocation | 4 |
| Deferral method | 6 |
| Tax rate changes | 2 |
| Discounting deferred taxes | 3 |
| NOL carryforward tax benefits | 5 |
| Tax credits | 4 |
| Others | 2 |
| None of the above | 6 |
| Respondents | 17 |

## Classification and Use of Deferred Tax Information

Questions 12 through 21 of the user questionnaire were designed to determine how users view deferred taxes in the financial statements and how they incorporate them in their financial analyses. On the question of defining a deferred tax credit balance in the balance sheet (Question 12), the users varied widely in their responses. The choices of the user group are summarized below.

| Choice | Number Selecting |
|---|---|
| Payable | 8 |
| Reduction in an asset | 3 |
| Paid-in capital | 0 |
| Quasi-equity | 4 |
| No comparable account | 2 |
| Total | 17 |

While four users considered the deferred tax credit account to most resemble a quasi-equity account, none of the preparer respondents reported their deferred tax credit accounts in the owners' equity section of their financial statements. In a related question, the users were asked how they applied deferred tax credit account balances in their computation of debt/equity ratios (Question 13). Their responses were as follows:

| Deferred Account Treated As | Number Selecting |
|---|---|
| Entire balance as debt | 3 |
| Entire balance as equity | 2 |
| Does not enter computation | 10 |
| Entire balance is apportioned between debt and equity | 1 |
| A portion of the balance is included as debt/equity | 1 |
| Total | 17 |

Those users who allocated the credit balance between debt and equity or who allocated only a portion of the balance, based this decision on the likelihood of payment of each of the published components of the account balance. This data, however, is rarely (if ever) published. Accounts that tended to roll over (such as depreciation) were treated as either equity or ignored, while accounts from isolated transactions that would reverse were treated as debt.

Of the eight persons who stated that the deferred tax credit balance account most resembled a payable, only two included the balance as debt in debt/equity ratios. Five of the eight did not include the balance in the ratio at all.

The users were asked the same questions on account definition and use in the debt/equity ratios regarding the unamortized investment tax credit in the balance sheet. With respect to account definition (Question 15), the users described the unamortized ITC account as most resembling the following:

| Choice | Number Selecting |
|---|---|
| Payable | 2 |
| Reduction | 5 |
| Paid-in capital | 0 |
| Quasi-equity | 9 |
| No comparable account | 1 |
| Total | 17 |

As with the definition of the deferred tax credit account, the users view of the unamortized ITC account conflicts with the preparers' balance sheet classification. Nine users view the unamortized ITC account as quasi-equity, although less than 1 percent of the preparers classified that account in owners' equity (see analysis of Question 15 in Chapter 4).

When computing debt/equity ratios, the majority of the respondents reported that they did not use any part of the unamortized ITC account balance in the ratio. Of those who did use the balance in the ratio, three-quarters of the respondents classified the account as equity. The responses to the debt/equity question (Question 16) are summarized below.

| Unamortized ITC Treated as | Number Selecting |
|---|---|
| Entire balance as debt | 2 |
| Entire balance as equity | 6 |
| Does not enter computation | 9 |
| Entire balance is apportioned between debt/equity | 0 |
| A portion of the balance is included as debt/equity | 0 |
| Total | 17 |

All but one user stated that their debt/equity ratio computation was the same for both rate-regulated and nonregulated corporations (Question 18). The one respondent who stated that the computations were different noted that the computations should be the same but that regulators do not always look at the same numbers. Therefore, adjustments are made based on the regulatory commission's policy.

When considering the application of the deferred tax account in their analysis of a company's cash flow position (Question 19), almost one-half of the users responded that they considered the deferred account in their analysis in all cases. Only one of the respondents said that the account does not enter into any cash flow analysis. A summary of the responses to this question are summarized below.

| Use of the Deferred Tax Account in Cash Flow Analysis | Number Selecting |
|---|---|
| All cases | 8 |
| Liquidation analysis only | 2 |
| When balance exceeds a prescribed % of equity (assets) | 1 |
| When account balance growth trend reverses | 5 |
| Only in particular industries | 0 |
| Not used in cash flow analysis | 1 |
| Total | 17 |

Those users who commented on their method of determining the cash flow effect from changes in the deferred tax account (Question 21) indicated that they had no formal technique with which to analyze the deferred tax account. Several respondents used trends in the growth of the deferred account to forecast future cash effects. One user confirmed his assumptions by contacting the financial officers of the companies being analyzed. Another admitted that many of his assumptions were pure guesses. The most frequent change in reporting cited by the users was an inclusion in the income taxes footnote of a listing of the expected payment dates for individual components of the deferred tax account. This is similar to the current requirement for long-term debt.

## User Opinions of the Information Provided by Interperiod Income Tax Allocation

### Relevant and Reliable Information

As users of accounting information, this sample of analysts is in a unique position to provide opinions on the value of the information currently provided by interperiod tax allocation for decision making. Statement of Financial Accounting Concepts No. 2 states that "relevance and reliability are the two primary qualities that make accounting information useful for decision making."[1] Reliability is defined to exist when "users can depend on it to represent the economic conditions or events that it purports to represent" (para. 62). Information is deemed to be relevant when it is "capable of making a difference in a decision by helping users to form predictions about the outcomes of past, present and future events or to confirm or correct expectations" (para. 47).

Within this context the users in this study were first asked if they felt that the current method of accounting for income taxes produced information that was "reliable" (Question 22) and "relevant" (Question 23). The responses of each of the two groups to these questions are summarized below.

| Quality of Information Provided Under Current Rules | Agree | Disagree | No Opinion |
|---|---|---|---|
| Reliable (Question 22) | 11 | 5 | 1 |
| Relevant (Question 23) | 11 | 5 | 1 |

The responses indicate general satisfaction with the value of the interperiod income tax information currently being presented. On the reliability issue, several of the respondents expressed concern that the income tax expense is not an accurate reflection of the current or future cash outflows. As for relevance, some users felt that current rules allowed for too much latitude in measuring the deferred tax, thus diminishing its predictive value.

## Possible Reporting Method Alternatives

A second set of questions in this section (Questions 24-29) asked the users to indicate that the adoption of any of the alternatives being considered by the FASB would result

---

[1]FASB Concepts Statement No. 2, Qualitative Characteristics of Accounting Information (Stamford, Conn.: FASB, 1980), p.x.

in information that was more relevant than that which is currently provided and was also cost justified.

In general, the respondents did not view any of the changes as providing information that was more relevant than the status quo or was cost justified if more relevant. The change that was viewed most favorably by the users was the adjustment of deferred tax accounts for subsequent changes in tax laws or rates (i.e., a switch to the liability method). Thirteen of the sixteen persons rendering an opinion on this issue stated that the liability method was a more relevant method than deferral. However, six of these thirteen respondents felt that a change to the liability method might not be cost justified.

One issue with little support suggested a separate set of accounting requirements for income taxes for private and small public companies (Question 28). A respondent opposed to this change stated that a different set of rules would be a "license for abuse." Despite the overall disfavor of the group toward two sets of rules, it should be pointed out that four of the eleven respondents offering an opinion stated that such a differentiation by company size would provide more relevant information and be cost justified.

The issue on the change from interperiod tax allocation to a taxes currently payable approach (Question 24) revealed several responses from the user group. Seven of the seventeen respondents stated that such a change would provide more relevant information and be cost justified. Six of the seventeen were on the other end of the opinion scale, stating that such a change would provide less relevant information. Of the remaining four respondents, two felt the change would provide more relevant information but would not be cost justified and two felt there would be no change in the relevance of the information produced.

The users were reluctant to favor changes that would allow for discounting (Question 26), recognition of the tax benefits of net operating losses (Question 27), and the adoption of the partial allocation method (Question 29). This resistance stems from a concern that such changes might allow the accounting numbers to become too subjective. On the NOL tax benefit issue, one respondent wrote that such a change would result in "just guesswork" and be "a terrible rule." Phrases used to describe a proposed change to allow discounting included "more complexity," "confusing," and "too much manipulation if management chose the discount rate."

This concern over the degree to which management judgment should be reflected in the accounting for income tax process is reflected in five users' responses to Question 30. When asked if such an infusion of management judgment into the reporting process would be beneficial or detrimental, these five users said "beneficial," eleven said "detrimental," and one said "no effect."

## Criteria for Current and Proposed Allocation Methods

The third set of questions in this section (Questions 31 through 38) dealt with conceptual issues related to criteria that are part of the evaluation process of current and proposed allocation methods. Questions 31 through 33 asked the users to describe their general level of agreement with statements concerning financial statement priority, cash flow considerations, and the relationship between book and taxable income.

On the issue of financial statement priority (Question 31), the users were very polarized in their responses. Of the 17 responses, eight persons believed that the income statement should be accorded primary emphasis in all cases, while seven persons believed that the income statement should never be accorded more emphasis than the balance sheet. This low consensus is similar to the consensus level exhibited by the preparers on the same issue (see analysis of Question 40 in Chapter 5).

When questioned whether cash flow considerations should take precedence over the matching criterion even when a liability will not be paid within a relatively short period of time, there was little consensus among the respondents (Question 32). Nine respondents agreed with the statement (six agreed in all cases), while seven respondents disagreed with the statements (six disagreed in all cases). While the opinions of the users lacked conformity on Question 32, the preparers generally disagreed with the cash flow precedence concept. The rate-regulated group, in particular, was almost unanimous in its disagreement with the statement (see analysis of Question 31 in Chapter 5).

Finally, the users were evenly split over whether the relationship between book income and taxable income has been so distorted by recent tax law changes that the relevancy of information produced by comprehensive allocation has diminished (Question 33). Responses tended to be at both extremes, with either emphatic agreement or emphatic disagreement.

Questions 34 and 35 asked the users to select the tax allocation method and the investment credit reporting method that would provide them with the most relevant information. With regard to the tax allocation method, the users made the following selections:

| Preferred Tax Allocation Method | Number Selecting |
|---|---|
| Deferred | 1 |
| Liability | 4 |
| Net-of-tax | 2 |
| Combination of liability and net-of-tax | 2 |
| No preference | 4 |
| No opinion | 4 |
| Total | 17 |

The preferences for a method of recording investment credits can be summarized as follows:

| Preferred ITC Reporting Method | Number Selecting |
|---|---|
| Deferred | 2 |
| Flow-through | 4 |
| Either, but make it required | 9 |
| Either, with the choice left to management | 2 |
| No opinion | 0 |
| Total | 17 |

Over one-half of the users did not have a preference for a method but did prefer that only one method be allowed. Only a two users were in favor of the status quo. This is consistent with users' preferences for comparability over flexibility in reporting accounting numbers.

On the issue of an appropriate discounting rate should discounting of deferred tax accounts be required (allowed), the users were divided on which rate to use (Question 36). The first choice was for some risk-free market rate, followed by any method provided it was consistent, and the third choices were the company's internal rate of return and the company's incremental borrowing rate. No user wanted the discounting rate to be determined by management.

The last two questions in this section of the questionnaire asked the users for their definitions of the corporate income tax and the investment credit. The choices for a definition of both items were the same as those given by the preparer group. (Questions 37 and 38 of the user questionnaire were asked as Questions 76 and 77, respectively, in the preparer questionnaire.)

The responses of the users to the income tax question were heavily in favor of the "expense" classification (15 of 17). One vote each was cast for a "cost of doing business" and an "anomalous item." The users' choices of an ITC classification can be summarized as follows:

1st choice: reduction of the effective tax rate (8 votes)
2nd choice: reduction in the cost of the asset (7 votes)
3rd choice: contribution to capital by government (2 votes)

This ordering of ITC descriptions parallels the ranking given by the nonregulated preparers, except that the third choice of the users was a cash subsidy. None of the preparers voted for the cash subsidy classification.

Despite the small number of respondents, it is evident that many diverse opinions and practices in accounting for income taxes exist between these users. With many valuable insights to bring to this issue, it is unfortunate that more users did not choose to participate in this survey.

## An Evaluation of Information Provided in a Selected Annual Report

The remaining questions in the user questionnaire (39-51) dealt with information relating to income taxes that was excerpted from a published financial statement. The intent of the questions was to determine if the users interpreted the information provided in a uniform manner.

One-half of the respondents believed that the increase in the deferred tax account signaled an increase in future cash outflows for the company. The remaining respondents felt that such an increase was unrelated to current or future cash outflows. Approximately two-thirds of the users misinterpreted the reported "effective" tax rate and/or the reported current portion of the tax provision. The existence of an increase in the tax provision coupled with a simultaneous increase in a tax net operating loss was also perplexing to many of the respondents. Finally, most of the users (15 of 17) believed that the disclosures of the investment credits were not adequate. A majority wanted more explicit information on the expiration dates of the ITC carryforwards.

## Summary

In general, the users in this study were fairly satisfied with the status quo in accounting for income taxes. As might be expected, they would favor more disclosure of certain items (the expiration dates of credits, the source of a tax NOL). They would also strongly oppose any changes that would reduce the comparability of financial statements within an industry.

Despite their stated satisfaction with existing rules, the users provided very different interpretations of the accounting for income taxes provided in the financial statement case study. Such disparities are an indication that there is room for improvement in the articulation of income tax information, especially in circumstances where book and taxable income are very different.

# 4 Financial Statement Data and Current Interperiod Income Tax Accounting Practices

The first two sections of the preparer questionnaire (Questions 3 through 19) were designed to obtain some basic corporate data on the financial statement results of allocating interperiod income taxes and to survey current interperiod income tax allocation practices. The results of these two sections are presented in this chapter.

## Financial Statement Data

### Question 3 — Individual Company Financial Data

The first information provided by the respondents was the total net deferred tax charge or credit in the balance sheet from both income tax timing differences, and deferrals of the investment credit for the years 1977 and 1982. A summary of these data are provided in Tables 4.1 and 4.2. More detailed information is provided in Appendix B, Tables B.1 and B.2. The table information is analyzed by SIC code, asset size, and rate-regulated status.

The deferred tax charge/credit account balance information is contained in Table 4.1. From this table, it can be observed that the average deferred tax credits exceeded the average deferred tax charges for each classification group (but not for each corporation in the groups) in both 1977 and 1982. Thus, there was always a net deferred tax credit balance for the three measurement classifications (SIC groups, asset size, and regulatory status). In addition, only SIC group number 6 (wholesale trade) failed to show an increase in net deferred tax credits from 1977 to 1982. Five of the nine SIC groups had increases in net deferred tax credits of over 100 percent with the largest group, manufacturing, having a 237 percent increase from 1977 to 1982. Both of the asset size groups and both of the regulatory status groups showed increases in excess of 100 percent for net deferred tax credits from 1977 to 1982. For all of the corporations combined, the average percentage increase of net deferred tax credits for 1982 over 1977 was 140 percent, or almost 2-1/2 times the 1977 net deferred tax credits. These data reflect a substantial growth in dollars of net deferred tax credits on the balance sheets of these corporations.

TABLE 4.1 *Average Net Deferred Tax Credits*

| Description | Average Net Deferred Tax Credits 1977 (000) | Average Net Deferred Tax Credits 1982 (000) | Percentage Increase from 1977 to 1982 |
|---|---|---|---|
| Agriculture, Forest, & Fishing [4] | 179,160 | 520,340 | 190% |
| Mining [11] | 425,820 | 1,160,200 | 172% |
| Construction [1] | 1,034 | 1,900 | 84% |
| Manufacturing [112, 114] | 31,371 | 105,750 | 237% |
| Transportation, Communication, & Other Public Utilities [66] | 222,620 | 491,110 | 121% |
| Wholesale Trade [5, 6] | 81,645 | 53,440 | (35%) |
| Retail Trade [6, 7] | 77,232 | 113,670 | 47% |
| Finance, Insurance, & Real Estate [25, 26] | 58,955 | 135,370 | 130% |
| Services [8, 9] | 12,796 | 24,805 | 94% |
| * * * * * * * * * * * * * * * * | | | |
| Assets under $250 million [54, 56] | 1,465 | 2,994 | 104% |
| Assets over $250 million [184, 188] | 141,180 | 340,460 | 141% |
| Nonregulated Corporations [179, 184] | 65,085 | 174,280 | 168% |
| Regulated Corporations [59, 60] | 244,170 | 535,090 | 119% |
| All Corporations Aggregated [238, 244] | 109,480 | 263,004 | 140% |

[ ] Denotes the number of corporations in each computation. Where two numbers are shown, the first number is for 1977, the second for 1982.

Table B.1 in Appendix B shows the net deferred tax charges and net deferred tax credits separately for both 1977 and 1982 by each of the three measurement classifications (SIC codes, asset size, and regulatory status). Some individual corporations in the survey had deferred tax charges in excess of deferred tax credits, e.g., 15 in manufacturing for 1982, even though the aggregate deferred tax credits exceeded deferred tax charges for each measurement classification. Table B.1 in Appendix B also shows the range of deferred taxes; the average and the percentage increase or decrease in the mean from 1977 to 1982; and the number of corporations in each computation.

It should be noted that between 1977 and 1980, the number of firms with net deferred tax charges decreased from 30 to 27. For this same period, the number of companies (in the 258 total) that responded to Question 3 increased from 238 in 1977 to 244 in 1982. Some of the 20 corporations that did not furnish data for 1977 (or 14 for 1982) indicated that this was proprietary information, and that they had not separately shown their net deferred tax charges or credits on their balance sheets. In these cases, the deferred tax amounts are commingled with other assets or liabilities.

Table 4.1 of this chapter was compiled from data in Table B.1 of Appendix B. The average net deferred tax credits had increased 237 percent for SIC group 4 (manufacturing). These manufacturing firms with net deferred tax credits show an average increase of only 181.9 percent. In other words, part of the overall 237 percent increase for the manufacturing group can be attributed to a less rapid growth in net deferred tax charges (36.3 percent) for those manufacturing corporations with net deferred tax charge accounts.[1] It is also interesting to note that in 1977, the manufacturing group was the only classification in which the average net deferred tax charges ($49,188) exceeded the average net deferred tax credits ($46,798). For 1982, average net deferred tax credits exceeded the average net deferred tax charges for every classification, including manufacturing.

---

[1]Another reason for this result is that some companies having net deferred charge balances in 1977 had net deferred credit balances in 1982 resulting in an increase greater than 100 percent for those companies.

In the regulatory status classification, no regulated corporation had net deferred tax charges in 1977, but in 1982 two corporations in this subcategory had net deferred tax charges. In the nonregulated group, the number of respondents with net deferred tax charges decreased from 30 in 1977 to 25 in 1982.

## Investment Tax Credits in the Balance Sheets

Respondents to Question 3 also provided the amount of investment tax credits (ITC) in their balance sheets for the years 1977 and 1982. This data was used only if the responses to Question 12 indicated that the company was employing the deferral method of accounting for the ITC for some or all of its operations. Some corporations primarily use flow through, but are deferring the ITC for certain rate-regulated subsidiaries or operations.

Table 4.2 summarizes the ITC information for those corporations with deferred ITCs resulting from the use of the deferral method. SIC groups 1, 2, 3, 6, 7, and 9 contain too few observations to make the changes in averages meaningful. The manufacturing group once again showed the largest percentage increase from among those groups with sufficient observations (SIC groups 4, 5, and 8).

TABLE 4.2 *Average Deferred ITC*

| Description | Average Deferred ITC 1977 (000) | Average Deferred ITC 1982 (000) | Percentage Increase from 1977 to 1982 |
|---|---|---|---|
| Agriculture, Forest, & Fishing [2, 1] | 8,567 | 75,004 | 775% |
| Mining [2, 1] | 124,510 | 9,879 | (92%) |
| Construction [0] | -- | -- | -- |
| Manufacturing [12, 10] | 21,532 | 61,183 | 184% |
| Transportation, Communication, & Other Public Utilities [51, 53] | 112,010 | 255,250 | 128% |
| Wholesale Trade [0] | -- | -- | -- |
| Retail Trade [1, 0] | 1,375 | -- | -- |
| Finance, Insurance, & Real Estate [9, 11] | 25,736 | 59,553 | 131% |
| Services [1] | 54 | 1,942 | 3,496% |
| * * * * * * * * * * * * * * * | | | |
| Assets under $250 million [5, 6] | 1,581 | 2,973 | 88% |
| Assets over $250 million [73, 71] | 85,520 | 209,350 | 145% |
| Nonregulated Corporations [28, 25] | 27,422 | 54,729 | 100% |
| Regulated Corporations [50, 52] | 114,040 | 259,880 | 128% |
| All Corporations Aggregated [78, 77] | 82,946 | 192,273 | 133% |

[ ] Denotes the number of corporations in each computation. Where two numbers are shown, the first number is for 1977, the second for 1982.

See Table B.2 in Appendix B for further details.

## Individual Timing Differences

The second part of Question 3 requested the name and the dollar size of each of the five largest timing differences for the years 1977 and 1982. Table 4.3 was prepared from these responses and lists all of the principal timing differences reported. Unfortunately, there are no universally recognized titles for specific timing differences; therefore, classification of timing differences depended on name recognition. At times, this was quite difficult. For example, one respondent identified a timing difference as "basic." After searching the corporation's annual report and confirming the information by telephone, it was determined that "basic" was in fact depreciation.

Table 4.3 lists the 36 sources of reported timing differences and their related number (computer code for processing). Number 30 (miscellaneous items) was assigned to any uncommon timing difference, and numbers 2 and 3 (miscellaneous accruals) have been combined with number 30. Also, number 31 is now an empty classification because it has been combined with item number 13.

TABLE 4.3 *Classified Timing Differences*

| Related Number | Timing Differences |
|---|---|
| 1 | Accrual to cash method |
| 2 | Omitted (included in 30) |
| 3 | Omitted (included in 30) |
| 4 | Bad debt allowances (loan losses) |
| 5 | Capitalized interest |
| 6 | Contribution carryforwards |
| 7 | Coupon redemption |
| 8 | Deferred compension (not pensions) |
| 9 | Depreciation and amortization |
| 10 | DISC |
| 11 | Foreign currency translation |
| 12 | Installment sales |
| 13 | Intangible drilling costs (oil and gas exploration and development) |
| 14 | Intercompany profit |
| 15 | Inventory valuations |
| 16 | Investment tax credit |
| 17 | Leases |
| 18 | Long-term contracts |
| 19 | Net operating losses |
| 20 | Pensions |
| 21 | Plant shutdowns |
| 22 | Property tax |
| 23 | Self insurance |
| 24 | State tax deferrals |
| 25 | Stock options |
| 26 | U.K. stock relief |
| 27 | Unremitted equity method earnings |
| 28 | Vacation accruals |
| 29 | Warranty and repair expenses |
| 30 | Other items (miscellaneous) |
| 31 | Omitted (included in 13) |
| 32 | Purchased gas adjustment |
| 33 | Gain on debt retirement |
| 34 | Defense facilities |
| 35 | Allowance for borrowed funds |
| 36 | Revenue agents review adjustments |
| 37 | Cost of removal |
| 38 | Safe harbor lease transactions |
| 39 | Nuclear fuel storage |

## Major Sources of Frequently Mentioned Timing Differences

The ten most frequently mentioned timing differences for 1982 and 1977 are provided in Tables 4.4 and 4.5. The rankings are separated into three classifications--all companies in the survey, nonregulated companies only, and regulated companies only. A more comprehensive analysis of this data by SIC group and asset size, as well as regulatory status, is contained in Table B.3 of Appendix B. Only those sources of timing differences that are in the top ten of at least one of the classifications' lists are reported in Tables 4.4 and 4.5 of this chapter. The miscellaneous category (number 30) was omitted from the analysis.

Table 4.4 is restricted to those sources of timing differences that resulted in deferred charges to the respondents. Deferred compensation was by far the most frequently mentioned source of deferred charges, receiving more than twice the number of mentions than the second most frequent source, inventory valuations. In 1982, twenty-seven of the thirty-five mentions of deferred compensation came from the manufacturing SIC group (see Table B.3, Appendix B). Not surprisingly, the deferred compensation account was also the most frequently mentioned deferred charge by the nonregulated corporations. The most frequently mentioned deferred charge by the regulated corporations was item 39, nuclear fuel storage.

It is apparent from Table 4.4 that the number of corporations in this survey reporting deferred charges was relatively small. Very few regulated corporations reported any deferred charges among their top five deferred accounts. The manufacturing group was the only SIC group to have ten or more items of deferred charges listed in the members' top five largest deferred accounts.

Finally, the only deferred charge item to significantly change in its relative ordering from 1977 to 1982 was item 21, plant shutdowns. This item was ranked ninth overall in 1977 and third overall in 1982. In all but one case, the plant shutdown account was listed by a nonregulated corporation. Regulated corporations tended to report plant shutdowns as a source of a deferred credit (see Table 4.5).

TABLE 4.4 *The Ten Most Frequently Mentioned Sources of Timing Difference: Deferred Charges*

| Timing Differences | Ranking in 1982 | | | Ranking in 1977 | | |
|---|---|---|---|---|---|---|
| | All Companies | Nonregulated | Regulated | All Companies | Nonregulated | Regulated |
| Deferred compensation | 1[35] | 1[33] | 2[2] | 1[29] | 1[27] | 2[2] |
| Inventory valuations | 2[16] | 2[16] | | 2[18] | 2[18] | |
| Plant shutdowns | 3[14] | 3[13] | 3[1] | 10[6] | 9[6] | |
| State tax deferrals | 4[13] | 3[13] | | 4[13] | 4[13] | |
| Warranty and repair expenses | 5[12] | 6[11] | 3[1] | 2[18] | 3[17] | 3[1] |
| Bad debt allowances | 5[12] | 5[12] | | 5[12] | 5[12] | |
| Pensions | 7[9] | 7[9] | | 7[8] | 7[8] | |
| Depreciation & amortization | 7[9] | 7[9] | | 8[7] | 9[6] | 3[1] |
| Self insurance | 7[9] | 7[9] | | 6[9] | 6[9] | |
| Net operating loss | 7[9] | 10[8] | 3[1] | | | |
| Nuclear fuel storage | | | 1[8] | | | 1[3] |
| Investment tax credit | | | 3[1] | 8[7] | 8[7] | |
| Cost of removal | | | 3[1] | | | |
| Intercompany profit | | | | 10[6] | 9[6] | |
| Gain on debt retirement | | | | | | 3[1] |

[ ] Denotes the number of corporations reporting this timing difference in their top 5 timing differences.

See Tables B.3 and B.5 in Appendix B for more details.

The single most frequently mentioned source of a deferred credit (from Table 4.5) was depreciation and amortization. One hundred ninety-four respondents listed depreciation as a source of one of their five largest deferred tax accounts in 1982. This represents 69 percent of the nonregulated corporations and 97 percent of the regulated corporations. Depreciation also was included in the top five deferred accounts as a deferred charge, but much less frequently than as a credit (9 mentions in 1982).

When the responses are segregated by regulatory status, it is clear that the sources of deferred credits that create large deferred tax balances are different between nonregulated and regulated corporations. The two groups share only four items in their respective lists--depreciation, intangible drilling costs, pensions, and the investment credit. In some instances, the differences are due to the various natures of their respective operations, e.g., DISCs, installment sales, and purchased gas adjustments. Other times, the dissimilarities are due to different accounting treatment of the same item. For example, plant shutdowns were reported as sources of deferred charges by nonregulated corporations and sources of deferred credits by regulated corporations. This is a result of different accounting treatment by both groups. Nonregulated corporations write off plant shutdowns for financial statement purposes when anticipated and for tax purposes when incurred. Regulated corporations spread losses from plant shutdowns over future years for financial reporting (unless the loss is not recoverable from its customers through increased rates) while deducting the loss for tax purposes in the year incurred.

The most dramatic change in relative and absolute occurrence of a timing difference from 1977 to 1982 was capitalized interest. This item appears as a deferred credit in Table 4.5 seven times in 1977 (all nonregulated companies), and 26 times in 1982 (all nonregulated companies). This increase is likely the result of Financial Accounting Statement 34, which first became effective for years beginning after December 15, 1979.

TABLE 4.5 *The Ten Most Frequently Mentioned Sources of Timing Differences: Deferred Credits*

| Timing Differences | Ranking in 1982: All Companies | Ranking in 1982: Nonregulated | Ranking in 1982: Regulated | Ranking in 1977: All Companies | Ranking in 1977: Nonregulated | Ranking in 1977: Regulated |
|---|---|---|---|---|---|---|
| Depreciation and amortization | 1[194] | 1[137] | 1[57] | 1[181] | 1[127] | 1[54] |
| Intangible drilling costs | 2[37] | 4[23] | 2[14] | 2[33] | 2[20] | 2[13] |
| Pensions | 3[28] | 5[22] | 8[6] | 3[22] | 3[18] | 7[4] |
| Capitalized interest | 4[26] | 2[26] | | | 10[7] | |
| Installment sales | 5[24] | 3[24] | | 7[15] | 6[15] | |
| Investment tax credit* | 6[23] | 10[12] | 4[11] | 4[20] | 8[8] | 3[12] |
| DISC | 7[20] | 6[20] | | 6[18] | 3[18] | |
| Unremitted equity method earnings | 8[16] | 7[16] | | 5[19] | 3[18] | |
| Leases | 9[13] | 8[13] | | | 10[7] | |
| Long-term contracts | 9[13] | 8[13] | | | | |
| Inventory valuations | | 10[12] | | 8[14] | 7[14] | |
| Warranty and repair expenses | | | 3[12] | 9[10] | | 4[10] |
| Purchased gas adjustment | | | 4[11] | 9[10] | | 5[9] |
| Plant shutdowns | | | 6[9] | | | 7[4] |
| Allowance for borrowed funds | | | 7[7] | | | 6[5] |
| Property tax | | | 8[6] | | | 7[4] |
| Cost of removal | | | 10[5] | | | 7[4] |
| Bad debt allowances | | | | | 8[8] | |
| Gain on debt retirement | | | | | | 7[4] |

[ ] Denotes the number of corporations reporting this timing difference in their top 5 timing differences.

See Table B.3 in Appendix B for more details.

* If this represents unamortized ITC amounts, which is likely, this is not really a timing difference because the ITC is neither a source of timing nor a permanent difference (as explained in Chapter 1).

## Major Sources of Timing Differences Based on Average Size

The rankings of the ten largest deferred charge accounts and deferred credit accounts are provided in Tables 4.6 and 4.7, respectively. As in previous tables, the information is provided for the years 1977 and 1982 and is delineated by regulatory status. The actual dollar amounts of the average balance in each of the separate timing difference accounts are contained in Table B.4 of Appendix B.

The actual account balances of some of the deferred credit accounts may be understated. The official literature [APB Opinion No. 11, Paragraph 48] requires the reduction in net deferred credits to the extent that they would reverse (on an item-by-item basis) within the carryforward period of a NOL (but not in excess of the tax effect of the NOL) if there is not "assurance beyond any reasonable doubt" that the NOL will be used. Most corporations accomplish this by reducing deferred credit balances instead of establishing deferred charge accounts for the tax effect of the NOL carryforward.[2] This would preclude a deferred charge balance for NOL carryforwards and may eliminate some or all deferred tax credit balances. Because the deferred charges and credits are usually netted (if both are either current or noncurrent) in the balance sheet, either technique may result in the same balance sheet presentation.

It should also be noted that if there are NOL deferred charge accounts there will often be ITC deferred charge accounts. These again result from the separate account technique for achieving a reduction in the deferred tax credits for the tax effects of the carryforward tax attributes (by recording the ITC carryforward as a deferred charge and netting it against deferred credits). There are 7 such deferred charge accounts for ITCs in 1982, compared to 9 NOL deferred charges. In average size rankings, these accounts were ninth and second, respectively. In 1977, a deferred charge for NOLs and ITCs only appeared in the

---

[2]See Table B.5 in Appendix B where 9 companies in 1982 have shown NOLs as deferred charges. It should be noted that the NOL deferred charge is not really a timing difference; it is really the effect of a permanent difference as explained in Chapter 1.

manufacturing group (SIC group 4). The ITCs exceeded the tax effect of the NOLs in number of companies (7 to 3, respectively) and in average size (second to seventh, respectively, see Table B.5 in Appendix B). It should be realized that all of the NOL deductions must be taken before any ITCs can be used in a carryforward year. This would not be true however, if the NOLs and ITCs were in different corporations that were filing separate rather than consolidated tax returns. The impact of the change in carryforwards for NOLs and ITCs from 7 years to 15 years may have also increased the amount of deferred charge accounts for these items in 1982. This change arose in the Economic Recovery Tax Act (ERTA) enacted in 1981 but with retroactive tax effects back to 1976. This would not affect financial reporting in 1977 but it could have significant effects in 1982 financial reporting.

*The Largest Deferred Charges* Table 4.6 lists the ten largest deferred charge accounts by average size. The actual average balances are provided in Table B.5 of Appendix B. As was the case in the frequency tabulation in Table 4.4 of this chapter, the top ten largest deferred charge accounts are primarily from the nonregulated corporations.

The largest deferred charge account for 1982 was inventory valuations. This item had been ranked sixth in 1977. The jump in its ranking can be attributed to one company which had a very large adjustment to this account in 1982. The second ranked account in 1982, net operating losses, moved from the 7th position in 1977. The third ranked account, nuclear fuel storage, also had a significant ranking change in 1982 compared to 1977. In 1977, this account was not among the top ten accounts on an "all-companies" ranking, although it was the second largest item among regulated respondents.

One-half of the top ten accounts listed in Table 4.4 for 1982 deferred charges also made the top ten average size list in Table 4.6 (inventory valuations, state tax deferrals, warranty and repair expenses, depreciation, and net operating loss). The most frequently mentioned deferred charge, deferred compensation, did not make the overall average size list. Accounts that were rarely mentioned but had large average account balances included intercompany profit, revenue agents review adjustments, cost of removal, and coupon redemptions.

TABLE 4.6 *The Ten Largest (by Average Size) Deferred Tax Charges*

| | Ranking in 1982 | | | Ranking in 1977 | | |
|---|---|---|---|---|---|---|
| Timing Differences | All Companies | Nonregulated | Regulated | All Companies | Nonregulated | Regulated |
| Inventory valuations | 1[16] | 1[16] | | 6[18] | 6[18] | |
| Net operating losses | 2[9] | 2[8] | 1[1] | 7[3] | 7[3] | |
| Nuclear fuel storage | 3[8] | | 2[8] | | | 2[3] |
| Intercompany profit | 4[6] | 3[6] | | 4[6] | 4[6] | |
| Revenue agents review adjustments | 5[2] | 4[2] | | 1[3] | 1[3] | |
| Cost of removal | 6[1] | | 3[1] | | | |
| Warranty and repair expenses | 7[12] | 5[11] | 6[1] | 5[18] | 5[17] | 4[1] |
| State tax deferrals | 8[13] | 6[13] | | 8[13] | 8[13] | |
| Depreciation and amortization | 9[9] | 7[9] | | 3[7] | 3[6] | 5[1] |
| Coupon redemption | 10[2] | 8[2] | | | | |
| Investment tax credit | | 9[6] | 5[1] | 2[7] | 2[7] | |
| Plant shutdowns | | 10[13] | 4[1] | | | |
| Deferred compensation | | | 7[2] | | | 1[2] |
| Foreign currency translation | | | | 9[3] | 9[3] | |
| Vacation accruals | | | | 10[5] | 10[5] | |
| Gain on debt retirement | | | | | | 3[1] |

[ ] Denotes the number of corporations reporting this timing difference in their top 5 timing differences.

See Tables B.4 and B.5 in Appendix B for further details.

***The Largest Deferred Credits*** Table 4.7 lists the ten largest deferred credit accounts by average size. Again, the actual average balances are provided in Table B.5 of Appendix B.

The largest deferred credit account for 1982 was intangible drilling costs with an average balance of $285.1 million.[3] Depreciation was a close second with an average balance of $247.4 million.[4] These two accounts were also one and two (in reverse order) in the Table 4.5 frequency tabulation, indicating that these accounts are a large component of the deferred tax balance of many companies. It can be seen more clearly in Table B.5 of Appendix B that the intangible drilling costs account balance was much larger among nonregulated companies than regulated companies. Depreciation, on the other hand, was almost three times larger among regulated companies than among nonregulated companies.

The biggest change in rankings for an account occurred in long-term contracts. This account was "unranked" among all companies in 1977, but was ranked fourth overall in 1982. The average account balance increased from $13.3 million for 7 companies in 1977 to $81.9 million for 13 companies in 1982.

---

[3]From Table B.5:
($403,890,000 x 23 + $89,946,000 x 14) /37 = $285.1 million.

[4]From Table B.5:
($159,930,000 x 137 + $457,770,000 x 57) /194= $247.4 million.

TABLE 4.7 *The Ten Largest (by Average Size) Deferred Tax Credits*

| Timing Differences | Ranking in 1982: All Companies | Ranking in 1982: Nonregulated | Ranking in 1982: Regulated | Ranking in 1977: All Companies | Ranking in 1977: Nonregulated | Ranking in 1977: Regulated |
|---|---|---|---|---|---|---|
| Intangible drilling costs | 1[37] | 1[23] | 4[14] | 2[33] | 2[20] | 5[13] |
| Depreciation and | 2[194] | 3[137] | 1[57] | 1[179] | 3[127] | 1[54] |
| amortization | | | | | | 2[3] |
| Vacation accruals | 3[4] | | 2[2] | 4[4] | 9[7] | |
| Long-term contracts | 4[13] | 4[13] | | | 10[8] | 3[12] |
| Investment tax credit | 5[23] | | 3[11] | 7[20] | 1[1] | |
| Plant shutdowns | 6[10] | | 5[9] | 3[1] | 8[1] | 8[9] |
| Purchased gas adjustment | 7[12] | 2[1] | 6[11] | | 4[15] | |
| Installment sales | 8[24] | 5[24] | | 5[15] | 5[7] | |
| Capitalized interest | 9[28] | 6[26] | | 9[10] | 6[7] | |
| Leases | 10[14] | 7[13] | | 8[7] | | |
| Safe harbor lease | | 8[11] | | | | 10[3] |
| transactions | | | | | | |
| Unremitted equity | | 9[16] | 7[3] | | | |
| method earnings | | | | | | 4[2] |
| State tax deferrals | | 10[5] | | | | 9[5] |
| Intercompany profit | | | 8[2] | 6[2] | | 6[11] |
| Allowable for borrowed funds | | | 9[7] | | 7[5] | |
| Warranty and repair expenses | | | 10[12] | | | 7[1] |
| U.K. stock relief | | | | 10[5] | | |
| Accrual to cash method | | | | | | |

[ ] Denotes the number of corporations reporting this timing difference in their top 5 timing differences.

See Tables B.4 and B.5 in Appendix B for details.

There was more consistency between the frequency rankings of Table 4.5 and the size rankings of Table 4.7 for the deferred credits than there was for the deferred charges. Seven of the most frequently mentioned deferred credits were also among the ten largest deferred credits (depreciation, intangible drilling costs, capitalized interest, installment sales, investment credit, leases, and long-term contracts). This compares to five deferred charges that appeared on both lists. Pensions, DISC, and unremitted equity method earnings were replaced by vacation accruals, plant shutdowns, and purchased gas adjustment on the ten largest by average size listing.

Another interesting analysis that can be made from the data contained in Table B.5 of Appendix B is to compare the percentage growth (decline) in individual deferred credit accounts for both regulated and nonregulated companies from 1977 to 1982. Those accounts with changes in excess of 100 percent are listed in Table 4.8.

The nonregulated companies reported increases in excess of 100 percent for eight individual deferred credit account balances. The greatest increase occurred in long-term contracts where the average balance increased 515 percent, from $13.3 million to $81.9 million. State tax deferrals increased substantially, from an average balance of $3.1 million in 1977 to $16.1 million in 1982, a growth of 411 percent. This growth occurred despite the fact that many states did not allow corporations the benefits of ACRS on the state tax return. The two largest accounts, depreciation and intangible drilling costs, both increased in excess of 100 percent (118 percent and 250 percent, respectively). The other accounts to increase in excess of 100 percent were accrual to cash method, DISC, pensions, and unremitted equity method earnings.

The 515 percent increase in long-term contracts is not surprising. The U.S. Treasury Department released very favorable final regulations in 1976 which, for the first time, allowed manufacturers to qualify. The magnitude of the increase in this deferred item reflects the fact that many companies availed themselves of the opportunity to adopt the completed contract method and for many companies this was a very significant change. At least one company, that changed methods in 1976, received a refund of the prior three years' federal income taxes due to the generation of a large NOL carryback through this change in accounting methods.

For regulated companies, the largest reported deferred tax credit increase was 638 percent for plant shutdowns. This is a deferred tax credit item due to regulatory rules which spread the shutdown amounts over future years. For nonregulated corporations, this item results in a deferred tax charge.

TABLE 4.8 *Percentage Changes in Deferred Credit Balances, 1977 to 1982*

| Timing Difference | Nonregulated | Regulated |
|---|---|---|
| Accrual to cash method | 102% | |
| Capitalized interest | | 283% |
| Depreciation and amortization | 118% | 109% |
| DISC | 127% | |
| Intangible drilling costs | 250% | 272% |
| Investment tax credit | | 187% |
| Long-term contracts | 515% | |
| Pensions | 127% | |
| Plant shutdowns | | 638% |
| Property tax | | 237% |
| State tax deferrals | 411% | |
| Unremitted equity method earnings | 123% | 311% |
| Purchased gas adjustment | | 334% |
| Allowance for borrowed funds | | 209% |

Note: Only those accounts with changes in excess of 100% are listed. To be considered, an account had to be listed by a minimum of three companies in both 1977 and 1982.

## Estimates of Growth in Deferred Tax Accounts

Responses to the final part of Question 3 indicate that there are only three deferred tax credit items impacting both nonregulated and regulated corporations with increases from 1977 to 1982 of over 100 percent with at least 3 observations in each year. These items are depreciation, intangible drilling costs, and unremitted equity method earnings (see Table 4.8). Only the first two of these items are really substantial in terms of numbers of observations. The projections of change for these two items from 1982 to 1987 show conservatism.

Reviewing only the depreciation deferred credits (not netted with deferred charges) that project increases (not netted with those that projected decreases), there is an estimated increase of only 85 percent from 1982 to 1987 for all usable responses in the sample. For nonregulated respondents, the average increase was 78 percent and 103 percent for regulated respondents. Even though ACRS would impact the entire period from 1982 through 1987 (assuming no tax law changes), these estimates are less than the 1977 to 1982 history of 118 percent and 109 percent, respectively. (See Table 4.8.) Given the significantly increased depreciation under ACRS rules, it cannot be determined from this data whether this change is due to projected changes in depreciable asset acquisitions, lack of knowledge concerning ACRS, movement of facilities overseas, or even other possibilities not readily seen. In an analysis of these results, consideration would have to be given to the severe recession that existed during and preceding the period in which the questionnaires were completed.

Even greater conservatism is seen in regard to intangible drilling and development costs. (This may imply that ACRS was fully considered in the depreciation estimates.) The average increase from 1982 to 1987 for all respondents was 80 percent. The percentage increase from 1982 to 1987 for nonregulated corporations was 65 percent, and 108 percent for regulated corporations. As seen in Table 4.8, these percentages from 1977 to 1982 for nonregulated and regulated corporations were 250 and 272 percent, respectively. Again, the data does not supply rationale to explain these differences.

## Deferred Tax Accounts as a Percentage of Total Assets and Owners' Equity

Previous sections of this chapter discussed the growth of the deferred tax accounts from 1977 to 1982 in absolute dollar terms. Another way in which to measure the growth of these accounts is to compare their growth over this five-year period as a percentage of other balance sheet accounts, in particular total assets and owners' equity. This analysis is presented in Table 4.9 for both net deferred charges and net deferred credits. Consistent with the previous format, the analysis is presented by regulatory status, with more detailed analysis reserved for Table B.6 of Appendix B.

As Table 4.9 shows, there has been a more stable growth trend for deferred credits as a percentage of total assets and owners' equity than for deferred charges. As a percentage of owners' equity, the deferred credit accounts have increased from 12.0 percent in 1977 to 16.8 percent in 1982, a 40 percent increase. In every year except 1981, the percentage has increased. As a percentage of total assets, the deferred credit accounts increased from 4.7 percent in 1977 to 6.2 percent in 1982, a 32 percent increase.

When the deferred credit analysis is delineated by regulatory status, it is apparent that the deferred credit accounts comprise a much higher proportion of the right side of the balance sheet for the regulated companies than for the nonregulated companies. For 1982, the deferred credit accounts averaged 24.5 percent of owners' equity for the regulated companies and 14.0 percent for the nonregulated companies. The growth rate for the two groups from 1977 through 1982 was comparable, however, averaging 41.4 percent for the nonregulated companies and 42.4 percent for the regulated companies. As one would expect, the comparative ratios for total assets paralleled the ratios for owners' equity. The total asset ratio was higher for the regulated companies (8.9 percent to 5.2 percent in 1982), but the growth trends for the six-year period were comparable (36.9 percent for regulated companies, 30.0 percent for nonregulated companies).

TABLE 4.9 *Deferred Tax Accounts as an Annual Percentage of Total Assets and Owners' Equity, 1977 to 1982*

Deferred Charges

| Year | Percentage of Owners' Equity: All Companies | Percentage of Owners' Equity: Nonregulated | Percentage of Owners' Equity: Regulated | Percentage of Total Assets: All Companies | Percentage of Total Assets: Nonregulated | Percentage of Total Assets: Regulated |
|---|---|---|---|---|---|---|
| 1977 | 7.0 | 6.6 | 20.0 | 1.5 | 1.3 | 7.0 |
| 1978 | 4.9 | 4.7 | 8.0 | 1.6 | 1.4 | 3.0 |
| 1979 | 4.0 | 3.4 | 13.0 | 1.4 | 1.3 | 4.5 |
| 1980 | 5.4 | 4.8 | 11.3 | 1.7 | 1.5 | 4.0 |
| 1981 | 11.0 | 10.8 | 12.3 | 1.8 | 1.6 | 4.0 |
| 1982 | 7.8 | 7.5 | 9.5 | 2.0 | 1.8 | 3.0 |

Deferred Credits

| Year | Percentage of Owners' Equity: All Companies | Percentage of Owners' Equity: Nonregulated | Percentage of Owners' Equity: Regulated | Percentage of Total Assets: All Companies | Percentage of Total Assets: Nonregulated | Percentage of Total Assets: Regulated |
|---|---|---|---|---|---|---|
| 1977 | 12.0 | 9.9 | 17.2 | 4.7 | 4.0 | 6.5 |
| 1978 | 13.1 | 11.0 | 18.6 | 5.0 | 4.2 | 7.1 |
| 1979 | 13.9 | 11.6 | 19.8 | 5.2 | 4.3 | 7.4 |
| 1980 | 16.1 | 14.0 | 21.7 | 5.4 | 4.4 | 7.9 |
| 1981 | 15.9 | 13.2 | 22.9 | 5.9 | 4.9 | 8.4 |
| 1982 | 16.8 | 14.0 | 24.5 | 6.2 | 5.2 | 8.9 |

Note: Net deferred credits exclude unamortized ITC.

See Table B.6 in Appendix B for more detail.

The growth in the ratios for deferred charges was erratic and less significant than the increases in the ratios for deferred credits, even though for this six-year period an increase is reflected. As a percentage of owners' equity for all corporations, the deferred charge accounts increased from an average of 7 percent in 1977 to an average of 7.8 percent in 1982, an increase of 11.4 percent. In three of the six years, however, the ratio actually declined. The deferred charge ratio to total assets increased from 1.5 to 2.0 percent, a growth of 33.3 percent. In this case, the growth was more stable, with increases occurring in five of the six years.

A comparison of deferred charge ratios by regulatory status is less meaningful than the deferred credit comparison because of the small number of regulated companies with a net deferred charge position (one to four companies each year from 1977-1982). The nonregulated companies parallel the aggregate experience, while the regulated companies exhibit highly fluctuating ratios.

## Current Interperiod Income Tax Allocation Practices

### Accounting for Timing Differences

The remainder of this chapter is devoted to an analysis of the current income tax allocation practices of the responding companies. The data analyzed were received in responses to Questions 5 through 19 of the questionnaire. The detail for these responses is in Tables B.7 and B.8 of Appendix B.

The respondents were first asked to describe their current method of income tax allocation for the tax effects of material timing differences (Question 5). The usable responses by regulatory status are presented below.

| Method | Percentage Using: All Companies | Nonregulated | Regulated |
|---|---|---|---|
| Comprehensive | 86.3 | 91.9 | 67.8 |
| Partial | 4.7 | 4.6 | 5.1 |
| Taxes currently payable | 2.3 | 3.0 | 0.0 |
| Combination of methods | 6.6 | 0.5 | 27.1 |

Despite the mandate of APB 11 to use the comprehensive method, not all of the respondents are adhering to that pronouncement. A high percentage of regulated companies that identified themselves as using a combination of methods stated that they were required by their regulatory commission to use a flow-through method for rate-making purposes. As a result, many of these companies were applying the comprehensive method to the nonregulated segments of their company and flow-through (taxes currently payable) to the regulated segments.

In conjunction with the question relating to overall income tax allocation methods, the respondents were asked to identify their current method of measuring the change in a timing difference (Question 6). The usable responses were as follows:

| Method | Percentage Using: All Companies | Nonregulated | Regulated |
|---|---|---|---|
| Gross change | 9.8 | 6.6 | 20.7 |
| Net change | 57.1 | 65.8 | 27.6 |
| Specific identification | 15.4 | 14.3 | 19.0 |
| Combination of methods | 17.7 | 13.3 | 32.7 |

It is interesting to note that the gross change method is cited least in this list of most frequently used methods, even though it is theoretically the most compatible with comprehensive allocation and the deferral method. The most widely used method overall (and for the nonregulated companies) is the net change method, which is theoretically most compatible with the liability method. Ease of computation is undoubtedly a contributing factor in the preference for the net change method.

For those companies using a combination of methods, a follow-up question was asked to determine which method was primary and which was secondary (Question 7). Of the 26 nonregulated companies using a combination of methods, twenty-two (84.6 percent) identified the net change method as the primary method, three (11.5 percent) identified the gross change method, and one (3.9 percent) identified the specific identification method. The specific identification method was selected as the secondary method 21 times, the gross change method was selected 6 times, and the net change method was selected twice.

The regulated companies were evenly divided between the gross and net change methods as being primary (each was selected by 42 percent of those companies using a combination of methods). Once again, specific identification was the most popular secondary method (9 responses), followed by the gross change method (6 responses), and the net change method (4 responses).

Question 8 asked the companies to identify their current method of accounting for the tax effects of changes in timing differences. A summary of their responses follows.

| | Percentage Using | | |
|---|---|---|---|
| Method | All Companies | Nonregulated | Regulated |
| Deferred | 85.5 | 86.3 | 83.1 |
| Liability | 9.0 | 11.2 | 1.7 |
| Net-of-tax | 1.2 | 1.5 | 0.0 |
| Combination of methods | 4.3 | 1.0 | 15.2 |

The GAAP required deferred method is the predominant choice of both groups of companies, although some companies (primarily nonregulated companies) are using the liability method. The percentage of regulated companies using the deferred method is actually closer to 97 percent because eight of the nine regulated companies that use a combination of methods classified the deferred method as their primary method in Question 9. The most prevalent secondary method used by the regulated companies was the net-of-tax method. Eighty-six percent of the regulated companies using a secondary method use the net-of-tax method. Several of the regulated companies stated that net-of-tax was used for the debt component of allowance for funds used during construction.

Closely related to the choice of an allocation method is the choice of a balance sheet classification of the deferred tax accounts that result from the allocation process. Much of the current controversy over deferred tax accounting revolves around the balance sheet nature of the deferred tax accounts, in particular, whether deferred tax credit accounts meet the definition of "liabilities." Questions 10 and 11 of the questionnaire asked for the company's balance sheet presentation of deferred tax credit accounts and deferred tax debit accounts. Their responses are summarized below.

Deferred Tax Credit Accounts

| | Percentage Using | | |
|---|---|---|---|
| Classification | All Companies | Nonregulated | Regulated |
| Liabilities | 58.3 | 68.0 | 25.9 |
| Contra-assets | 2.0 | 1.6 | 3.4 |
| Owners' equity | 0.0 | 0.0 | 0.0 |
| Separate classification | 29.8 | 22.7 | 53.4 |
| Combination of above | 9.9 | 7.7 | 17.3 |

Deferred Tax Debit Accounts

| | Percentage Using | | |
|---|---|---|---|
| Classification | All Companies | Nonregulated | Regulated |
| Assets | 48.7 | 50.6 | 42.6 |
| Contra-liabilities | 32.5 | 33.3 | 29.6 |
| Reductions in owner's equity | 0.0 | 0.0 | 0.0 |
| Combination of above | 18.8 | 16.1 | 27.8 |

As the tables show, there is a method difference between the responses of the nonregulated and regulated companies with regard to deferred tax credit account classification. Two-thirds of the nonregulated companies include the deferred tax credit accounts with other liabilities. Only one-quarter of the regulated companies classified these accounts with liabilities. Over one-half of the regulated companies segregated the deferred tax credit accounts as a separate classification on the balance sheet, compared to 22.7 percent of the nonregulated companies. Those companies using a combination of methods most often stated that they classified the current portion of deferred tax credit accounts with current liabilities and presented the noncurrent portion as a separate classification. Some of the regulated companies netted property-related deferred income taxes with plant investment.

In the classification of deferred tax debit accounts, the respondents preferred asset designation, although a rather high percentage of both groups selected contra-liability designation. Judging from accompanying comments, it appears that many of those selecting the contra-liability designation viewed deferred tax debits as offsets to deferred tax credits, resulting in a net deferred tax credit. For those companies that classify a net deferred tax credit as a liability, the netting of deferred charges against that account would be treating deferred taxes as a contra-liability. There certainly is no corresponding support to classify deferred tax credit accounts as contra-assets.

## Investment Credits

Questions 12 through 16 dealt with the accounting for, and the classification of, investment credits. This area has been particularly troublesome from a consistency standpoint, especially since the Congress prohibited the APB from mandating one particular accounting method in the Revenue Act of 1971. To compound matters, regulated companies are now virtually required to use a deferral method for the investment credit by Section 46(f) of the Internal Revenue Code. Thus, any decision by a regulatory body such as the FASB to require one method over another will need Congressional approval.

As one would expect, the regulated and nonregulated companies differed significantly in their choice of an accounting method for the investment credit. The nonregulated companies heavily favored the flow-through method (90.2 percent), while the regulated companies heavily favored the deferral and amortization method (78.6 percent). When these companies were asked to justify their choice of an accounting method (Question 14), 70.8 percent of the nonregulated companies and 56 percent of the regulated companies stated that the method was, for them, most conceptually correct. (It conforms to what they considered to be the nature of the investment credit.) The fact that opposite choices were supported with the same rationale illustrates the nature of the problem in developing a conceptual framework in the accounting for income taxes area.

A tabulation of the rationale responses of each group to Question 14 is presented below.

Rationale for Selecting ITC Method

| Rationale | Percentage Citing | |
|---|---|---|
| | Nonregulated | Regulated |
| Most conceptually correct | 70.8 | 56.1 |
| Lower cost of compliance | 8.7 | 1.8 |
| Advocated by APB opinions | 7.6 | 5.2 |
| Reduces earnings volatility | 2.6 | 1.8 |
| Other | 10.3 | 35.1 |

For those nonregulated companies citing "other" for their rationale, the most frequent reason given was to conform to their industry's practice. Regulated companies that chose "other" most often stated that they were required to use deferral for tax purposes by the Internal Revenue Code.

Respondents were also asked if they had changed methods of accounting for the investment credit and for the year of change. These changes are summarized in Table 4.10. Thirty-five of the corporations in this survey reported a change in accounting method for the ITC.

Of those 33 corporations reporting a year of change, eighteen were nonregulated companies and fifteen were regulated. Fifteen of the eighteen nonregulated companies changed to the flow-through method (83 percent), while ten of the fifteen regulated companies changed to deferral (66.7 percent). The years with the most frequent changes were 1971 and 1981 (seven changes) and 1982 (four changes). Both 1971 and 1981 are years in which major tax legislation was passed that directly affected accounting for the ITC. (A summary of the history of the ITC and some of its complexity is presented in Appendix F.)

The issue of balance sheet classification for deferred ITC balances was addressed in Question 15. The choices available and the responses of each group are presented below.

| | Percentage Classifying | | |
|---|---|---|---|
| Classification | All Companies | Nonregulated | Regulated |
| Liabilities | 15.4 | 13.0 | 22.0 |
| Contra-assets | 1.8 | 2.4 | 0.0 |
| Owners' equity | 0.4 | 0.6 | 0.0 |
| Separate classification | 18.9 | 3.0 | 64.4 |
| Not applicable | 63.6 | 81.0 | 13.6 |

The classification responses are very similar to the classification responses to the deferred tax credit balance question (Question 10). The nonregulated companies tended to classify the deferred ITC account as a liability, while the regulated companies favored separate classification.

One final ITC question was directed at those companies currently using the deferral method (Question 16). These companies were asked to describe how they chose the period over which to amortize the ITC. Sixteen of the eighteen nonregulated companies (89 percent) and 38 of the 44 regulated companies (86 percent) utilized the useful life of the related asset as the determining factor. Those companies not using the asset's useful life reported using criteria such as average useful life of all assets qualifying for the ITC or an arbitrary 20- to 30-year period.

TABLE 4.10 *Corporations Changing Accounting Methods for the ITC and the Year of Change*

| Change to | 1982 | 1981 | 1980 | 1979 | 1978 | 1977 | 1975 | 1972 | 1971 | 1964 | Total |
|---|---|---|---|---|---|---|---|---|---|---|---|
| Deferral | | | | | | | | | | | |
| Nonregulated | 0 | 0 | 0 | 1 | 0 | 1 | 1 | 0 | 0 | 0 | 3 |
| Regulated | 2 | 3 | 1 | 0 | 0 | 0 | 1 | 0 | 3 | 0 | 10 |
| Total | 2 | 3 | 1 | 1 | 0 | 1 | 2 | 0 | 3 | 0 | 13 |
| Flow-through | | | | | | | | | | | |
| Nonregulated | 2 | 3 | 0 | 1 | 2 | 1 | 1 | 0 | 1 | 3 | 15 |
| Regulated | 0 | 1 | 0 | 1 | 0 | 0 | 0 | 0 | 3 | 0 | 5 |
| Total | 2 | 4 | 0 | 2 | 2 | 1 | 1 | 0 | 4 | 3 | 20 |

See Table B.9 in Appendix B for more details.

## Tax Attribute Carryforwards

Questions 17 and 18 of the questionnaire dealt with the respondents' experiences with the tax attribute carryforwards of net operating losses (NOLs), investment credits, and foreign tax credits. These areas produce some of the most difficult problems in the income tax allocation process, and the experience of the respondents in these areas varied widely.

Question 17 asked the respondents if they had ever encountered an ITC, NOL or foreign tax credit carryforward for tax purposes, or an ITC or foreign tax credit carryforward for book purposes. As the following results indicate, many more of the respondents had experienced an attribute carryforward on their tax returns than they did on their financial statements. This may have been partially due to the NOL for which there is no corresponding carryover of book losses.

Percentage Experiencing Carryforward for Tax Purposes

| All Companies | Nonregulated | Regulated |
|---|---|---|
| 65.4 | 66.7 | 61.0 |

Percentage Experiencing Carryforward for Book Purposes

| All Companies | Nonregulated | Regulated |
|---|---|---|
| 38.5 | 37.9 | 40.4 |

Question 18 asked the respondents if they had encountered the situation where prior deferred tax credits had to be drawn down for the tax effects of tax attribute carryforwards. Since carryforwards normally exist only after exhausting all carryback opportunities, it was surprising that almost 30 percent of the respondents had experienced this aspect of interperiod tax allocation. As the table indicates, more of the nonregulated respondents experienced this drawn down situation than did regulated respondents.

Percentage Experiencing Draw Downs due to Carryforwards

| All Companies | Nonregulated | Regulated |
|---|---|---|
| 29.9 | 32.8 | 20.3 |

Finally, the respondents were asked to describe their level of agreement with the current accounting rules for recording the tax benefits of loss and tax credit carryforwards (Question 19). Slightly more than half of the nonregulated companies (51.8 percent) and not quite two-thirds (64.4 percent) of the regulated companies agreed in total with the current rules. An additional 27.5 percent of the nonregulated and 18.6 percent of the regulated agreed with the rules in most situations, bringing the agreement ratios to 79.4 percent and 83.0 percent, respectively. Only 6.2 percent and 3.4 percent, respectively, disagreed with the current rules. (The remainder did not express an opinion.)

Despite the relatively high level of agreement expressed by the respondents, this question also generated a lot of comments (56 companies attached a written comment to this question). In general, respondents supplying comments were critical of the complexity of the NOL carryforward rules, the perceived restrictiveness of the "beyond any reasonable doubt" criterion of APB 11, and the classification of the benefit realization of a loss carryforward as an extraordinary item. Selected comments received on this question will be presented in Chapter 5.

# 5 An Analysis of Preparer Opinions on Interperiod Income Tax Allocation

Questions 20 through 72 of the preparer questionnaire were intended to elicit opinions about issues for reconsideration under accounting for income taxes that have been identified by the FASB.

## Overall Satisfaction with Existing Rules

The responses to Questions 20 through 22 are presented in Tables 5.1, 5.2, and 5.3. For each of these questions, the number and percentage of responses to each satisfaction level are listed along with an overall mean (average) response by each group. In addition, a measure of consensus (the coefficient of variation[1] was computed to determine the degree of uniformity among the respondents. In all cases, the mean and coefficient of variation were computed for only those respondents expressing an opinion.

The responses indicate a relatively high degree of satisfaction with existing rules for allocating the effects of timing differences between periods and an even higher level of satisfaction with the investment credit rules. However, a somewhat lower level of satisfaction with the absence of accounting pronouncements governing the foreign tax credit is revealed. A large percentage of both groups of respondents (30 percent of the nonregulated and 75 percent of the regulated) expressed no opinion on the foreign income tax credit question.

The mean response of the nonregulated group was quite low (indicating a rather high level of satisfaction) for the question dealing with overall satisfaction with the accounting for timing differences (Question 20). It is important to note that only 26 percent of the respondents were satisfied to the point that they felt no changes were necessary. Fully 72 percent of the nonregulated group favored some form of change in the existing rules (65 percent of this group characterized the changes they advocated as being "minor"). Conversely, 66 percent of the regulated group were satisfied with the current income tax allocation rules to the extent that they felt no changes were necessary. Slightly more than one-third of this group (34 percent) favored some changes, of which 95 percent characterized the changes advocated as being "minor." The disparity in the responses of these two groups to Question 20 is reflected in the responses of these two groups to many of the questions in the questionnaire.

---

[1]The coefficient of variation can be defined in several ways. In this study, the coefficient was defined as the sample variance divided by the sample mean. The lower the coefficient, the higher the degree of consensus.

TABLE 5.1 *Question 20*

How would you describe your current level of satisfaction with the existing rules for allocating the effects of timing differences between accounting periods?

1. Very satisfied, no changes are necessary
2. Generally satisfied, but minor changes are necessary
3. Generally dissatisfied, major changes are necessary
4. Very dissatisfied, a complete revision is necessary
5. No opinion

| | Nonregulated | Regulated |
|---|---|---|
| Very Satisfied | 51 (26%) | 39 (66%) |
| Generally Satisfied | 92 (46%) | 19 (32%) |
| Generally Dissatisfied | 35 (18%) | 0 (0%) |
| Very Dissatisfied | 15 (8%) | 1 (2%) |
| No Opinion | 5 (2%) | 0 (0%) |
| Total | 198 | 59 |
| $\bar{x}$ (mean) | 2.07 | 1.37 |
| Consensus Level | Moderate | High |

TABLE 5.2 *Question 21*

How would you describe your current level of satisfaction with the existing rules for accounting for the investment tax credit, disregarding the new rules for basis reduction under the Tax Equity and Fiscal Responsibility Act of 1982?

1. Very satisfied, no changes are necessary
2. Generally satisfied, but minor changes are necessary
3. Generally dissatisfied, major changes are necessary
4. Very dissatisfied, a complete revision is necessary
5. No opinion

| | Nonregulated | Regulated |
|---|---|---|
| Very Satisfied | 126 (64%) | 46 (78%) |
| Generally Satisfied | 51 (26%) | 11 (18%) |
| Generally Dissatisfied | 11 (6%) | 1 (2%) |
| Very Dissatisfied | 3 (1%) | 1 (2%) |
| No Opinion | 7 (3%) | 0 (0%) |
| Total | 198 | 59 |
| $\bar{x}$ (mean) | 1.43 | 1.27 |
| Consensus Level | High | High |

TABLE 5.3 *Question 22*

How would you describe your current level of satisfaction with the absence of formal rules to guide accounting for the foreign income tax credit?

1. Very satisfied, no changes are necessary
2. Generally satisfied, but guidelines in certain complex situations would be desirable
3. Generally dissatisfied, this is a complex area in which rules could be helpful
4. Very dissatisfied, this area is very complex and rules are needed
5. No opinion

| | Nonregulated | Regulated |
|---|---|---|
| Very Satisfied | 45 (23%) | 5 (9%) |
| Generally Satisfied | 49 (25%) | 5 (9%) |
| Generally Dissatisfied | 30 (15%) | 4 (7%) |
| Very Dissatisfied | 14 (7%) | 0 (0%) |
| No Opinion | 59 (30%) | 43 (75%) |
| Total | 197 | 57 |
| $\bar{x}$ (mean) | 2.09 | 1.93 |
| Consensus Level | Moderate | Moderate |

## Issues Identified as Needing Reconsideration

Question 23 asked the respondents to identify those issues of accounting for income taxes that they felt were most in need of immediate reconsideration.

The issues listed for them to consider were patterned after the topics identified by the FASB in its drafts leading to the current discussion memorandum. The list consisted of the following:

1. The allocation requirement itself
2. The comprehensive allocation concept
3. The deferred method requirement for tax allocation
4. The appropriate response to changes in tax rates
5. The proscription against discounting deferred tax accounts
6. The accounting for the expected future benefits of net operating loss carryforwards
7. The accounting for tax credits
8. Others (please list)
9. None of the above

An analysis of the responses to this question is contained in Tables 5.4, 5.5, and 5.6.

Upon inspection of the data contained in Table 5.4, it is apparent that every issue on the list was identified by respondents in both groups as needing reconsideration. However, no one issue was a consensus choice for reconsideration. The tax rates issue was the most frequently selected issue, yet it only received recognition from 35 percent of the nonregulated group and 37 percent of the regulated group. It is also obvious that the existing accounting for income taxes rules troubled more of the nonregulated respondents than the regulated respondents. Only 13 percent of the nonregulated respondents felt that none of the issues needed reconsideration whereas 42 percent of the regulated group chose "none of the above." This is consistent with the analysis of the level of overall satisfaction question presented in the previous section (Question 20). The nonregulated group was also distinguished from the regulated group in the number of multiple issues identified as needing reconsideration.

TABLE 5.4 *Issues Identified as Needing Reconsideration (Question 23)*

| Issue | Nonregulated | Regulated | Total |
|---|---|---|---|
| Allocation Requirement | 40 (20%) | 2 (3%) | 42 |
| Comprehensive Allocation | 46 (23%) | 4 (7%) | 50 |
| Deferred Method | 45 (23%) | 6 (10%) | 51 |
| Tax Rate Changes | 70 (35%) | 22 (37%) | 92 |
| Discounting Deferred Taxes | 26 (13%) | 5 (8%) | 31 |
| NOL Carryforward Tax Benefits | 52 (26%) | 6 (10%) | 58 |
| Tax Credits | 33 (17%) | 7 (12%) | 40 |
| Others | 16 (8%) | 5 (8%) | 21 |
| None of the Above | 25 (13%) | 25 (42%) | 50 |

## An Analysis of Responses to Individual Issues

Questions 24 through 72 of the questionnaire were subdivided by the specific issues identified in Question 23 plus some additional questions relating to acquisitions and consolidations. For each of the two groups of respondents, the following descriptive statistics were computed for each question:

$\bar{x}$: the mean (average) response of those who expressed an opinion (i.e., those circling "no opinion" were excluded)

% Agree: the percentage of those who supported a specific statement (both "in all cases" and "in general") out of those who expressed an opinion

% Opinion: the percentage of respondents who expressed an opinion on this question

Consensus: the coefficient of variation (variance/mean) as a measure of group consensus; defined for this study as "high" (0-.33), "moderate" (.34-.67), and "low" (above .67)

X 2: chi-square (a measure of comparability of the responses of the two groups)

signif: the level of significance at which the hypothesis, that the two groups are similar with respect to their response, may be rejected

Each statement provided for written comments to clarify a respondent's position. Representative comments from each question are included in Appendix A.

## The Allocation Requirement

The issue of whether to apply interperiod tax allocation to at least some timing differences or to base the current period expense on taxes currently payable has rightly been labelled the "threshold" issue in any reconsideration of accounting for income taxes.[2] If allocation is deemed to no longer be appropriate, each of the other income tax related issues becomes irrelevant.

The arguments for and against interperiod tax allocation have been well documented.[3] Some have contended the issue revolves around whether the income tax meets the definition of an expense and as such, should be matched against current period revenues. Others, however, argue that interperiod allocation does not hinge on whether the income tax meets the financial accounting definition of an expense.[4]

The questions related to the allocation issue primarily dealt with the perceived relationship between financial accounting net income and taxable income. The questions and a statistical summary of the responses are contained in Table 5.6.

---

[2]Financial Accounting Standards Board, Accounting for Income Taxes Discussion Memorandum, August 29, 1983, para. 36 (hereafter referred to as FASB).

[3]Dennis R. Beresford, Lawrence C. Best, Paul W. Craig, and Joseph V. Weber, Accounting for Income Taxes: A Review of Alternatives (Stamford: Financial Accounting Standards Board, 1983), pp. 19-27 (hereafter referred to as Beresford, et. al.).

[4]James E. Wheeler and Williard H. Galliart, An Approval of Interperiod Income Tax Allocation (New York: Financial Executives Research Foundation, 1974), pp. 62-63.

Looking at Table 5.6, it is apparent that a large majority of both groups of respondents is still in favor of some form of interperiod tax allocation. Eighty-three percent of the nonregulated respondents and 98 percent of the regulated respondents felt that interperiod income tax allocation should still be required (Question 24). The degree of consensus was higher among the regulated respondents than it was among the nonregulated respondents, primarily because of the tendency of the nonregulated respondents to qualify their responses while the regulated respondents were unequivocal in theirs. Many of the qualifying comments from the nonregulated companies dealt with their preference for an allocation method (such as partial allocation), stating that interperiod tax allocation should be restricted rather than abolished. This issue is dealt with in the next section.

The question as to whether the income tax meets the definition of an expense was answered affirmably by both groups of respondents (Question 26). When subsequently asked to classify the income tax (Question 76), 81 percent of the nonregulated respondents and 95 percent of the regulated respondents selected the "expense" category. The second choice was a "cost of doing business other than an expense or loss" (11 percent and 3 percent), followed by "a distribution of earnings" (7 percent and 0 percent) and "an anomalous item" (1 percent and 2 percent). None of the respondents classified the income tax as a "loss." On a closely related issue, 85 percent of the nonregulated respondents and 100 percent of the regulated respondents felt that the federal income tax was still a tax on "income" (Question 28).

Despite the conceptual appropriateness of interperiod income tax allocation, the usefulness of such an accounting measure must also be evaluated. In particular, the information provided should be relevant ("capable of making a difference in a decision by helping users to form predictions about the outcomes of past, present and future events or to confirm or correct expectations"[5]), and the benefit of providing such information should exceed the cost to provide

---

[5]FASB Concepts Statement No. 2, Qualitative Characteristics of Accounting Information (Stamford, Conn.: FASB, 1980), p. 21.

it. When asked if they felt that the relevancy of the information provided by the current allocation rules had diminished in recent years, 32 percent of the non regulated companies but only 2 percent of the regulated companies agreed that it had (Question 25). Almost the same percentage of each group felt that the cost of presenting the allocation information exceeded the benefit derived by users of the financial statements (Question 27). Judging from the comments to this question it would appear that either the cost of compliance with the allocation rules varies widely from company to company or the perception of benefits differ.

The questions dealing with the allocation issue generated many comments. Selected representative comments for each question are presented in Appendix A.

## The Comprehensive Allocation Concept

If it is agreed that some form of interperiod allocation is appropriate (which is the case in this survey), the next issue is to determine the extent to which the allocation should be applied to transactions resulting in timing differences. The choice is to provide allocation for all timing differences (comprehensive allocation) or for selected timing differences based on their probability of realization over some time horizon (partial allocation). Those who endorse partial allocation face the additional considerations of either deciding on guidelines to determine the transactions (and time horizon) that will be subject to the allocation process or letting individual company managements make such a decision.

TABLE 5.5 *The Allocation Requirement*

| | Nonregulated | | | | Regulated | | | | | |
|---|---|---|---|---|---|---|---|---|---|---|
| Question | $\bar{x}$ | % Agree | % Opinion | Consensus | $\bar{x}$ | % Agree | % Opinion | Consensus | X 2 | Signif. |
| 24 | 1.69 | 83 | 98 | Moderate | 1.14 | 98 | 100 | High | 9.39 | .01 |
| 25 | 3.03 | 32 | 89 | Moderate | 3.86 | 2 | 97 | High | 22.03 | .001 |
| 26 | 1.80 | 77 | 98 | Low | 1.12 | 98 | 100 | High | 18.17 | .001 |
| 27 | 3.16 | 26 | 93 | Moderate | 3.86 | 2 | 98 | High | 14.8 | .01 |
| 28 | 3.48 | 15 | 95 | High | 3.95 | 0 | 100 | High | 12.6 | .01 |

24. Differences between taxable income and pretax accounting net income, after adjustment for permanent differences, are due to the timing of income and expense recognition, and, therefore, interperiod income tax allocation should be required.

25. Recent tax law changes (in particular, the Economic Recovery Tax Act of 1981) have so distorted the relationship between taxable income and pretax accounting net income that the relevancy of the information produced by comprehensive allocation has diminished.

26. The federal income tax meets the definition of an expense, and, therefore, the matching process requires that it be computed based on pretax book income (after the recognition of permanent differences) regardless of the period in which it can be expected to result in a cash outflow.

27. The cost of measuring and presenting the income tax allocation exceeds the benefit derived by users of the financial statements.

28. The federal income tax is so distorted by economic incentive provisions, social provisions, etc., that it should not be considered a tax on income.

The arguments for and against comprehensive allocation are numerous.[6] A primary concern appears to be over the growing balances in the deferred tax balance sheet accounts of a majority of companies. This is largely due to recurring timing difference accounts such as depreciation (see Chapter IV). A serious point of contention between those who favor one allocation method over another involves the question of whether the allocation process should focus on reversals of individual transactions within an account or on aggregate reversal of an account balance. Disagreement on this point is very evident in the responses to the questions relating to the issue of comprehensive allocation.

The questions relating to the comprehensive allocation issue (Questions 29 through 36) and the corresponding statistical summary are presented in Table 5.6. As was the case with respect to the allocation issue, the nonregulated and regulated groups were significantly different in their responses and their degrees of consensus. This is not surprising in that regulated respondents would be adversely impacted in their rate-making process if comprehensive allocation is eroded.

The aversion of the regulated group to any change in the current method of allocation is evident in their responses to Questions 29, 32, and 33. The regulated group unanimously agreed that comprehensive allocation was preferable to partial allocation (Question 29). Only a small percentage (7 percent) were even willing to allow the partial allocation method as an acceptable alternative to comprehensive (Question 32). The nonregulated group was more divided on the preferability of the comprehensive method. Although 72 percent of the nonregulated group agreed that comprehensive was preferable to partial, only 57 percent agreed unequivocally (Question 29). This compares to an unequivocal agreement by 97 percent of the regulated respondents. Of the 43 percent of the nonregulated respondents who do not support comprehensive allocation in all cases, almost one-half (44 percent) would prefer to replace comprehensive allocation with partial allocation. Less than 20 percent of this group voted to preclude the comprehensive method as an alternative method (Question 33).

---

[6]Beresford, _et. al_., pp. 35-43.

The question that elicited the greatest disparity between the responses of the two groups dealt with whether the comprehensive method resulted in the creation of deferred tax accounts in which turnaround was postponed indefinitely (Question 30). Seventy-six percent of the nonregulated respondents agreed that it did, while only 12 percent of the regulated group agreed with this statement. The source of the inconsistent responses appears to be in each group's interpretation of the statement. Written comments (presented in Appendix A) indicated that nonregulated respondents were looking at reversal (net changes of similar timing differences within the same group) while regulated respondents emphasized turnaround (net change of an individual timing difference).

This difference in perspective is also evident in the responses of these two groups to a subsequent question that asked if there was a significant conceptual difference between the roll over concept of a timing difference such as from depreciation and the indefinite reversal concept for reinvestment of a subsidiary's undistributed earnings (Question 75). One-half of the nonregulated respondents felt there was no significant conceptual difference between the two, whereas 89 percent of the regulated respondents felt there was a significant conceptual difference. Those who felt there was a significant difference stressed that the degree of management control over the two types of transactions was very different. This conflict over whether to focus on individual timing differences or changes in group account balances could be the most controversial and difficult issue to resolve if partial allocation is adopted.[7]

On the issue of whether the indefinite reversal criteria of APB Opinion 23 should also be applied to undistributed earnings of investees (Question 34), more than three-quarters (76 percent) of the nonregulated respondents agreed that the current rule was too restrictive. The consensus on this question was low because most respondents qualified their answers, stating that it was a function of the degree of control of the investor over the investee in each case. The regulated respondents were evenly divided over whether to extend APB Opinion 23 to investees (48 percent said yes).

---

[7]Beresford, <u>et. al.</u>, p. 33.

There was little support for including deferred tax credits and unamortized ITCs in the numerator of debt to equity ratios (Question 35). Those who did support the classification of some deferred accounts as liabilities generally agreed that unamortized ITCs should be excluded from such classification.

Finally, on the question as to whether a switch to partial allocation would likely result in higher reported net incomes (Question 36), most of the respondents in both groups (86 percent of the nonregulated and 91 percent of the regulated) agreed that it would. Several of the rate-regulated respondents felt that a switch to partial would lower net income because of the negative effect such a switch would have on rates charged to their customers.

As one might expect on such a controversial issue, this set of questions generated numerous comments. Selected representative comments for each question are presented in the Appendix A.

TABLE 5.6 *The Comprehensive Allocation Requirement*

| | Nonregulated | | | | Regulated | | | | | |
|---|---|---|---|---|---|---|---|---|---|---|
| Question | $\bar{x}$ | % Agree | % Opinion | Consensus | $\bar{x}$ | % Agree | % Opinion | Consensus | X 2 | Signif. |
| 29 | 1.90 | 72 | 95 | Low | 1.03 | 100 | 98 | High | 22.4 | .001 |
| 30 | 1.87 | 76 | 96 | Low | 3.61 | 12 | 100 | High | 79.6 | .001 |
| 31 | 2.88 | 37 | 94 | Moderate | 3.86 | 8 | 100 | High | 27.43 | .001 |
| 32 | 2.90 | 38 | 83 | Moderate | 3.73 | 7 | 95 | High | 22.6 | .001 |
| 33 | 3.41 | 19 | 83 | Moderate | 3.95 | 2 | 97 | High | 14.9 | .001 |
| 34 | 1.91 | 76 | 61 | Low | 2.52 | 48 | 49 | Low | 8.0 | .02 |
| 35 | 3.10 | 31 | 88 | Moderate | 3.53 | 16 | 93 | High | 5.49 | .10 |
| 36 | 1.64 | 86 | 75 | Moderate | 1.47 | 91 | 90 | Moderate | 5.5 | .10 |

29. The comprehensive allocation approach results in a more accurate determination of the income tax provision than does the partial allocation approach, and, therefore, is the preferred method of income tax allocation.

30. The use of comprehensive allocation often results in the creation of deferred tax credit (or debit) accounts that represent liabilities (or assets), the payment (or recovery) of which is, for all intents and purposes, postponed indefinitely.

31. The nature of the income tax provision is sufficiently different from the nature of accounting operating expenses that cash flow considerations should take precedence over the matching criterion when payment of the tax liability (a net decrease in the deferred tax credit account) or recovery of the tax asset (a net decrease in the deferred tax charge account) cannot be reasonably foreseen in a relatively short period of time.

32. The partial allocation method should be allowable as an acceptable alternative to the comprehensive allocation method.

33. The partial allocation method should replace the comprehensive allocation method as the only acceptable accounting method.

34. The indefinite reversal criteria (of APB Opinion 23) should be equally available to be applied to the undistributed earnings of investees (generally 20% to 50% owned) as well as subsidiaries (51% to 100% owned).

35. Deferred tax credits and unamortized ITCs should be considered as liabilities in debt to equity computations.

36. A change from comprehensive to partial allocation would likely result in higher reported net incomes.

## The Deferred Method Requirement

A second consideration that must be addressed if interperiod tax allocation is retained is the appropriate method for measuring and classifying the income statement and balance sheet effects of accounting for timing differences. The deferred method, which is prescribed by APB Opinion No. 11, attempts to spread the tax effects of an originating timing difference over the accounting periods during which the difference reverses. This method, which was a compromise choice by the APB members in 1969 because it was the "most useful and practical approach" at that time, has come under renewed attack because of the assertion in FASB Concepts Statement 3 (paragraph 164) that the balance sheet accounts resulting from the deferred method do not meet the definitions of assets and liabilities. As a result, the FASB has reopened the discussion as to whether the liability or net-of-tax methods, or some combination of methods, should replace the deferred method.

The arguments in favor of retaining the deferred method or for adopting the liability and/or net-of-tax methods have not evolved beyond those advanced during the discussion of APB Opinion 11 to any great extent.[8] Even the "death sentence" imposed on the deferred method by Concepts Statement 3 was accompanied by a "reprieve" in footnote 45.[9] In addition, there were many observers who believed that this measurement/classification issue could not

---

[8]Beresford, et. al., pp. 59-63.

[9]In footnote 45, the FASB noted that the deferred method has been held out to be a variation of the net-of-tax method by some advocates of the deferred method. Such an argument contends that the difference between the two methods is in the "geographical" location of the accounts on the financial statements.

be satisfactorily resolved until the FASB completed its concepts statement on recognition and measurement.[10]

Coincident with the discussion about the theoretical and practical merits of each method are the issues of financial statement priority and financial statement account definition, classification, and purity. An objective of the survey questions dealing with the deferred method requirement was to elicit responses about these related issues as well.

The questions related to the deferred method requirement (Questions 37 through 46) and the corresponding statistical summary are presented in Table 5.7. The respondents from both groups continued to favor the status quo for the most part, although the degree of consensus declined among the groups from the previous sets of questions. This was particularly true among the regulated group.

On the question as to whether the deferred method should continue to be required, an almost unanimous (97 percent) concurrence was voiced by the regulated group compared to 69 percent by the nonregulated group (Question 37). Of the nonregulated respondents who agreed with the statement, one-third qualified their support by stating that the other methods might be appropriate in certain circumstances, such as where major rate changes occur or for small companies. Twenty percent of the regulated group qualified their support for the deferred method.

Question 38 asked the respondents if the FASB's indictment of the deferred method in Concepts Statement 3 provided justification for either allowing the liability and/or net-of-tax methods as alternatives to deferred or replacements for deferred. A larger percentage favored the allowance of the liability and net-of-tax methods as

---

[10]For examples, see Philip L. Defliese, "Deferred taxes-forever," Journal of Accountancy, August 1983, p. 94 and Coopers & Lybrand, Interperiod Allocation of Income Taxes (A Study Sponsored by the Edison Electric Institute and the American Gas Association) February 1983, p. 74.

alternatives to deferred (42 percent of the nonregulated and 25 percent of the regulated) as opposed to replacing the deferred method (23 percent and 13 percent, respectively). When the overlap between those who voted in favor of both allowing another method as an alternative or replacing deferred is eliminated, more than half of the nonregulated respondents who expressed an opinion favored a method other than the deferred method in certain situations. Judging from the written comments, there was much stronger support for the liability method than there was for the net-of-tax method.

Although each of the three methods can be conceptually supported, the respondents felt that it would be preferable to require all companies to use the same method (Question 39). The major concern expressed by those in favor of uniformity was retaining the comparability of financial statements of companies, particularly those within the same industry. Very few of the respondents qualified their answers to this question. Ninety-three percent of the nonregulated respondents who supported uniformity were unequivocal in their support, as were 95 percent of the regulated respondents.

Given the high level of support for uniformity of method, it was not unexpected that the respondents would not be in favor of allowing a combination of methods within a company (Question 41). Those who did support the use of more than one method within the same company frequently stated that definite criteria should first be proposed by the FASB in order to retain intercompany comparability.

At the center of the arguments in favor of or against an allocation method are the nature and classification of the financial statement (particularly the balance sheet) accounts that result from using that method. Several of the questions in this section of the questionnaire dealt with the respondents' opinions concerning the financial statement "consequences" of using the deferred method or an alternative method. A frequent distinction made between the deferred method and the liability method is that the former is income statement oriented while the latter is balance sheet oriented. Question 40 dealt with the respondents' opinions as to which financial statement should receive priority when considering the propriety of an income tax allocation method. Most of the respondents agreed in general that it should be the income statement, although many of those providing comments indicated that both should receive equal consideration. As a check for consistency among the opinions of the respondents, the responses to question 40 were segregated by those who favored deferred and those who favored the liability method. Conceptually, those who favored deferred should be more in agreement with this statement than those who favored the liability method. This was in fact the case, but to a lesser degree than was expected. Seventy-five percent of those who favored the deferred method felt priority should be given to the income statement compared to 60 percent of those who favored the liability method.

The issue of whether or not deferred tax accounts meet the definitions of assets, liabilities or contra-accounts has received significant attention in the allocation discussion.[10] Almost three-quarters of the nonregulated group and 64 percent of the regulated group agreed that deferred accounts met the definitions of assets or liabilities in many cases, but very few respondents in either group supported the contra-account format (Questions 43 and 44). These questions generated many qualifying comments, the most frequent of which stressed that the reversal period should be the determining factor in the classification criteria (three to five years was most often mentioned as the appropriate time range).

An unexpected response was received from both groups to the question relating to the appropriate criteria to use in designating deferred accounts as current or noncurrent (Question 45). Present rules require that the designation be made based on the classification of the asset or liability that gave rise to the deferred account. Yet little more than one-third of the nonregulated group and less than one-half of the regulated group supported that criterion. The majority favored using the length of the reversal period of the timing difference as the standard. This response was unexpected in that the "asset test" is consistent with deferred while the "reversal test" is more consistent with the liability method.

Finally, a high percentage of the respondents were in favor of continuing to allow companies to use either the gross change, net change, or specific identification methods of measuring a change in a timing difference (Question 42). Those who objected to the choice of methods were more concerned over the loss of comparability between financial statements than with conceptual inconsistencies (such as

Wheeler and Galliart's argument that the deferred method with the net change method is a "gross inconsistency").[11] Similarly, a large majority of both groups (more so the nonregulated respondents than the regulated respondents, 91 percent to 69 percent) supported the practice of netting deferred tax credits with deferred tax charges provided they are both classified as either current or noncurrent (Question 46). Those who qualified their response stipulated that the accounts would have to be related to the same asset before netting would be acceptable.

Representative responses from the many that were received on this set of questions are in the Appendix A.

---

[11]Paul Rosenfield and William C. Dent, "No More Deferred Taxes," Journal of Accountancy, February 1983, pp. 44-55.

[12]Wheeler and Galliart, p. 78.

TABLE 5.7 *The Deferral Method Requirement*

| | Nonregulated | | | | Regulated | | | | | |
|---|---|---|---|---|---|---|---|---|---|---|
| Question | $\bar{x}$ | % Agree | % Opinion | Consensus | $\bar{x}$ | % Agree | % Opinion | Consensus | X 2 | Signif. |
| 37 | 2.06 | 69 | 97 | Low | 1.29 | 97 | 98 | High | 18.01 | .001 |
| 38(1) | 2.79 | 42 | 82 | Moderate | 3.32 | 25 | 95 | Moderate | 9.19 | .01 |
| 38(2) | 3.32 | 23 | 75 | Moderate | 3.73 | 13 | 93 | High | 7.45 | .05 |
| 39 | 1.69 | 77 | 95 | Low | 1.81 | 73 | 100 | Low | 2.59 | .30 |
| 40 | 2.00 | 68 | 94 | Low | 1.84 | 79 | 95 | Low | 2.43 | .30 |
| 41 | 3.45 | 21 | 95 | High | 3.42 | 19 | 100 | Moderate | 2.27 | .30 |
| 42 | 1.51 | 84 | 92 | Low | 1.39 | 90 | 100 | Moderate | 5.02 | .10 |
| 43 | 1.86 | 74 | 95 | Low | 2.17 | 64 | 100 | Low | 3.65 | .20 |
| 44 | 3.71 | 7 | 95 | High | 3.59 | 17 | 98 | High | 5.17 | .10 |
| 45 | 2.98 | 34 | 93 | Moderate | 2.66 | 47 | 100 | Low | 6.90 | .05 |
| 46 | 1.32 | 91 | 95 | Moderate | 1.97 | 69 | 100 | Low | 19.60 | .001 |

37. The deferred method of income tax allocation "provides the most useful and practical approach to interperiod tax allocation and the presentation of income taxes in financial statements." (quoted from APB 11 paragraph 35) and, therefore, should be the required method of tax allocation.

38. FASB Concepts Statement No. 3, Elements of Financial Statements of Business Enterprises, states that both the liability method and the net-of-tax method produce a view of deferred income tax credits that is consistent with the definitions of the Statement (paragraph 163), whereas the deferred

method produces a view of deferred income tax credits that is not consistent with the Statement (paragraph 164).

1. In light of their compatibility with Concepts Statement No. 3, both the liability method and the net-of-tax method should be acceptable as alternative methods of income tax allocation along with deferred.

2. In light of their compatibility with concepts Statement No. 3, the liability method and the net-of-tax method should replace the deferred method as acceptable accounting methods.

39. Although arguments can be made for each allocation method, it would be preferable that only one method be made acceptable.

40. When considering the propriety of one income tax allocation method over another, primary emphasis should be given to the effects on the income statement, with secondary emphasis on the balance sheet.

41. The method of tax allocation should be determined separately for each timing difference item, thereby allowing for a combination of the methods within the company.

42. The election to use either the "gross change," "net change," or "specific identification" methods to measure a change in a timing difference should continue to be acceptable, regardless of any changes in the acceptability of a method of tax allocation such as the deferral method.

43. Deferred tax credits (charges) from timing differences meets the definition of a "liability" (asset) and should be presented as such on the balance sheet.

44. Deferred tax credits (charges) arising from timing differences are attributed to assets (liabilities), and should be presented as contra-accounts to such assets (liabilities) on the balance sheet.

45. If deferred tax credits were required to be recorded as liabilities, their designation as current or noncurrent should be determined by the related asset that gave rise to their existence rather than by the time period required for their reversal.

46. It is acceptable to net deferred tax credits with deferred tax charges provided they are both classified as either current or noncurrent.

## Tax Rate Issues

The issue of which tax rates to use in establishing a current period addition to a deferred tax account, and whether such addition should be adjusted if the rates subsequently change (Questions 47 through 49), is closely related to the choice of a preferred allocation method (deferred, liability, or net-of-tax) and to the issue of discounting. It is interesting to note, especially in the case of regulated respondents, that the tax rate issue was the most frequently mentioned as needing reconsideration (see previous analysis of Question 23). In light of their overwhelming support for deferral and their disapproval of discounting, it is surprising that the regulated respondents would identify this issue with a much higher frequency (37 percent) than any other issue.

The questions relating to the tax rates issue and the corresponding statistical summary are presented in Table 5.8. The responses of the two groups are not statistically different for the first two questions (.01 level of significance), but they are very different on the issue of adjusting for changes in tax rates.

Both groups were almost unanimous in their agreement that the current period addition to a deferred tax account should be based on the current tax rate rather than on expected future tax rates (Question 47). Those who qualified their answers felt that future rates should be considered only where the rate has been already legislated. Several regulated companies commented that taking future tax rates into consideration would only be appropriate with deferred charges, where the transaction had not yet impacted the tax return.

On the question of whether reductions in deferred accounts should be measured using a FIFO flow assumption, slightly more than one-half of each group agreed that it should (Question 48). Those against FIFO cited a preference for weighted average, current rates, or specific identification. Many of the written comments noted the administrative complexities that a FIFO system would entail.

The most controversial question dealt with whether prior deferred tax credits or charges should be adjusted for tax rate changes (Question 49). Approximately one-half of the nonregulated group agreed that they should be adjusted as compared to one-fifth of the regulated group. The level of support for this statement is consistent with each of the group's previous support for the liability or net-of-tax method (Question 38 analysis). The mean score of those who favored deferred was 2.96 on this question, while the mean of those who favored/tolerated other methods was 1.95. In other words, those who favored deferred were opposed to the idea of adjusting for rate changes, whereas those who supported an alternative method were more positive to such adjustments. (This is evidence of the internal consistency of those who participated in the survey). Several of the regulated respondents reiterated the opinion that deferred tax charge accounts could be adjusted for rate changes, but not deferred tax credits (see appendix for examples).

TABLE 5.8 *Tax Rates*

| | Nonregulated | | | | Regulated | | | | | |
|---|---|---|---|---|---|---|---|---|---|---|
| Question | $\bar{x}$ | % Agree | % Opinion | Consensus | $\bar{x}$ | % Agree | % Opinion | Consensus | X 2 | Signif. |
| 47 | 1.16 | 98 | 98 | High | 1.10 | 100 | 100 | High | 1.18 | .70 |
| 48 | 2.36 | 58 | 90 | Low | 2.56 | 51 | 97 | Moderate | 2.35 | .50 |
| 49 | 2.49 | 51 | 96 | Low | 3.40 | 19 | 98 | High | 18.99 | .001 |

47. The creation of a current period addition to a deferred tax credit or deferred tax charge account should be based on the current tax rate rather than on expected future tax rates.

48. The reduction in a deferred tax credit or charge account under the deferred method should be measured by assuming a FIFO flow of prior deferrals and rates.

49. All prior deferred tax charges and credits should be adjusted to the current tax rate whenever the rates change.

## Discounting

The issue of discounting deferred tax accounts has arisen as part of a larger scale concern over the appropriateness of discounting any or all longterm liabilities or receivables. With some precedent for discounting already established for payables and receivables (APB No. 21), pensions (APB No. 8), and leases (FASB Statement No. 13), it seems natural that the issue of discounting deferred tax accounts would surface in the interperiod allocation discussion.

The discounting discussion can be divided into two parts. First, there is the threshold issue of whether discounting is compatible with interperiod tax allocation. Conceptually, this question would be dependent on the choice of an allocation method. If the deferred method is retained, the argument in favor of discounting is far weaker than if the liability method is adopted. This is largely due to the nature of the balance sheet accounts that each method produces. If partial allocation is adopted, some have suggested that discounting may be "much less significant" than if comprehensive is retained[13] while others have contended that a switch to partial would "require" discounting if combined with the liability method.[14] The second issue is the implementation issue. If discounting is required, what becomes the appropriate discount rate and time period to use in making the computation?

Both the threshold and implementation aspects of discounting were included in the questionnaire. The questions and the corresponding statistical analysis are presented in Table 5.9.

It is evident from the responses to Question 50 that there was very little support for discounting in both groups of respondents. As could be expected, the consensus of the groups was also very high. Those who provided written

---

[13]FASB, para. 108 c.

[14]R. D. Nair and Jerry J. Weygandt, "Let's Fix Deferred Taxes," Journal of Accountancy, November 1981, p. 102.

comments cited complexity, subjectivity, and lack of a comprehensive conceptual statement on discounting as the predominant reasons for their negative reaction to discounting.

If discounting were implemented, most of the respondents would rather use a company's incremental borrowing rate or a weighted cost of capital as the appropriate interest rate, as opposed to the company's internal rate of return (Question 51). Many of the respondents had not given the discounting period question (Question 52) much thought (30 percent had no opinion). Those who did respond were divided over whether the aggregate amounts of the deferred tax accounts or the individual items within the account should determine the reversal period over which to discount the account (note the conflicting comments in the appendix).

TABLE 5.9 *Discounting*

| | Nonregulated | | | | Regulated | | | | | |
|---|---|---|---|---|---|---|---|---|---|---|
| Question | $\bar{x}$ | % Agree | % Opinion | Consensus | $\bar{x}$ | % Agree | % Opinion | Consensus | $X^2$ | Signif. |
| 50 | 3.45 | 20 | 92 | High | 3.82 | 5 | 93 | High | 6.43 | .05 |
| 51 | 3.13 | 29 | 69 | Moderate | 2.62 | 45 | 71 | Low | 3.80 | .20 |
| 52 | 2.53 | 51 | 67 | Low | 3.00 | 36 | 71 | Moderate | 3.67 | .20 |

50. Long-term deferred tax amounts should be recorded at present value (i.e., discounted).

51. If long-term deferred tax amounts were recorded at present value, the appropriate interest rate should be each company's internal rate of return.

52. The correct period to use in determining the present value of long-term deferred tax accounts is the period over which the aggregate amounts of the accounts (and not individual items within the the accounts) reverse.

## Loss and Tax Credit Carryforwards

The issue of when (and how) to recognize the tax benefits of a net operating loss (NOL) carryforward and/or a tax credit carryforward has received renewed attention due to the increase in the carryforward period from seven to fifteen years and from the well publicized controversy between Aetna Life and Casualty Co. and the Securities and Exchange Commission. Currently, APB Opinion No. 11 prohibits a company from recording the future tax benefits of an NOL carryforward unless those future benefits are assured "beyond any reasonable doubt." In its further elaboration on situations where the necessary level of assurance is achieved, APB 11 specifically rules out cases where the NOL is the result of operations. This proscription prevents the majority of companies experiencing a net operating loss from recognizing the tax benefits until they are actually realized in the future period. The "cost" of forgoing the benefit recognition in the current period can be substantial in its effect on net income. In the Aetna case, the tax benefits constituted almost 39 percent of reported net income.[15]

Conceptually, there is the question as to whether the future tax benefit meets the definition of an asset.[16] There is also the question as to the restrictiveness of the recognition criteria. Many critics of the current restrictions argue that the combination of an increased carryforward period and the "going concern" assumption provides justification for reducing the recognition threshold to a "reasonable assurance" test. Those who favor the current standard cite the increased level of subjectivity that is introduced if the rules are relaxed and its consequent diminishment of financial statement comparability.

Even if current rules are retained, there still exist questions about the reporting of the actual realization of the NOL tax benefits in the future years and the interaction of NOL carryforwards and unused credits with existing deferred tax accounts. In the former case, the recognition

---

[15]"Aetna Scrambles to Replace Net SEC Disallowed," The Wall Street Journal, February 10, 1983, p. 50.

[16] FASB, para. 155.

of the tax benefit in a future period must be recorded as an extraordinary item on the income statement even though the "event" producing the benefit was from continuing operations. In the latter case, a company must credit income and eliminate any net deferred tax credit (balance sheet) accounts arising from timing differences accumulated prior to the time the NOL carryforward or unused credit is created, and which are expected to reverse in the carryforward period. This draw-down process and the subsequent reinstatement of these accounts when the carryforwards are realized can be very complex, and according to one CPA's observation, "accounts for a large number of the practice problems that are encountered."[17]

The questions asked of the respondents on the NOL and tax credit carryforward issue dealt with the appropriateness of changing the current recognition rules and the reporting and draw-down rules that already exist. The questions themselves and the related statistical analysis are presented in Table 5.10. In addition to these questions, an earlier part of the questionnaire asked the respondents about their actual experience with NOL and credit carryforward. That information will also be reviewed again in this section.

It was stated in Chapter 4 that a majority of respondents to this survey had some exposure to NOL carryforwards and/or credit carryforwards. Two-thirds of the nonregulated respondents and 61 percent of the regulated respondents reported that their company had experienced an NOL or a foreign or ITC credit carryforward for tax purposes (Question 17). These percentages dropped to 38 percent and 40 percent, respectively, of the respondents who reported that they had experienced an investment credit or foreign credit carryforward for book purposes. One-third of the nonregulated respondents and one-fifth of the regulated respondents had also encountered the situation where they had to draw down prior deferred credits because of a loss carryforward or because of unused investment credits or foreign credits (Questions 18).

Along with the experience questions, the respondents were also asked to assess their overall level of agreement with the current rules governing NOL and credit carryforwards (Question 19). A very high percentage of both groups were in

---

[17]Beresford, <u>et. al.</u>, p. 106.

full or general agreement with the current carryforward rules. Ninety-three percent of the nonregulated group and 96 percent of the regulated group were in general support of the current rules, out of which 61 percent and 75 percent, respectively, were in full agreement with the rules. Fourteen percent of each group did not render an opinion on this issue. Those who cited disagreement or lack of full agreement with the rules most often mentioned complexity and the treatment of the realization of the NOL carryforward as an extraordinary item in the income statement as aspects needing reconsideration.

Despite the high level of support for the current carryforward rules, a relatively high percentage of the respondents (44 percent of the nonregulated and 34 percent of the regulated) were in favor of relaxing the NOL recognition rules (Question 53). Those companies in support of the relaxation would substitute either "probable" or "reasonably assured" in place of "beyond any reasonable doubt" in the current language of APB Opinion No. 11. Those who favored maintaining the current language cited conservatism as justification for the more stringent criteria.

The remainder of the carryforward questions dealt with the more technical mechanics of balance sheet presentation and deferred credit draw downs. Due to the technical complexity of this aspect of carryforwards, a rather high percentage of respondents did not express an opinion on these questions (the range was 20-70 percent, with Question 58 receiving the most "no opinions").

On the question of recording acquired loss or tax credit carryforwards (Question 54), two-thirds of the nonregulated respondents and almost two-thirds of the regulated respondents (sixty-two percent) favored setting up a separate asset for these benefits rather than recording them as part of goodwill, as is currently required by FASB Technical Bulletin 81-2 for investment credits. Many of the respondents qualified their answers by adding a "reasonable assurance" test to whether the acquirer expects to realize the benefits of the carryforwards. The draw-down questions (55-59) received mixed responses, with some of the current rules being supported and some not. For example, approximately two-thirds of both groups did not want the excess ITC available over the recognized ITC (for book purposes) to be recorded as an asset, but rather supported the current drawn-down rules (Question 55). A slightly smaller percentage of both groups (61 percent of the nonregulated and 59 percent of the regulated) also agreed that only those deferred credits existing at the creation of the carryforward should be considered in the draw-down process (Question 57). On the other hand, 71 percent of the nonregulated respondents and 58 percent of the regulated respondents favored adjusting a draw down of deferred tax credits to current tax rates (Question 56), a procedure which is not currently permitted.

The questions of which deferred tax credit accounts to offset in the draw-down process were addressed in Questions 58 and 59. More than three-quarters of each group agreed that draw downs should be restricted to the deferred tax credits of the company(ies) appearing on the tax return of the corporation experiencing the loss or unused credit (Question 59). A majority of both groups also favored restricting the draw downs from foreign tax credit carryforwards or losses to foreign deferred tax credit accounts (Question 58). Several of the response comments indicated that the restriction should apply to foreign NOLs but not foreign tax credit carryforwards (see Appendix A). There are no current rules that prescribe one accounting treatment over the other in this area.

TABLE 5.10 *Loss and Tax Credit Carryforwards*

| | Nonregulated | | | | Regulated | | | | | |
|---|---|---|---|---|---|---|---|---|---|---|
| Question | $\bar{x}$ | % Agree | % Opinion | Consensus | $\bar{x}$ | % Agree | % Opinion | Consensus | X 2 | Signif. |
| 53 | 2.78 | 44 | 90 | Moderate | 2.96 | 34 | 90 | Moderate | 1.74 | .50 |
| 54 | 2.08 | 67 | 77 | Low | 2.23 | 62 | 66 | Low | 4.17 | .20 |
| 55 | 2.99 | 35 | 80 | Moderate | 3.11 | 30 | 78 | Moderate | 0.39 | .90 |
| 56 | 1.95 | 71 | 62 | Low | 2.35 | 58 | 73 | Low | 4.44 | .20 |
| 57 | 2.21 | 61 | 71 | Low | 2.25 | 59 | 75 | Low | 0.10 | .95 |
| 58 | 2.30 | 58 | 55 | Low | 2.00 | 67 | 20 | Low | 23.73 | .001 |
| 59 | 1.73 | 77 | 80 | Low | 1.59 | 80 | 69 | Low | 4.13 | .20 |

53. With the increase in the NOL carryforward period from seven to fifteen years, a company should now be permitted to recognize the benefits of an incurred NOL carryforward in the year incurred in all cases except where the future viability of the company is in doubt.

54. In accounting for future tax benefits of acquired loss or tax credit carryforwards (acquired through acquisitions) a separate asset should be recorded for these benefits rather than recording this as a part of goodwill with subsequent adjustments to goodwill as the loss or tax credit carryforward is used (FASB Technical Bulletin 81-2).

55. If the investment tax credit available exceeds the amount applicable to the tax on the book equivalent of taxable income, the resulting excess ITC should be recorded as an asset rather than drawing down net deferred tax credits from timing differences.

56. In an actual reversal (under the deferral method) of a deferred tax credit arising from a timing difference the tax rate at which it was originally recorded, at least theoretically should be used for the reversal. But there is also an adjustment to the income taxprovision for any difference between that historical rate and the current tax rate incurred as a result of an actual reversal. A draw down of deferred tax credits should therefore be adjusted to current tax rates in determining the increase in tax liability that an actual drawdown (reversal) would create for purposes of recording ITC carryforwards.

57. Recognition of the excess available ITC over the recognized based on the book equivalent of taxable income should be limited to the increase in tax liability due to reversals of timing differences in the ITC carryforward period, with <u>no recognition</u> given to deferred credits that are likely to be created in this 15-year carryforward period.

58. Draw downs of deferred tax credits (from timing differences) in accounting for foreign tax credit carryforwards or foreign net operating loss carryforwards should be restricted to foreign deferred tax credit accounts.

59. Draw downs of deferred tax credits (from timing differences) for losses (or tax credits) should be restricted to the deferred tax credits of the company or companies appearing on the tax return of the corporation incurring the loss (or having the unused credit).

## Tax Credits

In addition to the conceptual and technical problems related to unused credit carryforwards, there are also conceptual differences over which method should be used to account for the investment credit and other credits. Currently, both the flow-through method (full recognition of the credit in the period it originates) and the deferral method (amortization of the credit over the life of the related asset) are acceptable methods of accounting for the investment credit. There are no rules that directly address the accounting for any other credits (foreign tax credit, jobs credit, etc.).

The issue of which accounting method is preferable has been subject to debate since the enactment of the investment credit in 1962. Those who would argue for one method over the other are confronted with the compounding intrusion of the U.S. Congress, which has legislated (in 1971) that either method is acceptable in reports to federal agencies, but also that deferral (normalization) is required for all public utility property (beginning in 1981). As a result, any pronouncement that would mandate one method over the other must first secure Congressional action before it could be effective.

The vast majority of nonregulated companies use the flow-through method for accounting for investment credits. According to the Ernst & Whinney report, the 1982 issue of _Accounting Trends & Techniques_ indicated that 90 percent of the 600 companies surveyed in 1981 used the flow-through method.[18]

In this sample, 174 out of 194 (90 percent) nonregulated respondents reported using flow-through, which corresponds almost exactly to the _Accounting Trends & Techniques_ survey. Of the regulated companies, 44 out of 56 respondents (83 percent) reported using the deferral method.

---

[18]Beresford, _et. al._, p. 110.

The major conceptual argument used to support one method over another is one's perception of the nature of the investment credit. Those who argue for deferral contend that the investment credit should be viewed as a reduction in the cost of the asset that generates it. Those who argue for flow-through maintain that the investment credit is a selective reduction in the current year's taxes. Others believe that the credit could be viewed as a contribution to a company's capital account by the federal government.

As part of this questionnaire, companies were asked to rank, by order of preference, four statements that described the investment credit. The four choices were:

1. The ITC is a contribution to the capital of the respective taxpayer by the federal government similar in many respects to the gift of land by a state or local government in attracting industry to an industrial park.

2. The ITC is a selective method for reducing the effective income tax rates for the firm acquiring qualified assets.

3. The ITC is a reduction in the cost of acquiring a qualifying asset.

4. The ITC is an administrative procedure to permit the taxpayer to withhold the cash equivalent of the credit from taxes otherwise payable. The responses were organized by the companies' current method of accounting for the investment credit.

The most preferred description of the investment credit by the flow-through companies was statement number 2, the reduction in the effective tax rate. Almost half of the respondents (85 out of 186) selected this statement as their first choice. Next in preference were statements 3 (cost reduction), 4 (cash subsidy), and 1 (capital contribution).

The most preferred description of the investment credit by the deferral companies was statement number 3, the reduction in the cost of the asset. However, only one-third of the respondents (21 out of 62) selected this statement as their first choice. Next in preference were statements 4 (cash subsidy), 2 (reduction in effective tax rate), and 1 (capital contribution). The distinction between the first three choices was much weaker among the deferral companies than it was among the flow-through companies.

The attitudinal questions related to the credits issue were intended to elicit companies' opinions about the existence of multiple methods and financial statement presentation. The questions themselves and the related statistical analysis are presented in Table 5.11.

A large majority of the respondents in both groups (77 percent of the nonregulated and 84 percent of the regulated) felt that there existed a need for more formal guidance on accounting for tax credits other than the investment credit (Question 60). Many of the comments recommended that guidelines be established but were not in favor of definitive rules. Interestingly, the responses to this question were more polarized than most of the other responses. The responses were either an unequivocal yes or no (with the yes' outnumbering the no's by 3 to 1).

Two-thirds of the nonregulated companies, but only one-half of the regulated companies, favored a continuance of alternative accounting methods for the investment credit (Question 61). As might be expected, those in favor of allowing one method supported their current method. Few (21 percent) of the nonregulated respondents, but a good many (61 percent) of the regulated respondents felt that consistency would require that companies using the deferred method for timing differences should also use the deferred method for investment credits (Question 63). Those disagreeing with the statement argued that the nature of a timing difference was not similar to that of the investment credit; therefore, there was no requirement that the two be accorded similar accounting treatment.

For those companies using the deferred method there is a further question about the balance sheet classification of the unamortized credit. The choices are either as a liability, a reduction in the related assets cost, a deferred credit, or as a part of equity. The majority of both groups favored the classification of the unamortized credit as a liability over a contra-asset account (Question 62). Such support contradicts Concepts Statement No. 3, paragraph 166, which specifically precludes the credit account from being a liability, and defines it as a reduction in the acquisition cost of the asset. Few of the respondents in both groups were influenced by the reduction in basis requirement for the investment credit that was enacted by the Tax Equity and Fiscal Responsibility Act of 1982 (Question 64).

Finally, concerning the reporting of the investment credit used in the financial statements, less than one-half (49 percent) of the nonregulated and about one-quarter (26 percent) of the regulated groups felt that the number should be based on book income rather than taxable income (Question 65). A higher percentage of both groups (58 percent and 49 percent, respectively) were in favor of disclosing both the book and tax ITC carryforward in the notes to the financial statement (Question 66). Most of those in disagreement with the disclosure of both numbers would exclude the book ITC carryforward because it is, in their opinion, meaningless.

TABLE 5.11 *Tax Credits*

| | Nonregulated | | | | Regulated | | | | | |
|---|---|---|---|---|---|---|---|---|---|---|
| Question | $\bar{x}$ | % Agree | % Opinion | Consensus | $\bar{x}$ | % Agree | % Opinion | Consensus | X 2 | Signif. |
| 60 | 1.73 | 77 | 90 | Low | 1.50 | 84 | 75 | Low | 15.66 | .001 |
| 61 | 1.99 | 67 | 97 | Low | 2.50 | 50 | 98 | Low | 5.89 | .05 |
| 62 | 2.05 | 65 | 80 | Low | 1.86 | 72 | 98 | Low | 10.99 | .01 |
| 63 | 3.38 | 21 | 92 | Moderate | 2.24 | 61 | 100 | Low | 38.00 | .001 |
| 64 | 3.38 | 21 | 93 | Moderate | 3.61 | 14 | 97 | High | 1.88 | .50 |
| 65 | 2.51 | 49 | 91 | Low | 3.22 | 26 | 91 | Moderate | 9.44 | .01 |
| 66 | 2.33 | 58 | 87 | Low | 2.56 | 49 | 97 | Low | 4.87 | .10 |

60. Definitive allocation rules should be developed to account for all tax credits (e.g., the foreign tax credit) as they are as much a part of the tax liability computation as is the ITC.

61. The choice between "deferral and amortization" or "flow-through" as acceptable methods of accounting for investment tax credits should be maintained.

62. The deferred investment tax credit is more properly classified as a liability rather than as the reduction in the acquisition cost of the related asset.

63. Consistency would require that companies using the deferral method to account for timing differences also use the "deferral and amortization" method to account for investment tax credits and vice versa.

64. The requirement in the Tax Equity and Fiscal Responsibility Act of 1982 that, for tax purposes, a company claiming the full investment credit must reduce the cost recovery basis by one-half the amount of the credit is sufficient to argue that investment credits could, for financial accounting purposes, be recorded as contra-accounts to the related assets.

65. The recognition, for financial reporting, of the amount of the ITC used should be based on the book tax provision before the ITC rather than on the actual tax liability before the ITC.

66. In regard to Question (65) above, both the book ITC carryforward and the actual tax ITC carryforward should be shown in the notes to the financial statement.

## Acquisitions and Consolidations

Although the specific issue of accounting for the tax effects of acquisitions and consolidations is not part of the FASB Discussion Memorandum, there are some pertinent aspects of this subject that relate to accounting for income taxes. In particular, the requirement in APB Opinion No. 16, paragraph 89, that assets acquired in a business combination be recorded using a net-of-tax method is not wholeheartedly endorsed. In addition, business combinations often result in a company having a dual basis for the acquired assets, one for tax and one for book. This creates a situation where the same asset could cause both a timing and a permanent difference. If the tax basis exceeds the book basis, there are complex accounting issues related to recognizing the tax effect of this permanent difference (balance sheet presentation and period(s) of recognition).

The final set of opinion questions directed to all respondents dealt with some of the accounting for income tax problems related to business combinations. Due to the complexity and infrequency of several of the questions asked, the "no opinion" response rate tended to be high for both groups. The questions and the related statistical analysis are presented in Table 5.12.

The classification of purchased goodwill as a permanent difference was not seen as a controversial item by the respondents (Question 67), even where it was anticipated that the business segment containing the goodwill would be sold. Those who qualified their response emphasized that for goodwill to qualify as a timing difference, the disposition would have to be planned and consumated in a short period of time.

The net-of-tax approach to recording assets acquired through a stock purchase required by APB Opinion No. 16 was not viewed as supporting the arguments favoring the net-of-tax accounting concept by a majority of both groups (Question 68). Several of the respondents felt that a business combination was sufficiently different from normal operations and that the use of one method for a combination did not require the use of the same method for ongoing operations.

With respect to business combinations that result in dual basis assets, a majority of nonregulated respondents (57 percent), but not of regulated respondents (37 percent), felt that if the tax basis exceeded the book basis, the excess tax basis should be accounted for using the current NOL recognition criteria. Those who objected to such treatment frequently argued that the excess should be treated as a permanent difference. Along these lines, approximately two-thirds of each group agreed that the difference between the tax basis and the book basis of an asset meets the definition of a permanent difference even though this difference will turn around as the asset is written off or sold (Question 70). Over 80 percent of both groups agreed that the net result of such treatment was to recognize the permanent difference over the book life rather than the tax life of the asset (Question 71).

With respect to consolidations, not quite half of each group felt that eliminating the equity method of accounting for subsidiaries in favor of consolidation would improve accounting for income taxes (Question 72). Of those who do file a consolidated tax return, 31 percent of the nonregulated group and 19 percent of the regulated group employ different methods for book and tax for allocating the consolidated corporate income tax liability between the parent corporation and its subsidiaries (Question 73). Proposals for uniformity of methods for both book and tax purposes were made by both the FASB and the Accounting Standards Executive Committee, but no action has been taken on this issue. From an economic standpoint, most of the respondents (71 percent and 67 percent) did not feel that the allocation of the consolidated tax liability for financial reporting would impair or enhance the potential of a corporation to later absorb NOLs or tax credits (Question 74).

TABLE 5.12 *Acquisitions and Consolidations*

| | Nonregulated | | | | Regulated | | | | | |
|---|---|---|---|---|---|---|---|---|---|---|
| Question | $\bar{x}$ | % Agree | % Opinion | Consensus | x | % Agree | % Opinion | Consensus | X 2 | Signif. |
| 67 | 1.41 | 87 | 88 | Moderate | 1.14 | 97 | 63 | High | 26.20 | .001 |
| 68 | 2.80 | 41 | 70 | Moderate | 3.11 | 31 | 61 | Moderate | 3.94 | .20 |
| 69 | 2.37 | 57 | 69 | Low | 3.00 | 37 | 51 | Moderate | 11.26 | .01 |
| 70 | 2.01 | 67 | 76 | Low | 2.11 | 63 | 64 | Low | 4.20 | .20 |
| 71 | 1.53 | 84 | 64 | Low | 1.54 | 83 | 59 | Low | 2.18 | .50 |
| 72 | 2.61 | 48 | 70 | Low | 2.68 | 43 | 68 | Low | 0.71 | .70 |

67. The amortization of purchased goodwill is correctly designated as a permanent difference even in situations where it is anticipated that a business segment containing goodwill will be sold.

68. The requirement (in APB Opinion No. 16 paragraph 89) that the reported fair value of an asset, acquired as a result of the purchase of stock of another corporation, should reflect the asset's tax deductibility basis supports the arguments favoring the net-of-tax accounting concept.

69. Referring to statement (68) above, if the tax basis were in excess of an asset's fair value, the reported amount of the asset should be limited to the fair value, with the excess tax basis accounted for as a NOL would be treated.

70. Referring again to statement (68) above, the basis difference between book and tax is a permanent rather than a timing difference even though it will turn around as the asset is written off or sold.

71. Referring to statement (70) above, if the basic difference is a permanent difference then adjusting the recorded basis of a depreciable asset for the tax effect forces the recognition of a permanent difference over the book life rather than the life of the asset.

72. Elimination of the equity method of accounting for subsidiaries (owned over 50 percent) in favor of consolidation would improve accounting for income tax (these subsidiaries are often considered for tax purposes when owned 80 percent or more).

## Questions for Rate-Regulated Corporations Only

The final set of questions (Questions 80 through 87) in the preparer questionnaire was directed at rate-regulated corporations only. It has been previously discussed that the rate-regulated companies would, as a group, suffer the most adverse economic consequences in the near term should major changes be made in the interperiod income tax allocation rules. For this reason, it was felt that additional questions related to the effects of any accounting changes should be addressed to this group of respondents.

Several of the questions in this section were designed to assess the current impact of the allocation rules on the financial statements of rate-regulated companies. The majority of firms answering these questions use the cost of service normalization method for accounting for the ITC (71 percent). Eleven percent use rate base normalization, seven percent use flow-through, and eleven percent use both flow-through and one or more of the normalization methods (based on responses to Question 80).

Table 5.13 summarizes the balance sheet impact of deferred tax accounts (credits or charges) and unamortized ITCs as a percentage of net public utility property over the years 1973-1982 (Question 81). The average ratio for each year has fluctuated during the ten year period for those firms with deferred credits and those with deferred charges. In both cases, the largest ratio occurred in 1982, at a ratio in excess of eleven percent of net utility property. The range of ratios for firms with either deferred credits or deferred charges extended as high as 20 percent in some years.

Earlier in this chapter it was noted in the discussion of comprehensive versus partial allocation that regulated corporations tended to focus on the reversal of individual timing differences within an account when asked if the payment of deferred credits was postponed indefinitely (Question 30). Nonregulated corporations, on the other hand, tended to focus on roll-over of entire account balances. This difference in focus was evident in the groups' responses to the indefinite postponement question. When the regulated companies were asked if they forsaw any net turnaround in their deferred credit account within the next five years, eighty-nine percent responded that they did not anticipate any net turnaround in that period (Question 82). Seven percent anticipated turnaround of less than 10 percent, two percent anticipated less than 20 percent, and two percent said that more than 50 percent was expected. This would indicate that if roll-over were subject to partial allocation, and partial allocation were adopted, the regulated industry would experience a significant decrease in reported tax expense figure.

Those companies that did anticipate a net turnaround listed the following reasons for the projection:

1. Fewer current property additions

2. Purchased gas adjustment clause

3. Reduction in capital budget

TABLE 5.13 *Deferred Tax Credits (Charges) and Unamortized ITCs as a Percentage of Net Public Utility Property, 1973 to 1982*

| Year | Deferred Charges | | Deferred Credits and Unamortized ITCs | |
|---|---|---|---|---|
| | Range | Average | Range | Average |
| 1973 | 0-14% | 5.9% | 0-12% | 5.2% |
| 1974 | 0-18% | 10.1% | 1-18% | 8.8% |
| 1975 | 0-12% | 6.4% | 0-13% | 5.7% |
| 1976 | 0-18% | 10.8% | 2-19% | 9.4% |
| 1977 | 0-19% | 7.7% | 1-16% | 6.5% |
| 1978 | 0-17% | 11.1% | 1-21% | 9.9% |
| 1979 | 0-19% | 8.9% | 1-16% | 7.4% |
| 1980 | 0-18% | 11.4% | 1-21% | 10.5% |
| 1981 | 0-18% | 9.2% | 1-17% | 8.0% |
| 1982 | 0-20% | 11.6% | 1-21% | 11.1% |

In conjunction with the net turnaround question, the companies were also asked to assess the impact of a change to partial allocation or ITC flow-through on rates charged to their customers (Question 84). Thirty-eight percent of the respondents projected a significant reduction in rates, and an additional 43 percent projected a slight reduction. Seventeen percent projected an increase in rates (eight percent said a slight increase, nine percent said a significant increase).

Some of the reasons given for the anticipated changes are as follows:

- "A significant decrease in the short-term, but a significant increase in the long-term."

- "Loss of interest-free loan."

- "There would be some reduction in the short term, but in the long term the effect would be an increase in rates because of an increase in the rate base and a decrease in the future benefit of investment tax credits."

- "Difficult to determine because although the cost of service would decrease, the rate base would increase (deferral is presently deducted from rate base). Over a period of time, customers would probably pay more."

- "Assuming IRS normalization requirements are continued, the benefits would be lost so there would be a significant increase in rates. Assuming IRS normalization requirements were rescinded there would be a short-term reduction but a long-term increase due to the increase in cost of capital resulting from the replacement of the lost cash flow. The adverse effects on financial condition and earning coverage would require allowing higher rates of return to permit issuance of additional securities, thus further diluting the immediate reduction in rates."

In light of the perceived adverse economic effect that would ensue from a change to partial allocation or ITC flow-through, it is not surprising that eighty-eight percent of the regulated respondents felt that an exception should be made for regulated industries if flow-through was adopted (Question 85). The strength of the reaction against flow-through is evident from the fact that 54 of the 57 responding companies added a written comment to their response. Selected written comments to this question are provided below. Interestingly, many of the comments are altruistic, stating that a change would be detrimental to the customers, not the company.

- "Utilities would lose a substantial capital formation device and would result in higher rates to customers."

- "The same accounting policies should apply to regulated industries as apply to nonregulated industries. However, the economics of rate regulation at times create assets and liabilities of regulated industries that do not exist in nonregulated industries and vice versa. Also, under current tax law, regulated industries are required to use interperiod tax allocation for most timing differences and the deferral and amortization method for investment credits."

- "Could set unfair rates. Benefits current customers at the expense of future customers."

- "Normalization stabilizes customer rates by avoiding fluctuations due to changes in statutory income tax regulations."

- "The rate-making process requires certain unique accounting treatments, especially in the area of deferred costs."

- "This is inequitable to future rate-payers because all tax benefits would accrue to current rate-payers. In addition, flow-through would not provide incentives for capital investments by utilities."

- "Utilities are already hard pressed to earn a rate sufficient to support book values. Unless regulatory commissions granted higher returns to offset the losses from reduced revenue requirements, it would damage utilities even further."

- "Loss of this treatment would adversely affect utilities' cash flow and financial positions."

On a related issue, eighty percent of the respondents felt that the use of flow-through in the rate-making process should impact the accounting for timing differences (Question 86). The rationale to support this opinion was most often that "financial statements should reflect what has occurred in the rate-making process."

Finally, when asked if there should be a different set of "generally accepted accounting principles" for rate regulated as opposed to nonregulated companies, seventy-five percent of the respondents said no (Question 87). Many of the written comments noted that the economic effects unique to rate-making are adequately covered in SFAS No. 71. Other comments were similar to this one: "GAAP should be defined as accounting and reporting principles that accurately reflect economic effects of financial transactions. Accounting requirements must be flexible enough to reflect different economic circumstances. This does not imply two different standards, only one that is flexible enough to accurately record and report economic reality."

# Appendix A
# Selected Written Comments to Questions

The numbers in the left-hand margin are the questionnaire numbers. An "R" after the number indicates a response by a rate-regulated company.

## The Allocation Requirement (Questions 24-28)

Question 24

Should interperiod allocation be required?

Agree

[58R] Except for items under a specific dollar amount.

[222R] Immaterial differences should be excepted as provided by GAAP.

[279] Income tax allocation is justified in limited instances in which taxes will probably be paid in the future based on present obligations.

[347] Interperiod income tax allocation should be required only where it is probable that those taxes would ultimately be paid.

[407] Allocation should be required only if the difference will result in payment [refund] in 3 to 5 years.

[1040R] From ARB #23 to the present, this has been the treatment and should not be destroyed--perhaps minor modifications are in order.

[1502] It would be inappropriate to ignore the income tax effects of transactions affecting pretax accounting income merely because of timing considerations.

[1805] While it is generally agreed that some form of interperiod income tax allocation should be required, it is acknowledged that existing procedures for interperiod allocation may require some modification so as to better reflect expenses and liabilities resulting from interperiod tax allocation.

[145R] Individually large items which will turn around within a short period of time should require interperiod tax allocation. Otherwise, interperiod income tax allocation seems no longer useful.

Disagree

[1528] Serious consideration must be given to the flow-through concept especially since recent emphasis has been on cash-flow considerations.

Question 25

Is the interperiod allocation information relevant?

Agree

[1426] The concept of matching taxes with income and expense is more important now than before.

[83] Capital recovery (depreciation) timing/items have cost relevancy.

Disagree

[641R] Enterprises and their accountants must do a better job of explaining the long-term nature of tax deferrals, and should consider disclosing the components of the deferred income tax balances as of year-end in the annual report.

[66R] Major distortion is due to ACRS depreciation.

Question 26

The federal income tax is an expense that should be based on pretax book income.

Agree

[58R] Minor monetary timing differences should be excepted from the requirement of interperiod tax allocation.

[379] In those cases where turn around is 5 years or more in the future, usefulness of information is more important than matching.

Disagree

[1771] The matching concept as presently used in the conceptual framework would not encompass income tax considerations.

[1893] The matching process cannot override the reality of the transaction. The tax return is the basis of book expense.

Question 27

Does the benefit of interperiod allocation exceed the cost?

Agree

[33] Cost is high but probably justified for timing differences that will impact cash flow in the forseeable future.

[296] Only true benefit is from a cash flow standpoint.

[724] Cost of measuring tax allocation is minor.

[995] Cost is not excessive to measure the allocation. However, the value is questionable.

[1462R] Current allocation procedures have been in existence for 16 years. A change in methods at this time would prove costly.

[1793] The costs rise disproportionately to the increasing complexity of the tax law. However, such information is very useful.

Disagree

[593] Few readers understand the information provided and for preparers of financial statements, rules appear to be unnecessarily complex with no common conceptual objective.

[1378] The current tax effect of certain timing differences can be difficult and often expensive to complete with accuracy prior to financial reporting deadlines.

[185] Level of sophistication needed to understand tax accounting is lacking in many users.

Question 28

Can the federal income tax still be considered a tax on income?

Agree

[988] The basic premise is income. Governmental problems of revenue vs. social objectives are not relevant to financial statement presentation.

[1462R] It increases the complexity of computation, but does not change the nature of the expense.

[145R] Many items are still based on income. Distortions are a fact of life and should be accepted in that light.

Disagree

[178] It is not a tax on accounting determined (book) income. It is a tax based on complex tax laws which are further complicated by Treasury regulations, IRS interpretations, court decisions, etc., which have severed any relationship to book income.

## The Comprehensive Allocation Concept (Question 29-36 and 75)

Question 29

Comprehensive allocation is the preferred method of income tax allocation.

Agree

[735] Except as to special circumstances resulting from inclusion of subs in reporting earnings.

[1040R] Otherwise, too many opinions would exist as to what warranted partial allocation.

[1432] It should be an all or none requirement.

[1473] We generally agree that the comprehensive allocation method is, in most cases, the most appropriate method of interperiod tax allocation. However, there are certain situations with respect to major items which do not tend to roll over in total--especially those which management can control--i.e., accelerated depreciation on capital investments, which may warrant different accounting treatment. In such cases, we believe it is appropriate for management to be able to use its best judgment regarding the ultimate requirement to actually pay those taxes in determining the necessity to record deferred tax liabilities (a methodology similar to that used at present in the U.K. under their Statement of Standard Accounting Practice #15). In this regard, however, we suggest that certain standardized criterion be established to assist managements in making those judgments.

[1538] With partial allocation, unless specifically defined, management could manipulate earnings, thus affecting "accuracy".

Disagree

[686] Partial allocation may be more accurate over a period of years.

[1509] A better relationship between future cash requirements and the deferred tax provision is needed.

[1536] The comprehensive approach does not reasonably approximate future cash flows and therefore is not representative of actual taxes expected to be paid.

[5] Partial allocation is generally superior especially in situations where a company's asset base is growing and some deferred taxes will never reverse.

[178] Both are going the wrong direction from reality. Partial allocation is only slightly less wrong then comprehensive allocation.

Question 30

Does comprehensive allocation result in indefinite postponement of reversals of deferred tax accounts?

Nonregulated responses

[211] This may be true in the aggregate but it is not true of the individual items.

[296] Many allocations for specific items reverse rapidly and are not indefinite in nature.

[457] We agree in general with some exceptions, for instance, when there are business contractions or interruptions.

[553] In most cases, the items revolve so that new assets and liabilities are being created and old ones are being extinguished--even though net balance is stable or increasing.

[635] If the business continues to grow, postponement indefinitely will probably occur, but if the firm stagnates reversal will occur.

[723] Yes, if you consider an item such as depreciation on a going concern basis, but many items will roll over completely such as plant rearrangement costs.

[988] Assuming a constant level of activity, the deferred tax account in total will remain constant even though the component tax originating items continually roll over. Maximizing the deferral is the goal of tax planning and taxpayer election and only appears to postpone the payment indefinitely. Actually, the deferral is continually eroded by the reversal of the component items.

[1213] This is generally true for differences between book and tax depreciation. However, timing of cash flows, such as pension payments, often results in turnaround recognition.

[1574] General agreement prompted by tax vs. book depreciation difference which significantly exceeds all other timing differences combined.

[1893] Agree for depreciation but not for other specific areas such as accounting changes amortized for tax purposes.

Rate-regulated responses

[55R] Items subject to continual rollover, such as accelerated depreciation, appear to result in recording a liability which would be realized only in liquidation. This may not be necessary for financial statements intended to show financial position on a going concern basis.

[508R] Excess of tax over book expense for depreciable assets postponed indefinitely assuming continual equal or increasing property acquisitions.

[641R] In aggregate, the statement is true. However, on an individual item basis, all timing differences will reverse; however, they are in many cases offset by new timing differences. The effect is to give the appearance of indefinite postponement of tax payments. This indefinite postponement is not assured and thus should be measured and reflected in the financial statements.

[1040R] All you have to do is work with the detail that establishes these accounts and you realize such statements are not accurate.

[1462R] Indefinite postponement of payment is a myth. In a period of economic growth the reversal of old timing differences may be offset by the creation of new ones. However, individual timing differences are in fact paid as they reverse.

[1990R] Each timing difference by definition used in normalization reverses, i.e., over the life of a specific plant, etc. If a utility replaces a plant at an inflated cost over time and if no innovations reduce the cost of such plant, then the total net deferred tax balance remains relatively constant, similar to accounts payable. Deferred tax by definition is not postponed indefinitely. A nonregulated industry could arguably present the indefinitely postponed concept if not impacted by technology innovations.

[29R] Although the total in the deferred tax accounts grows, that does not mean that payment is postponed indefinitely. Payment for individual items does become due.

[169R] The fact that the reversal of a prior period deferral is more than offset by a new deferral does not hide the fact that the reversal did, in fact, occur.

Question 31

Should cash flow considerations take precedence over the matching criterion when reversal cannot be reasonably forseen in a relatively short period of time?

Agree

[1473] In cases where the ultimate tax liability is postponed indefinitely for extended periods, non-recognition of certain deferred tax liabilities under the partial allocation may be appropriate.

Disagree

[44] The income statement should never be used as a measure of cash flow.

[681] For planning purposes, but not for income reporting. The funds statement can separately deal with cash flow considerations.

[1538] Why change income tax accounting to reflect cash flow when the rest of the income statement does not?

Question 32

Should partial allocation be allowable as an acceptable alternative?

Agree

[192] Only if guidelines can be adopted to avoid subjectivity.

[588] With proper criteria.

[699] If this method produces more realistic results, it should be permitted.

[1045] It must have very definite rules to determine/estimate future taxes payable.

[1159R] For those cases where partial allocations make sense, they should be allowed, i.e., where timing differences are immaterial and ease of measurement is desirable.

[1473] We generally believe that the variations of partial allocation are appropriate,...but question whether alternative should be allowed in similar economic circumstances due to the overall desirability to maintain consistency/comparability among companies.

[1574] At least with regard to tax vs. book depreciation.

[1749R] Industry groups should employ similar accounting whether it be partial or comprehensive allocation.

Disagree

[591R] To allow alternative allocation approaches would distort comparability.

[907R] No conceptual basis for partial allocation. Could lead to manipulation of reported earnings.

[1040R] Too many differences of opinion and industries exist to make such an approach totally workable.

[1351] Alternative methods serve only to confuse the situation further.

[1538] One method must be specified for comparability.

[1771] Comparability would be lost if companies could choose between comprehensive and partial allocation.

Question 33

Partial allocation should replace the comprehensive allocation method as the only acceptable method of allocation?

Agree

[33] This makes the most sense theoretically, but presents significant practical problems (i.e., definition, determination of turnaround period, timing of establishment of the deferred tax, etc.).

[1704] Companies using the partial allocation method should disclose if there are material differences between partial and full allocations.

[5] In the absence of the taxes payable basis, agree.

Disagree

[153] Some situations may be so unpredictable that they require the comprehensive allocation to be employed.

Question 34

The indefinite reversal criteria for APB Opinion 23 should be equally available to the undistributed earnings of investors.

Agree

[33] This could have sufficient control with 20% ownership to cause indefinite reversal or all owners could mutually agree not to take future dividends.

[457] If investor has sufficient control over dividend policy.

[1473] If an investor (in 20% to 50% ownership range) can show sufficient control of the affiliate to impact payment of dividends,etc., then it may be appropriate to apply the indefinite reversal criterion under APB Opinion 23. A 50% associate may be an example.

Disagree

[1793] Too diverse an area for anybody to provide flexibility in the area.

[181] Control over an investee differs significantly from control by a parent over a subsidiary.

Question 35

Should deferred tax credits and unamortized ITCs be considered liabilities in debt to equity ratios?

Agree

[231] An unamortized ITC should not be considered a liability.

[591] Only to the extent they meet the definition of a liability outlined in the Financial Accounting Standards Board Concept Statement #3.

[641R] Only the portion expected to reverse should be included in the liabilities.

[988] Deferred taxes should be considered in all financial ratio computations when appropriate.

[1125] Unamortized ITC should be considered as equity in debt to equity calculations.

[1373] There may be cases where deferred tax credits are a significant factor in this ratio and should be included. Unamortized ITC does not belong in this computation.

[11] The liability for taxes should be treated the same as any other liability.

Disagree

[250R] Let investors, etc. decide.

[1432] It would cloud the definition of debt.

[1473] Under present accounting rules, deferred tax credits (the majority of which normally relate to accelerated matters) are so indefinite of payment in total (rollover concept) that they must be considered part of equity.

[1574] Disagree under current rules. Under partial allocation there is more justification for classification as a liability.

[1907] Absolutely not; if anything, they should be a part of stockholders equity.

[49] Since they have already reduced the equity, they should not be considered as a liability. Otherwise, their effect is compounded.

Question 36

A change from comprehensive to partial allocation would likely result in higher reported net incomes.

Agree

[591R] Initially, yes; however, if the assumption for indefinite reversal turns out to be wrong, it could result in lower reported net earnings.

[1448] It depends upon the type of company involved. For our company, a service company with a lot of deferred compensation, a change from comprehensive to partial would, until recently, have resulted in lower net income. Now it would result in higher net income.

[1536] Many enterprises will probably cease providing deferred taxes on depreciation timing differences and thereby, increase reported net income.

[1805] Unless rigid rules are established for partial allocation procedures, such as the reversal of prior year timing differences which is the result of a management decision in the current year, it is anticipated that partial allocation would result in higher reported net income.

Disagree

[250R] For this company, deferred federal tax expense would be reduced in the initial year with rate decreases equal to reduced expense in subsequent years.

[907R] For a utility, flow through would reduce revenues not increase net income. Furthermore, there would be increased capital costs due to the loss of these cash flow benefits.

[1329R] This may not be the case for regulated companies for which deferred taxes are a material component of rate making.

[124R] This statement would not be true for a utility as any decrease in operating expenses would be passed on to the customer in the form of lower rates.

Question 75

Is there a significant conceptual difference between the roll over concept of a timing difference and the indefinite reversal concept for reinvestment of a subsidiary's undistributed earnings?

Agree

[681] Recognition in one instance is highly assured while the other can be remote depending on numerous economic conditions.

[1073R] Rollover is a "continued renewal" while indefinite reversal is the "permanent deferral" of a tax.

[1462R] Reversal of timing differences related to subsidiary undistributed earnings cannot be predicted and is subject to the control of the taxpayer. The taxpayer is required to take specification in order for rollover to occur.

[1904] The rollover concept is subject to the element of time. The distribution of subsidiary earnings is based on tax planning and cash flow requirements.

Disagree

[1528] The result is somewhat the same, both are based upon management decisions.

[33] Under partial allocation there is no significant difference, but under comprehensive allocation there is a significant difference.

## The Deferral Method Requirement (Questions 37-46)

Question 37

The deferred method should continue to be required.

Agree

[907R] The deferred method could be considered a proxy for the net-of-tax or liability concept.

[1197] Yes for medium and large corporations, but not necessary for small businesses.

[1509] The nature of the item is not understood by users, and it does not result in suitable proxy for liability as measurement is overstated, but practically speaking the deferred method is acceptable.

[1904] Agree as regards matching concept, but we find difficulty in describing the balance sheet accounts as assets or liabilities.

Disagree

[33] The deferred method is faulty because adjustments to liability are not permitted to reflect the best knowledge (i.e., rate changes, turnaround period, etc.).

[279] The deferred method is impractical as to calculation and not meaningful as to definitions. Deferred tax credits are neither liabilities nor asset reductions.

[1071] The liability method is more realistic than the deferred method.

[1383] This may have been true when APB 11 was issued. The situation clearly needs current review.

[1744R] Deferred taxes which can be specifically related to an asset should be presented as a contra-asset to reflect expenditure of tax benefits. Flexibility should be provided to allow exceptions in situations where regulated rate making is based on a different accounting method.

[11R] Liability method is an acceptable alternative. A combination of the net-of-tax and either the liability or deferred methods would also be acceptable.

[75] The liability method requires less record keeping and would appear to be more practical.

Question 38

Should the liability/net-of-tax method(s) replace or be alternatives to the deferral method?

Agree

[33] We prefer the liability method but not the net-of-tax method. Net-of-taxes is merely a presentation approach. The net-of-tax method obscures important detail.

[409] The liability method should be the only acceptable method.

[907R] The valuation concept should be used if the income taxes relate to a recorded asset or liability. Use the liability method if there is no related asset or liability. The tax rate should be the rate in effect when the item is included in the tax return.

[1685] Net-of-tax is not appropriate since we do not view deferred taxes as valuation allowances. Liability may be appropriate in certain instances.

[1904] The liability method produces relevant balance sheet accounts, but the net-of-tax method would value assets and liabilities based on the sophistication of a company's tax department, thereby distorting comparability among companies. The net-of-tax method's only acceptable usage is in valuing assets and liabilities acquired in a business combination.

Disagree

[470R] The "elements project" is incomplete. The "accounting recognition" portion is yet to be developed. We would have to believe that the appropriateness of taxes entering into income will be addressed in that project.

[1040R] Why rebuild the house if it has existed for over 30 years?

[1073R] The results of the methods differ significantly. If all were acceptable methods, the comparability between financial statements would be lost.

[1159R] The deferral method should not be discarded because of "green eye shade" accounting.

Question 39

Only one allocation method should be made acceptable.

Agree

[250R] GAAP should mean consistency of accounting practices in all industries; the ultimate user of the financial statements, the stockholder, should be allowed to compare companies in different industries using the same accounting methods before making his investment decision.

[1462R] The existence of several acceptable methods is the same as having none.

Disagree

[522R] Different methods for different "industry groups" would be acceptable. For the utility industry the "deferral method" is the correct method, but may not be the acceptable method for some other industry.

[988] Uniformity of presentation should not be made at a sacrifice of otherwise supporting factors and circumstances.

[1744R] The economics of each timing difference should be assessed and accounted for independently. Flexibility should also be provided to allow accounting conformance with regulatory requirements.

[1844] Standards should allow accounting options to reflect economic differences when appropriate.

Question 40

Primary emphasis should be given to the effects on the income statement when evaluating the propriety of an income tax allocation method.

Agree

[407] If comprehensive allocation is continued, the income statement should have emphasis.

[995] Both statements are important in varying degrees to different users. However, if one must be selected, the income statement should be primary.

Disagree

[907R] It is not necessary to emphasize one over the other. Concepts Statements support comprehensive allocation from both the income statement and balance sheet point of view.

[1536] Emphasizing the income statement over the balance sheet is one reason for the problems now being considered. Both financial statements are equally important.

[1704] Both should be given approximately equal emphasis. If the balance sheet is meaningless it lends question to the income statement's accuracy.

[1990R] The balance sheet in regulated industries is important due to the rate-making process considerations.

[178] Tax allocation is a balance sheet problem. The deferred tax liability account on most balance sheets is grossly distorting debt/equity relationships, etc.

Question 41

A combination of allocation methods should be allowed within a company.

Agree

[533] Agree in principle; but application could leave room for abusers which would have to be controlled.

[11R] Although a combination of methods may be acceptable, the criteria that applies to each category of items to which such notions apply should be determined by the FASB.

Disagree

[1373] A combination including the net-of-tax method would be very misleading and confusing.

[1536] All timing differences are essentially alike and should be accounted for under a single method.

[172] This is theoretically sound, but may not be practical for many companies.

Question 42

Companies should continue to be able to elect either the gross change, net change, or specific identification method regardless of the allocation method.

Agree

[1536] Companies should be able to use whatever method makes sense considering the costs and benefits involved.

Disagree

[960] Only one method should be accepted, increasing comparability between companies.

[1473] The net change method should only be acceptable where it provides a reasonable estimate of the gross change effects (allowed for cost benefit reasons only).

[1844] The gross change is the most theoretically correct if the cost of implementation does not exceed benefits.

Question 43

Deferred tax accounts meet the definitions of assets and liabilities and should be presented as such on the balance sheet.

Agree

[347] Only partial allocation would produce amounts that could meet the definition of liability/ asset.

[641R] Only the tax currently due (within one year) and the deferred tax expected to reverse within the next three to four years should be classified as liabilities.

[995] Technically, yes. Practically, no.

[86] Items that reverse in 3-5 years are liabilities. Those that do not reverse are part of equity.

[1473] While the company recognizes that there is a question whether deferred tax credits meet the definition of a liability under the FASB concept statements as they are currently written, we believe that such credits do in fact have the characteristics of a liability (except...deferred tax credits which are so large that the ultimate payment of those taxes is indefinitely postponed) and should therefore be accounted for under the deferred method using partial allocation concepts.

[1793] Deferred taxes are no stranger than a number of other deferred items appearing in today's balance sheets.

Disagree

[33] Use of comprehensive allocation with the deferred method doesn't produce a "liability" as described by the conceptual framework.

[907R] Generally, deferred taxes are valuation accounts. However, if there is not a corresponding asset or liability, then the deferred taxes meet the definition of a liability.

[1536] Deferred tax credits, especially for recurring timing differences, do not constitute a probable sacrifice of resources, an essential quality of an accounting liability.

[1745R] Most deferred taxes are valuation accounts to related assets and liabilities. If there is no related asset or liability, the charge or credit represents a receivable or payable.

Question 44

Deferred tax accounts should be presented as contra-accounts on the balance sheet.

Agree

[1462R] This is conceptually correct but not practiced. It would require extensive supplemental disclosure to determine the effects of tax allocation.

[1745R] Agree for material amounts but minor amounts should be grouped and shown separately for simplicity in presentation.

[11R] This has considerable merit for significant balance sheet items.

Disagree

[522R] Should be separately identified on balance sheet, not lumped under "assets" and "liabilities."

[954] Contra asset accounts are too theoretical and the laymen reading the financials don't care.

Question 45

The designation of a deferred tax credit as current or noncurrent should be determined by the classification of the asset giving rise to the credit, not the time period required for the credit's reversal.

Agree

[222] Generally agree, but if there is no relationship to an asset, should refer to the operating cycle of the firm or some other means.

[124R] For utilities, deferred tax credits are amounts ultimately payable to the government or rate payers. The segregation of such amounts as current or noncurrent is not only impractical but of questionable value. It would seem appropriate that the generally accepted distinction between current and noncurrent be maintained.

Disagree

[995] This approach conflicts with cash flow objectives.

[1473] In general, we believe that better indications of cash flow requirements would be served by classification of the deferred tax accounts based on expected reversal dates.

Question 46

It is acceptable to net deferred tax credits with deferred tax charges provided they are both classified as either current or noncurrent.

Agree

[44] Current-yes. Noncurrent-no.

[1159R] Materiality or nature of reason for deferred might mean net could be acceptable.

[1744R] Netting should be allowed within related categories of deferred tax. Under the valuation concept, the credits and charges would have to be related to the same asset or liability in order to be netted.

Disagree

[907R] Under the valuation concept, the deferred tax credits and charges would have to be related to the same asset or liability in order to be netted.

[279] For clarity sake, show broad-more meaningful to see composition of the account.

## Tax Rates (Questions 47-49)

Question 47

Current period additions to deferred tax accounts should be based on the current tax rate rather than on expected future tax rates.

[33] If different future rates have been legislated, they should be used. However, estimated future rates should not be used.

[907R] The tax rate to use in computing an addition to deferred taxes should be the tax rate in effect when the transaction which resulted in the deferred taxes was or will be reflected on the tax return.

[1040R] If the timing difference has already hit a tax return then yes. If it has not, then provision to adjust to future tax rates is appropriate.

[1073R] Agree, with the exception of deferred tax charges, which should be recorded based upon the rate expected at the time of reversal, if the rate change is known.

Question 48

The reduction in a deferred tax account under the deferral method should be measured by assuming a FIFO flow of prior deferrals and rates.

Agree

[222] Generally agree, but should have option to use average rate assumption under gross change method, or measurement criteria specified for net change method.

[1365] Agree in theory, but a FIFO flow would be extremely difficult to implement.

Disagree

[192] For large companies, a booking nightmare.
[418] An average of set-up rates is much more workable than FIFO.
[87] Considering the various rates used over the years to establish the deferred tax credit or charge, average rates should be used for reduction.
[177] Should allow use of net change with average or current rates.
[1073R] Theoretically, FIFO or average is most appropriate but for practical application, it is most appropriate to use current rates.
[1713] FIFO is acceptable, but weighted average is preferable.
[1805] It is believed that the use of a weighted average tax rate would be reasonably accurate and much less burdensome.
[1932] Use of current rates should be an acceptable alternative.

Question 49

All prior deferred tax charges and credits should be adjusted to the current tax rate whenever the rates change.

Agree

[5] Yes, if the taxing authority changes the rates but not if the level of income causes changes in the rate bracket and future expectations are to return to the prior bracket.
[641R] Provided that in the case of regulated industries, the appropriate rate relief is concurrent with recording of the tax rate adjustment.
[960] Provides the most current estimate of the effect on current and future cash flow.

Disagree

[222R] Generally disagree, except in the case of an NOL carry forward.

[717] Perhaps a material unrecorded potential liability as a result of a rate increase should be disclosed.

[988] Cost prohibitive income statements for the year of change would be a disaster.

[1073R] Conservative accounting should require deferred items to be adjusted only if the liability increases.

[1704] The present method of adjusting through the tax cushion at the time of reversal and then determining the adequacy of the cushion is adequate.

[153] Should consider amortizing the rate change into income over the expected period of reversal.

## Discounting (Questions 50-52)

Question 50

Long-term deferred tax accounts should be discounted.

Agree

[379] If comprehensive allocation is to continue, then discounting deferred taxes seems preferable.

[5] Generally agree but only within the context of discounting other long-term assets and liabilities.

[995] If comprehensive allocation is retained, discounting may more accurately reflect real liability.

Disagree

[340] Too many subjective factors would be involved if discounting were required (i.e., time period, appropriate rate, change in rates).

[526R] This would further complicate an already complex situation, i.e., "interest" would have to be accrued on an annual basis.

[11R] The issue of the discounting of all liabilities to present value should be addressed as a separate question as part of the conceptual framework.

[1073R] Discounting is very proper in theory, but the application of this would be nearly impossible due to the unknown date of reversal.

[1574] Only if the liability method were adopted, and this complexity appears to be a negative of that method.

[1793] Administratively, this could be a quagmire under the net change method.

[1898R] In as much as accumulated deferred tax credits are deducted from the rate base, these funds are not 'tax-free." Thus, discounting is especially inappropriate for utilities.

Question 51

The appropriate discounting rate would be a company's internal rate of return.

Agree

[1705] Yes, but other rates such as a company's cost to acquire long-term funds in the current year should be considered.

Disagree

[340] Have problem defining "company's internal rate of return." Use of such would hinder comparability from company to company and/or industry to industry.

[522R] Rate used should be the weighted after tax cost of capital.

[526R] Incremental borrowing rate would be more appropriate.

[1473] The company recognized that there would be substantial implementation complexities if deferred taxes were discounted to present value, and therefore does not believe it would be cost justified. We generally believe that if such accounting were required, it should conceptually be the following net long-term assets should be discounted based on a company's internal rate of return, whereas net long-term liabilities should be discounted using either the company's incremental borrowing rate or its cost of capital, whichever is most appropriate.

[1932] Interest rate should be the same rate for all companies and should be a widely recognized rate, such as the prime rate.

Question 52

The discount period should be determined by the reversal period of the aggregate amounts of the deferred tax accounts rather than of the individual items within the account.

Agree

[995] Individual item basis is not necessary. There is no need to be so exact.

[1473] However, under the current accounting rules (comprehensive allocation), this would not be consistent with the overall theory for deferred tax accounting. Such a theory appears to be more consistent with the partial allocation concepts which more appropriately consider the overall rollover issues regarding certain deferred tax items.

Disagree

[1098] If the account contains a few major items of timing differences, then recognition should be given to those individual items.

[1793] If it is to be done, it should be done correctly. Averaging could lead to distortion.

## Loss and Tax Credit Carryforwards (Question 19 and 53-59)

Question 19

General level of agreement with current accounting rules for recording the tax benefits of loss and tax credit carryforwards.

Agree

[413R] Disagree with the method of accounting for investment credit carry forwards. The company also believes that the accounting rules for loss and tax credit carry forwards are extremely complex and difficult to apply. An effort should be made to simplify the method.

[457] Realization of the NOL should not be extraordinary.

[876] Benefit on realization of a loss carry forward should be classified as continuing operations, not an extraordinary item.

[1473] In general, the company agrees with the current rules on the recording of tax benefits of loss and tax carry forwards in most instances. However, there are specific portions of those rules which we believe are in need of revision. First, we believe that the realization of tax benefits in later years related to net operating loss carry forwards should not be treated as an extraordinary item. It does not seem appropriate to penalize continuing operations of a company in a loss year (by not being able to recognize the tax effect related to those operating losses) and then require that the subsequent accounting for the actual realization of those benefits later on be excluded from continuing operations...

Secondly, we believe the existing rules regarding the overall accounting recognition of net operating loss carry forwards are too complex and, as a result, incomprehensible to management in most cases. While some general realization criteria are appropriate, it is our general feeling that these rules are unnecessarily complex principally because of the very stringent recognition principles inherent in the literature, i.e., assurance beyond a reasonable doubt....In our view, many of these problems would be resolved if the rules were written more with larger or more complex companies in mind. For example, most larger corporations should be in a situation which allows them to immediately recognize the tax benefits of net operating loss carry forwards if a reasonableness test was used rather than an assured beyond a reasonable doubt test.

[1793] Ultimate realization rules are difficult to apply and are construed differently by the major accounting firms.

[37R] The lack of rules or guidelines pertaining to consolidated tax allocations pertaining to loss subsidiaries.

[1633] The guidelines for recognition of loss carry forwards are too restrictive, resulting in inappropriate treatment.

Question 53

In light of the increase in the NOL carry forward period to 15 years, a company should be permitted to recognize the benefits of a NOL carry forward in the year incurred, except where the future viability of the company is in doubt.

Agree

[211] Yes, but with full disclosure.

[907R] In situations where the utilization of the NOL carry forward is probable (as defined in Concepts Statement No. 3), then the NOL carry forward should be recorded as an asset.

[1473] We generally believe that the criteria should be loosened for recognition of the tax benefits of NOLs, but the company should still be able to support such recognition based on the economic facts and circumstance affecting it at the time.

[37R] For two reasons: 1.) Possible merger candidate, therefore it may be probable an asset exists, and 2.) Over 15 years a viable company should turnaround.

[87] Recognition of tax benefit, either partially or in full, should be permitted when utilization is reasonably assured.

Disagree

[1079] NOL carry forwards should be allowed only in cases where realization is certain.

[1509] This is a gain contingency and should be recognized when realized.

[1805] The recognition of the benefits of the NOL carry forward in the year incurred should have been and continue to be based upon a conservative estimate of the company's viability and probable recovery in the period allowed.

[178] This is inconsistent with our position on income tax as current year's taxes payable within one year. We shouldn't recognize NOL or ITC carry forwards until they can be used to offset current income taxes payable.

Question 54

Future tax benefits of losses or credits that are acquired through acquisitions should be recorded as a separate asset, not as goodwill.

Agree

[250] Only if probable of being used in the future.

[1071] No different than any other asset acquired.

[1685] Should be recorded in all cases except where likelihood of obtaining the tax benefit is in doubt.

Disagree

[1045] How could this be done without revealing to the IRS its judgment values?

[181] Continue to include in goodwill until realized with disclosure of NOL.

Question 55

The excess of ITC available over ITC recognized should be recorded as an asset, not as a draw-down of net deferred tax credits.

Agree

[1473] While the company believes that recognition of the asset is somewhat dependent on or related to the anticipated existence of significant deferred tax credits which reverse in the ITC carry forward period, we nevertheless feel that the recognition of that benefit as an asset would be much more practical as compared to a requirement to actually recognize the benefit through technical reversal of the deferred tax credits in the company's accounts.

[1756] If you have consistently used flow-through, then I agree.

[49] Agree, if excess is to be recorded. However, excess should be based on taxable income rather than accounting income after permanent difference.

Disagree

[413R] It is not at all clear that the ITC should even be recognized until utilized in tax returns.
[960] Should not affect balance sheet. Recognized when usable for tax purposes footnote disclosure of carry over.
[5] Too many balance sheet accounts are confusing to the reader.

Question 56

A draw-down of deferred tax credits should be adjusted to current tax rates in determining the increase in tax liability that an actual draw-down would create for purposes of recording ITC carryforwards.

Agree

[250R] It should be adjusted to current rates and discounted.
[1373] As long as the adjustment is recorded to the tax provision, rather than distorting the balance sheet.

Disagree

[192] Far too complicated.
[1131] Impractical and immaterial.
[1930] The difference between current tax rates and the historical rate should be identified as a permanent adjustment at the time of actual reversal.

Question 57

Draw-downs due to an unused ITC should be limited to the tax increase resulting from a reversal of timing differences existing at the time the unused ITC originates; no recognition should be given to deferred credits that are likely to arise in the carryforward period.

Agree

[1473] While we generally believe that the recognition principles regarding ITC carryforwards are required, we again believe that the existing principles in the literature are much too stringent. In this regard, we believe that the rules should be revised to allow recognition of such carryforwards when they arise if the company can conclude that such benefits are reasonably probable of realization.

[1574] Recognition should be given if new deferred credits are projected during the planning horizon.

[83] Certain deferred credits relate to the continued existence of a company (in capital improvements) and should be considered.

Disagree

[507R] ITC carry forwards should not be recognized in the financial statements.

[1351] This is a good example of the "Alice in Wonderland" type problems which arise under current tax allocation practices.

[49] Impossible to determine in practice.

Question 58

Draw-downs due to foreign losses or unused credits should be restricted to foreign deferred tax credit accounts.

Agree

[5] No for foreign tax credit carry forward; yes for foreign net operating loss.

[5]* To do otherwise would be illogical.

Disagree

[1473] Since the ability of the company to utilize excess FTC carry forwards in the future will depend significantly on its ability to generate sufficient foreign source income as well as sufficient domestic taxes otherwise payable, the company should be able to support recognition of such future benefits based on its reasonable expectations of its future income levels, i.e., both foreign source and otherwise.

[1805] If deferred tax credits have arisen as a result of the consolidation process, then such tax credits should be considered when draw-downs are made; thereby not restricting such draw-downs only to the deferred credits of an individual company.

Question 59

Draw-downs from losses or unused credits should be restricted to the deferred tax credits of the company(ies) appearing on the tax return of the company incurring the loss or unused credit.

Agree

[1685] Agree with the corporate tax return entity theory, but not with draw-down limitation.

[75] Draw-down should reflect overall change in consolidated liability.

Disagree

[181] Unless deferred tax credits are only available to certain companies.

## Tax Credits (Questions 60-66)

Question 60

Definitive allocation rules should be developed to account for all tax credits.

[457] This area is too complex for definitive rules, but conceptual guidelines would be helpful.

[553] There must be some flexibility in the rules due to the uncertain amount and nature of the foreign tax credit.

[988] Other credits are not as common as the ITC and they can be applied in a similar fashion to ITC without "cookbook" rules.

[1159R] Tax credits are so varied that definitive rules in many cases would cause undue complication.

---

*This response is from a bias sample company (actually No. 5-2) whereas the prior response was from the random sample group, company 5.

Question 61

Deferral and flow-through should continue to be acceptable methods of accounting for investment credits.

Agree

[7] Absolutely.

Disagree

[413R] Deferral and amortization should be required for all companies.

[717] Deferral and amortization is preferable. The APB dropped the ball a long time ago. It's too late to change.

[1071] Flow-through is the accepted method and should be prescribed.

[1473] The company believes the flow-through method is the most appropriate method since it most clearly recognizes the effects of the tax benefits associated with the credit. Therefore, comparability among companies would be improved by establishing an accounting requirement to use only that method.

Question 62

The deferred investment credit is more properly classified as a liability rather than as the reduction in the acquisition cost of the related asset.

[470R] We feel it would be more proper to classify it as a "deferred owners'equity" than a liability.

[995] The ITC is a rate reduction rather than an asset cost adjustment.

[29R] Investment credit should be reported separately as a deferred credit.

[174R] Deferred ITC is not a liability or a reduction in an acquisition cost.

Question 63

The deferred method for timing differences is consistent with the deferred method for investment credits.

[53R] One is a timing difference, the other is not.

[413R] The company believes the deferral method is correct for both timing differences and ITC; however, flow-through accounting for one does not necessarily dictate flow-through accounting for another.

[988] Applications and use are separate and need not be treated identically (a liquidated company would have reversal of all timing differences and be unable to use the deferred ITC-availability of the credit is not assured).

[1704] Although theoretically preferable, the record keeping is too burdensome for most companies.

Question 64

The tax basis adjustment required by TEFRA is sufficient to argue that investment credits should be recorded as contra-assets for financial purposes.

[413R] There are strong arguments for recording investment tax credits as contra-accounts to the related assets with or without reductions of basis for tax purposes.

[876] Details of the tax code should generally not control accounting treatment. For instance, in this case, how would you take into account the option to reduce the credit itself?

[1242] Tax and book accounting are "different" and one should not dictate the other.

[1536] Congress' intent in adopting tax legislation should not be viewed as a basis of establishing generally accepted accounting principles.

Question 65

The reported amount of ITC used should be based on the book tax provision rather than the actual tax liability.

Agree

[33] However, economic realities must prevail. If ITC expires on a tax but not a book basis, the expiration should be recognized for financial reporting.

[1427R] It should be recognized not only on the book tax provision, but also on deferred tax timing differences turning around in the carryforward period.

[1805] The statement would be true except to the extent that the credit available based on taxable income was greater than would be allowed based on book income, in which circumstances the larger current credit should flow through to net income since it represents a permanent difference.

Disagree

[413R] The tax carry forward is the only meaningful number. If ITC can never be used in tax returns, it will never be utilized and therefore should not be recorded for financial purposes until utilized in tax returns.

[988] The "amount of ITC used" should be based on the actual amount of the ITC used (which must be the tax liability figure).

Question 66

Both the book ITC carry forward and the actual tax ITC carry forward should be disclosed in the notes to the financial statement.

Agree

[1771] Both should be disclosed if material.

[1805] Footnote disclosure of book ITC carry forward and/or the actual tax ITC carry forward should be considered if it is expected that the recognition of such amounts in future periods will materially impact the earnings of such periods.

Disagree

[304] Only the actual tax ITC carry forwards should be shown in the notes to the financial statements.

[418R] Only actual tax ITC carry forward is relevant.

[1705] Book ITC carry over will only confuse readers.

[1716] Book ITC is meaningless.

[4] Only the book carry forward should be disclosed, when material.

[37R] The amount of ITC expected to be used should be recorded as an asset and any excess value above that amount disclosed in the footnotes as a possible gain contingency.

# Acquisitions and Consolidations (Questions 67-72)

Question 67

The amortization of purchased goodwill is correctly designated as a permanent difference, even where it is anticipated that the business segment containing it will be sold.

Agree

[526] There is always some doubt as to whether or not the segment will be sold until the sale actually occurs.

[1234] It is extremely rare that a company is acquired with the intent of reselling in the near term.

[1473] Generally, the question as to whether a divestiture will be made by sale of stock vs. sale of assets can be an important question that may affect value if the business is going to be sold. From the standpoint of goodwill specifically, this may significantly affect the ultimate deductibility of that intangible asset. Therefore, our general feeling is that it must be considered, at best, a contingent asset until it is actually realized through deductibility on the return.

Disagree

[192] While anticipation of a sale is not realization, recognition as a timing difference is justified.

[954] If facts warrant, i.e., planned dispositions, timing treatment should be allowed.

[995] The entire concept of amortizing goodwill is weak. The concentration should be placed on realization/going concern values.

[1445] Amortization of goodwill may be reflected as a timing difference if the sale will be structured such that goodwill is included in the tax basis of the assets sold.

Question 68

The requirement in APB Opinion No. 16 that the reported fair value of an asset acquired through a stock purchase should reflect the asset's tax deductibility basis supports the arguments favoring the net-of-tax accounting concept.

Agree

[1040] We feel the net-of-tax (valuation) method does fairly reflect certain business transactions. This is one.

Disagree

[44] It doesn't support the argument. It only highlights the need for the creation of a tax liability (asset) related to the basis.

[591R] Financial considerations in a business combination accounted for as a purchase are not necessarily the same for the acquisition of an asset.

[1242] The tax amount should be reported separately.

[1509] Normal accrual is not a valuation exercise. Allocation of purchase price is a valuation exercise.

[1793] APB No. 16 is not applied consistently with respect to this issues by all accounting firms. I would argue that APB No. 16 should be revisited on this issue.

Question 69

If the tax basis exceeded the asset's fair value, the reported amount of the asset should be limited to the fair value, with the excess tax basis accounted for as a NOL would be treated.

Agree

[1509] But it should be as a purchased NOL, not as an extraordinary credit.

[37] If this question means that the tax benefit of the excess taxbasis amortization would be recognized over the asset life, the answer is agree.

Disagree

[457] The excess should be treated like any other permanent difference with the resulting reduction in tax expense explained in the notes.

[907] The asset's fair value would include the value of its tax benefits. However, if the tax basis is somehow more than fair value,you would have an additional asset and if its utilization is probable (as used in Concepts Statement No. 3), then the excess basis should be recorded as an asset.

[11R] Tax basis is a factor to be considered in determining fair value. If fair value is properly determined, the excess of the tax basis is a permanent difference that need not be accounted for.

Question 70

The basis difference between book and tax is a permanent difference, even though it will turn around as the asset is written off or sold.

[1045] Financial benefit on difference should be recorded as it is utilized for tax return.

[1432] How can it be a permanent difference when it will turn around?

[192] It will not turn around.

Question 71

If the basis difference is a permanent difference, then adjusting the recorded basis of a depreciable asset for the tax effect forces the recognition of a permanent difference over the book life rather than the tax life of the asset.

[323R] The book life more properly reflects the earning potential of the assets. The tax life only reflects the tax sheltering potential of the assets via accelerated depreciation deductions.

[876] That's a tough one. Conceptually the statement appear accurate; but I wouldn't handle it as a basis reduction.

[1427R] The longer of the two depreciation lives.

[1805] If there is a difference between the book and tax life of an asset, then the matching principle would require that the amortization of a permanent difference would be recognized over the book life of the asset.

[145R] Believe recognition of difference over the shorter tax life would be more appropriate, because difference disappears when asset becomes fully depreciated for tax purposes.

Question 72

Elimination of the equity method (for subsidiaries owned over 50 percent) in favor of consolidation would improve accounting for income tax.

[593] Under APB No. 3 equity subs and consolidated subs are governed by the same rules. Therefore, I"m not sure that your point has been well taken.

[844] If the nature of the business of the sub varies from that of the parent, then I believe the equity basis is preferable.

[1071] This might improve tax accounting, but at a cost of misstating the rest of the financial statements.

[1771] Accounting for equity investments is a different issue. However, in practice many companies consolidate their equity investment on the income statement.

[11] The problem of accounting for taxes is the same for both the equity method and consolidation unless a consolidated tax return is filed.

[177] We agree with the statement but do not favor elimination of the equity method.

# Appendix B
# Tables of Data from the Preparer Questionnaire

This Appendix contains nine tables in which the data from Questions 3 through 19 from the preparers' questionnaire are analyzed. The analysis is generally shown separately for each of the three measurement classifications, i.e., for each of the nine basic SIC groups, for those respondents with assets under and over $250 million, and also for nonregulated and regulated respondents.

Tables B.3, B.4, and B.5 identify timing differences only by their identification numbers which are shown in the following table.

| Identification Number | Timing Differences |
|---|---|
| 1 | Accrual to cash method |
| 2 | Omitted (included in 30) |
| 3 | Omitted (included in 30) |
| 4 | Bad debt allowances (loan losses) |
| 5 | Capitalized interest |
| 6 | Contribution carryforwards |
| 7 | Coupon redemption |
| 8 | Deferred compensation (not pensions) |
| 9 | Depreciation and amortization |
| 10 | DISC |
| 11 | Foreign currency translation |
| 12 | Installment sales |
| 13 | Intangible drilling costs (oil and gas exploration and development) |
| 14 | Intercompany profit |
| 15 | Inventory valuations |
| 16 | Investment tax credit |
| 17 | Leases |
| 18 | Long-term contracts |
| 19 | Net operating losses |
| 20 | Pensions |
| 21 | Plant shutdowns |
| 22 | Property tax |
| 23 | Self insurance |
| 24 | State tax defferals |
| 25 | Stock options |
| 26 | U.K. stock relief |
| 27 | Unremitted equity method earnings |
| 28 | Vacation accruals |
| 29 | Warranty and repair expenses |
| 30 | Other items (miscellaneous) |
| 31 | Omitted (included in 13) |
| 32 | Purchased gas adjustment |
| 33 | Gain on debt retirement |
| 34 | Defense facilities |
| 35 | Allowance for borrowed funds |
| 36 | Revenue agents review adjustments |
| 37 | Cost of removal |
| 38 | Safe harbor lease transactions |
| 39 | Nuclear fuel storage |

TABLE B.1 *Net Deferred Tax Charges and Deferred Tax Credits (on a Separate Corporation Basis)*

| | | 1977 Net Deferred Tax Charges | | | | 1982 Net Deferred Tax Charges | | | | |
|---|---|---|---|---|---|---|---|---|---|---|
| | | Number of Corps. | *000* Minimum | *000* Maximum | *000* Mean | Number of Corps. | *000* Minimum | *000* Maximum | *000* Mean | Increase over 1977 |
| 1 | Agriculture, Forest, & Fishing | -- | -- | -- | -- | -0- | -- | -- | -- | -- |
| 2 | Mining | 1 | 23,416 | 23,416 | 23,416 | -0- | -- | -- | -- | -100% |
| 3 | Construction | -- | -- | -- | -- | -0- | -- | -- | -- | -- |
| 4 | Manufacturing | 18 | 38 | 628,600 | 49,188 | 15 | 34 | 683,030 | 67,050 | 36.3% |
| 5 | Transportation, Communication, & Other Public Utilities | 2 | 13,249 | 411,620 | 212,440 | 4 | 271 | 793,600 | 233,980 | 10.1% |
| 6 | Wholesale Trade | 2 | 32 | 4,265 | 2,149 | 1 | 2,284 | 2,284 | 2,284 | 6.3% |
| 7 | Retail Trade | 2 | 307 | 3,316 | 1,812 | 2 | 1,064 | 1,075 | 1,070 | -40.9% |
| 8 | Finance, Insurance, & Real Estate | 4 | 662 | 6,222 | 2,747 | 5 | 869 | 154,600 | 44,023 | 1,502.6% |
| 9 | Services | 1 | 1,249 | 1,249 | 1,249 | | -- | -- | -- | -100% |
| | Totals | 30 | | | | 27 | | | | |

| | | 1977 Net Deferred Tax Credits | | | | 1982 Net Deferred Tax Credits | | | | |
|---|---|---|---|---|---|---|---|---|---|---|
| | | Number of Corps. | *000* Minimum | *000* Maximum | *000* Mean | Number of Corps. | *000* Minimum | *000* Maximum | *000* Mean | Increase over 1977 |
| 1 | Agriculture, Forest, & Fishing | 4 | 2,128 | 544,690 | 179,160 | 4 | 29,700 | 1,291,000 | 520,340 | 190.4% |
| 2 | Mining | 10 | 450 | 2,422,800 | 470,740 | 11 | 7,762 | 5,782,000 | 1,160,200 | 146.5% |
| 3 | Construction | 1 | 1,034 | 1,034 | 1,034 | 1 | 1,900 | 1,900 | 1,900 | 83.8% |
| 4 | Manufacturing | 94 | 6 | 458,450 | 46,798 | 99 | 99 | 2,704,300 | 131,930 | 181.9% |
| 5 | Transportation, Communication, & Other Public Utilities | 64 | 175 | 6,210,100 | 236,220 | 62 | 1,713 | 14,385,000 | 537,890 | 127.7% |
| 6 | Wholesale Trade | 3 | 127 | 410,700 | 137,510 | 5 | 20 | 320,600 | 64,585 | -53.0% |
| 7 | Retail Trade | 4 | 908 | 457,000 | 116,750 | 5 | 4,093 | 772,000 | 159,560 | 36.7% |
| 8 | Finance, Insurance, & Real Estate | 21 | 7 | 239,760 | 70,707 | 21 | 64 | 770,730 | 178,080 | 151.9% |
| 9 | Services | 7 | 28 | 46,453 | 14,803 | 9 | 400 | 82,121 | 24,805 | 67.6% |
| | Totals | 208 | | | | 217 | | | | |
| | Total Corporations Represented | 238 | | | | 244 | | | | |

Table B.1 (Continued)

| | 1977 Net Deferred Tax Charges | | | | 1982 Net Deferred Tax Charges | | | | |
|---|---|---|---|---|---|---|---|---|---|
| | Number of Corps. | *000* Minimum | *000* Maximum | *000* Mean | Number of Corps. | *000* Minimum | *000* Maximum | *000* Mean | Percentage Increase for 1977 |
| Assets less than $250 million | 12 | 32 | 4,265 | 1,043 | 10 | 34 | 5,100 | 1,224 | 17.4% |
| Assets greater than $250 million | 18 | 609 | 628,600 | 74,517 | 17 | 248 | 793,600 | 126,700 | 70.0% |

| | 1977 Net Deferred Tax Credits | | | | 1982 Net Deferred Tax Credits | | | | |
|---|---|---|---|---|---|---|---|---|---|
| | Number of Corps. | *000* Minimum | *000* Maximum | *000* Mean | Number of Corps. | *000* Minimum | *000* Maximum | *000* Mean | Percentage Increase for 1977 |
| Assets less than $250 million | 42 | 6 | 15,298 | 2,181 | 46 | 20 | 25,022 | 3,911 | 79.3% |
| Assets greater than $250 million | 166 | 132 | 6,210,100 | 164,570 | 171 | 64 | 14,385,000 | 386,900 | 135.1% |

| | 1977 Net Deferred Tax Charges | | | | 1982 Net Deferred Tax Charges | | | | |
|---|---|---|---|---|---|---|---|---|---|
| | Number of Corps. | *000* Minimum | *000* Maximum | *000* Mean | Number of Corps. | *000* Minimum | *000* Maximum | *000* Mean | Percentage Increase for 1977 |
| Nonregulated Corporations | 30 | 32 | 628,600 | 45,127 | 25 | 34 | 793,600 | 80,966 | 79.4% |
| Regulated Corporations | -- | -- | -- | -- | 2 | 295 | 141,750 | 71,021 | N/A |

| | 1977 Net Deferred Tax Credits | | | | 1982 Net Deferred Tax Credits | | | | |
|---|---|---|---|---|---|---|---|---|---|
| | Number of Corps. | *000* Minimum | *000* Maximum | *000* Mean | Number of Corps. | *000* Minimum | *000* Maximum | *000* Mean | Percentage Increase for 1977 |
| Nonregulated Corporations | 149 | 6 | 2,422,800 | 87,275 | 159 | 20 | 5,782,000 | 214,413 | 145.7% |
| Regulated Corporations | 59 | 1,176 | 6,210,100 | 244,170 | 58 | 1,713 | 14,385,000 | 555,990 | 127.7% |

TABLE B.2 *Deferred ITC by Measurement Classifications for Corporations Using the Deferred Method for One or More Entities or Transactions Including Lease Transactions in 1977 or 1982*

| | 1977 | | | | 1982 | | | | |
|---|---|---|---|---|---|---|---|---|---|
| | Number of Corps. | *000* Minimum | *000* Maximum | *000* Mean | Number of Corps. | *000* Minimum | *000* Maximum | *000* Mean | Percentage Increase over 1977 |
| Agriculture, Forest, & Fishing | 2 | 677 | 16,456 | 8,567 | 1 | 75,004 | 75,004 | 75,004 | 775.5% |
| Mining | 2 | 3,410 | 245,600 | 124,510 | 1 | 9,879 | 9,879 | 9,879 | -92.1% |
| Construction | 0 | -- | -- | -- | 0 | -- | -- | -- | -- |
| Manufacturing | 12 | 40 | 114,000 | 21,532 | 10 | 38 | 306,000 | 61,183 | 184.1% |
| Transportation, Communication, & Other Public Utilities | 51 | 2,576 | 2,730,300 | 112,010 | 53 | 3,549 | 6,543,700 | 255,250 | 127.9% |
| Wholesale Trade | 0 | -- | -- | -- | 0 | -- | -- | -- | -- |
| Retail Trade | 1 | 1,375 | 1,375 | 1,375 | 0 | -- | -- | -- | -- |
| Finance, Insurance, & Real Estate | 9 | 67 | 156,110 | 25,736 | 11 | 239 | 468,590 | 59,553 | 131.4% |
| Services | 1 | 54 | 54 | 54 | 1 | 1,942 | 1,942 | 1,942 | 3,496.3% |
| Totals | 78 | | | | 77 | | | | |
| Assets less than $250 million | 5 | 40 | 3,274 | 1,581 | 6 | 38 | 6,337 | 2,973 | 88.0% |
| Assets over $250 million | 73 | 54 | 2,730,300 | 85,520 | 71 | 239 | 6,543,700 | 209,350 | 144.8% |
| Totals | 78 | | | | 77 | | | | |
| Nonregulated corporations | 28 | 40 | 245,600 | 27,422 | 25 | 38 | 468,590 | 54,729 | 99.6% |
| Regulated corporations | 50 | 2,576 | 2,730,300 | 114,040 | 52 | 3,549 | 6,543,700 | 259,880 | 127.9% |
| Totals | 78 | | | | 77 | | | | |

TABLE B.3 *The Ten Most Frequently Mentioned Sources of Timing Differences (Deferred Charges and Deferred Credits) by Measurement Classifications (for 1977 and 1982)*

1982 Deferred Charge Items of Timing Differences*

| Rank Order | SIC Groups 1 | 2 | 3 | 4 | 5 | 6 | 7 | 8 | 9 |
|---|---|---|---|---|---|---|---|---|---|
| 1 | 15[1] | 9[1] | -- | 8[27] | 39[8] | 20[2] | 17[2] | 4[3] | 8[2] |
| 2 | 20[1] | 15[1] | -- | 15[14] | 8[2] | 8[1] | 4[1] | 8[2] | 23[1] |
| 3 | 21[1] | 17[1] | -- | 21[11] | 16[2] | 9[1] | 8[1] | 9[2] | 25[1] |
| 4 | 23[1] | 27[1] | -- | 24[10] | 19[2] | 19[1] | 20[1] | 24[2] | |
| 5 | | | -- | 29[10] | 17[1] | 24[1] | 28[1] | 1[1] | |
| 6 | | | -- | 4[8] | 21[1] | 28[1] | | 11[1] | |
| 7 | | | -- | 14[6] | 23[1] | 29[1] | | 16[1] | |
| 8 | | | -- | 23[6] | 29[1] | | | 19[1] | |
| 9 | | | -- | 9[5] | 37[1] | | | 21[1] | |
| 10 | | | -- | 20[5] | | | | | |

1977 Deferred Charge Items of Timing Differences*

| Rank Order | SIC Groups 1 | 2 | 3 | 4 | 5 | 6 | 7 | 8 | 9 |
|---|---|---|---|---|---|---|---|---|---|
| 1 | 15[1] | 9[1] | -- | 8[25] | 39[3] | 24[1] | 17[1] | 4[3] | 8[1] |
| 2 | 20[1] | 15[1] | -- | 15[16] | 8[2] | 28[1] | | 1[1] | 23[1] |
| 3 | 23[1] | 17[1] | -- | 29[16] | 5[1] | 29[1] | | 8[1] | 25[1] |
| 4 | | 27[1] | -- | 24[11] | 9[1] | | | 9[1] | |
| 5 | | | -- | 4[9] | 23[1] | | | 17[1] | |
| 6 | | | -- | 16[7] | 29[1] | | | 24[1] | |
| 7 | | | -- | 20[7] | 33[1] | | | | |
| 8 | | | -- | 14[6] | | | | | |
| 9 | | | -- | 21[6] | | | | | |
| 10 | | | -- | 23[6] | | | | | |

[ ] Denotes the number of corporations reporting this timing difference in their list of top 5 timing differences.

* See second page of Appendix B for the list of timing differences shown in this table by identification numbers.

Table B.3 (Continued)

1982 Deferred Credit Items of Timing Differences*

| Rank | SIC Groups | | | | | | | | |
|---|---|---|---|---|---|---|---|---|---|
| Order | 1 | 2 | 3 | 4 | 5 | 6 | 7 | 8 | 9 |
| 1 | 9[4] | 9[8] | -- | 9[93] | 9[61] | 9[4] | 9[5] | 9[11] | 9[8] |
| 2 | 13[2] | 13[7] | -- | 10[18] | 13[14] | 10[1] | 12[5] | 17[8] | 1[3] |
| 3 | 5[1] | 5[4] | -- | 5[17] | 16[12] | 12[1] | 5[1] | 16[4] | 38[3] |
| 4 | 17[1] | 12[3] | -- | 20[17] | 29[12] | 13[1] | 15[1] | 4[3] | 4[1] |
| 5 | 18[1] | 1[2] | -- | 12[15] | 32[11] | 15[1] | 20[1] | 13[3] | 5[1] |
| 6 | 20[1] | 27[2] | -- | 18[11] | 21[9] | | | 5[2] | 10[1] |
| 7 | 24[1] | 18[1] | -- | 13[10] | 35[7] | | | 27[2] | 16[1] |
| 8 | 27[1] | 20[1] | -- | 15[10] | 20[6] | | | 1[1] | 20[1] |
| 9 | | 38[1] | -- | 27[9] | 22[6] | | | 11[1] | 24[1] |
| 10 | | | -- | 16[6] | 37[5] | | | 20[1] | 27[1] |
| | | | | | | | | 24[1] | |
| | | | | | | | | 32[1] | |
| | | | | | | | | 38[1] | |

1977 Deferred Credit Items of Timing Differences*

| Rank | SIC Groups | | | | | | | | |
|---|---|---|---|---|---|---|---|---|---|
| Order | 1 | 2 | 3 | 4 | 5 | 6 | 7 | 8 | 9 |
| 1 | 9[4] | 9[8] | -- | 9[88] | 9[59] | 9[2] | 9[4] | 9[10] | 9[6] |
| 2 | 13[2] | 13[7] | -- | 10[18] | 13[13] | 13[1] | 12[2] | 4[5] | 1[1] |
| 3 | 27[2] | 5[2] | -- | 20[13] | 16[12] | 15[1] | 5[1] | 17[4] | 4[1] |
| 4 | 1[1] | 12[1] | -- | 15[12] | 29[10] | 26[1] | 20[1] | 16[3] | 5[1] |
| 5 | 15[1] | 18[1] | -- | 12[11] | 32[9] | | | 1[2] | 20[1] |
| 6 | 18[1] | 20[1] | -- | 27[11] | 35[5] | | | 12[1] | 27[1] |
| 7 | 20[1] | | -- | 13[9] | 20[4] | | | 13[1] | 33[1] |
| 8 | 24[1] | | -- | 16[5] | 21[4] | | | 20[1] | |
| 9 | | | -- | 18[5] | 27[4] | | | 24[1] | |
| 10 | | | -- | 22[4] | 33[4] | | | 27[1] | |
| | | | -- | 26[4] | 37[4] | | | 32[1] | |

[ ] Denotes the number of corporations reporting this timing difference in their list of top 5 timing differences.

* See second page of Appendix B for the list of timing differences shown in this table by identification numbers.

Table B.3 (Continued)

By Asset Size

Items of Timing Differences*

| Rank Order | Deferred Charges 1982 Under 250 M | Deferred Charges 1982 Over 250 M | Deferred Charges 1977 Under 250 M | Deferred Charges 1977 Over 250 M | Deferred Credits 1982 Under 250 M | Deferred Credits 1982 Over 250 M | Deferred Credits 1977 Under 250 M | Deferred Credits 1977 Over 250 M |
|---|---|---|---|---|---|---|---|---|
| 1 | 8[11] | 8[24] | 8[5] | 8[24] | 9[44] | 9[150] | 9[38] | 9[143] |
| 2 | 9[5] | 15[12] | 15[5] | 29[15] | 12[9] | 13[36] | 10[5] | 13[33] |
| 3 | 20[5] | 21[12] | 4[4] | 15[13] | 10[8] | 5[25] | 4[3] | 27[21] |
| 4 | 24[5] | 29[10] | 24[4] | 24[9] | 15[5] | 20[23] | 15[3] | 20[19] |
| 5 | 15[4] | 4[9] | 9[3] | 4[8] | 20[5] | 16[20] | 16[3] | 16[17] |
| 6 | 4[3] | 19[8] | 20[3] | 23[7] | 1[4] | 27[17] | 20[3] | 10[13] |
| 7 | 10[2] | 23[8] | 29[3] | 14[6] | 4[4] | 12[15] | 22[3] | 12[13] |
| 8 | 21[2] | 24[8] | 23[2] | 16[6] | 5[3] | 17[13] | 24[3] | 15[11] |
| 9 | 25[2] | 39[8] | | 20[5] | 16[3] | 10[12] | 12[2] | 29[11] |
| 10 | 28[2] | 16[6] | | 21[5] | 38[3] | 29[12] | 18[2] | 5[9] |
| | 29[2] | 17[6] | | | | | | 32[9] |

By Regulatory Status

Items of Timing Differences*

| Rank Order | Deferred Charges 1982 Nonregulated | Deferred Charges 1982 Regulated | Deferred Charges 1977 Nonregulated | Deferred Charges 1977 Regulated | Deferred Credits 1982 Nonregulated | Deferred Credits 1982 Regulated | Deferred Credits 1977 Nonregulated | Deferred Credits 1977 Regulated |
|---|---|---|---|---|---|---|---|---|
| 1 | 8[33] | 39[8] | 8[27] | 39[3] | 9[137] | 9[57] | 9[127] | 9[54] |
| 2 | 15[16] | 8[2] | 15[18] | 8[2] | 5[26] | 13[14] | 13[20] | 13[13] |
| 3 | 21[13] | 16[1] | 29[17] | 9[1] | 12[24] | 29[12] | 10[18] | 16[12] |
| 4 | 24[13] | 19[1] | 24[13] | 29[1] | 13[23] | 16[11] | 20[18] | 29[10] |
| 5 | 4[12] | 21[1] | 4[12] | 33[1] | 20[22] | 32[11] | 27[18] | 32[9] |
| 6 | 29[11] | 29[1] | 23[9] | | 10[20] | 21[9] | 12[15] | 35[5] |
| 7 | 9[9] | 37[1] | 20[8] | | 27[16] | 35[7] | 15[14] | 20[4] |
| 8 | 20[9] | | 16[7] | | 17[13] | 20[6] | 4[8] | 21[4] |
| 9 | 23[9] | | 9[6] | | 18[13] | 22[6] | 16[8] | 22[4] |
| 10 | 19[8] | | 14[6] | | 15[12] | 37[5] | 5[7] | 33[4] |
| | | | 21[6] | | 16[12] | | 17[7] | 37[4] |

[ ] Denotes the number of corporations reporting this timing difference in their list of top 5 timing differences.

* See second page of Appendix B for the list of timing differences shown in this table by identification numbers.

TABLE B.4 *The Ten Largest (by Average Size) Deferred Tax Charges and Deferred Tax Credits (by Identification Number)*

1982 Deferred Tax Charges*

| Rank Order | SIC Groups 1 | 2 | 3 | 4 | 5 | 6 | 7 | 8 | 9 |
|---|---|---|---|---|---|---|---|---|---|
| 1 | 21[1] | 15[1] | -- | 19[5] | 19[2] | 19[1] | 17[2] | 19[1] | 23[1] |
| 2 | 20[1] | 9[1] | -- | 14[6] | 39[8] | 24[1] | 8[1] | 24[2] | 8[2] |
| 3 | 15[1] | 17[1] | -- | 36[2] | 37[1] | 29[1] | 28[1] | 21[1] | 25[1] |
| 4 | 23[1] | 27[1] | -- | 29[10] | 23[1] | 20[2] | 20[1] | 11[1] | |
| 5 | | | -- | 24[10] | 21[1] | 8[1] | 4[1] | 8[2] | |
| 6 | | | -- | 15[14] | 16[2] | 28[1] | | 9[2] | |
| 7 | | | -- | 7[2] | 29[1] | 9[1] | | 16[1] | |
| 8 | | | -- | 16[4] | 8[2] | | | 4[3] | |
| 9 | | | -- | 28[4] | 17[1] | | | 1[1] | |
| 10 | | | -- | 8[27] | | | | | |

1977 Deferred Tax Charges*

| Rank Order | SIC Groups 1 | 2 | 3 | 4 | 5 | 6 | 7 | 8 | 9 |
|---|---|---|---|---|---|---|---|---|---|
| 1 | 20[1] | 9[1] | -- | 36[3] | 8[2] | 29[1] | 17[1] | 24[1] | 8[1] |
| 2 | 15[1] | 15[1] | -- | 16[7] | 39[3] | 24[1] | | 8[1] | 23[1] |
| 3 | 23[1] | 17[1] | -- | 14[6] | 23[1] | 28[1] | | 4[3] | 25[1] |
| 4 | | 27[1] | -- | 29[16] | 33[1] | | | 9[1] | |
| 5 | | | -- | 19[3] | 29[1] | | | 17[1] | |
| 6 | | | -- | 15[16] | 9[1] | | | 1[1] | |
| 7 | | | -- | 24[11] | 5[1] | | | | |
| 8 | | | -- | 11[3] | | | | | |
| 9 | | | -- | 28[4] | | | | | |
| 10 | | | -- | 8[25] | | | | | |

[ ] Denotes the number of corporations in each SIC group reporting this timing difference in their list of top 5 timing differences.

* See second page of Appendix B for the list of timing differences shown in this table by identification numbers.

Table B.4 (Continued)

1982 Deferred Tax Credits*

| Rank Order | SIC Groups 1 | 2 | 3 | 4 | 5 | 6 | 7 | 8 | 9 |
|---|---|---|---|---|---|---|---|---|---|
| 1 | 18[1] | 9[8] | -- | 13[10] | 9[61] | 9[4] | 12[5] | 32[1] | 9[8] |
| 2 | 9[4] | 13[7] | -- | 9[93] | 28[2] | 13[1] | 9[5] | 13[3] | 5[1] |
| 3 | 13[2] | 18[1] | -- | 5[17] | 16[12] | 15[1] | 5[1] | 9[11] | 10[1] |
| 4 | 24[1] | 38[1] | -- | 18[11] | 13[14] | 12[1] | 20[1] | 17[8] | 16[1] |
| 5 | 5[1] | 5[4] | -- | 17[4] | 21[9] | 10[1] | 15[1] | 38[1] | 20[1] |
| 6 | 20[1] | 12[3] | -- | 12[15] | 32[11] | | | 16[4] | 1[3] |
| 7 | 27[1] | 27[2] | -- | 38[5] | 14[2] | | | 27[2] | 38[3] |
| 8 | 17[1] | 1[2] | -- | 24[1] | 35[7] | | | 5[2] | 27[1] |
| 9 | | 20[1] | -- | 20[17] | 29[12] | | | 11[1] | 24[1] |
| 10 | | | -- | 15[10] | 27[4] | | | 24[1] | 4[1] |

1977 Deferred Tax Credits*

| Rank Order | SIC Groups 1 | 2 | 3 | 4 | 5 | 6 | 7 | 8 | 9 |
|---|---|---|---|---|---|---|---|---|---|
| 1 | 9[4] | 9[8] | -- | 21[1] | 9[59] | 9[2] | 12[2] | 13[1] | 5[1] |
| 2 | 13[2] | 13[7] | -- | 13[9] | 28[3] | 26[1] | 9[4] | 9[10] | 9[6] |
| 3 | 18[1] | 12[1] | -- | 5[3] | 16[12] | 15[1] | 5[1] | 17[4] | 20[1] |
| 4 | 24[1] | 18[1] | -- | 9[88] | 14[2] | 13[1] | 20[1] | 32[1] | 33[1] |
| 5 | 20[1] | 27[2] | -- | 12[11] | 13[13] | | | 16[3] | 1[1] |
| 6 | 27[2] | 5[2] | -- | 26[4] | 29[10] | | | 4[5] | 27[1] |
| 7 | 15[1] | 20[1] | -- | 15[12] | 1[1] | | | 1[2] | 4[1] |
| 8 | 1[1] | | -- | 20[13] | 32[9] | | | 24[1] | |
| 9 | | | -- | 27[11] | 35[5] | | | 27[1] | |
| 10 | | | -- | 19[2] | 34[1] | | | 20[1] | |

[ ] Denotes the number of corporations in each SIC group reporting this timing difference in their list of top 5 timing differences.

* See second page of Appendix B for the list of timing differences shown in this table by identification numbers.

Table B.4 (Continued)

By Asset Size*

| Rank Order | Deferred Charges | | | | Deferred Credits | | | |
|---|---|---|---|---|---|---|---|---|
| | 1982 | | 1977 | | 1982 | | 1977 | |
| | Under 250 M | Over 250 M | Under 250 M | Over 250 M | Under 250 M | Over 250 M | Under 250 M | Over 250 M |
| 1 | 21[2] | 15[12] | 10[1] | 36[3] | 18[2] | 9[150] | 12[2] | 9[143] |
| 2 | 29[2] | 19[8] | 29[3] | 16[6] | 13[1] | 13[36] | 17[1] | 13[33] |
| 3 | 10[2] | 9[4] | 21[1] | 9[4] | 15[5] | 28[2] | 18[2] | 21[5] |
| 4 | 23[1] | 24[8] | 17[1] | 14[6] | 32[1] | 18[11] | 32[1] | 28[3] |
| 5 | 1[1] | 39[8] | 19[1] | 15[13] | 12[9] | 16[20] | 9[38] | 12[13] |
| 6 | 16[1] | 14[6] | 12[1] | 29[15] | 9[44] | 12[15] | 16[3] | 16[17] |
| 7 | 9[5] | 36[2] | 9[3] | 19[2] | 16[3] | 21[9] | 26[1] | 14[2] |
| 8 | 15[4] | 29[10] | 16[1] | 24[9] | 38[3] | 32[11] | 10[5] | 17[6] |
| 9 | 8[11] | 37[1] | 15[5] | 11[3] | 10[8] | 5[25] | 24[3] | 5[9] |
| 10 | 6[1] | 7[2] | 8[5] | 28[4] | 1[4] | 38[9] | 15[3] | 26[4] |

[ ] Denotes the number of corporations reporting this timing difference.

* See second page of Appendix B for the list of timing differences shown in this table by identification numbers.

Table B.4 (Continued)

By Regulatory Status*

| Rank | Deferred Charges | | | | Deferred Credits | | | |
|---|---|---|---|---|---|---|---|---|
| | 1982 | | 1977 | | 1982 | | 1977 | |
| Order | Nonregulated | Regulated | Nonregulated | Regulated | Nonregulated | Regulated | Nonregulated | Regulated |
| 1 | 15[16] | 19[1] | 36[3] | 8[2] | 13[23] | 9[57] | 21[1] | 9[54] |
| 2 | 19[8] | 39[8] | 16[7] | 39[3] | 32[1] | 28[2] | 13[20] | 28[3] |
| 3 | 14[6] | 37[1] | 9[6] | 33[1] | 9[137] | 16[11] | 9[127] | 16[12] |
| 4 | 36[2] | 21[1] | 14[6] | 29[1] | 18[13] | 13[14] | 12[15] | 14[2] |
| 5 | 29[11] | 16[1] | 29[17] | 9[1] | 12[24] | 21[9] | 5[7] | 13[13] |
| 6 | 24[13] | 29[1] | 15[18] | | 5[26] | 32[11] | 17[7] | 29[10] |
| 7 | 9[9] | 8[2] | 19[3] | | 17[13] | 27[3] | 26[5] | 1[1] |
| 8 | 7[2] | | 24[13] | | 38[11] | 14[2] | 32[1] | 32[9] |
| 9 | 16[6] | | 11[3] | | 27[16] | 35[7] | 18[7] | 35[5] |
| 10 | 21[13] | | 28[5] | | 24[5] | 29[12] | 16[8] | 27[3] |

[ ] Denotes the number of corporations reporting this timing difference.

* See second page of Appendix B for the list of timing differences shown in this table by identification numbers.

TABLE B.5 *The Average Size of Deferred Tax Charges and Credits by Each Source of Timing Difference by the Three Measurement Classifications (for 1977 and 1982) (in thousands of dollars)*

| Timing Differences | 1982 Mean Deferred Charges SIC Codes 1 | 2 | 3 | 4 | 5 | 6 | 7 | 8 | 9 |
|---|---|---|---|---|---|---|---|---|---|
| 1 | | | | 685[1] | | | | 489[1] | |
| 4 | | | | 2,277[8] | | | 154[1] | 656[3] | |
| 6 | | | | 403[1] | | | | | |
| 7 | | | | 12,297[2] | | | | | |
| 8 | | | | 6,185[27] | 5,419[2] | 59[1] | 1,906[1] | 13,034[2] | 2,879[2] |
| 9 | | 176,100[1] | | 1,921[5] | | 2[1] | | 9,415[2] | |
| 10 | | | | 733[2] | | | | | |
| 11 | | | | 1,112[2] | | | | 21,160[1] | |
| 12 | | | | 4,801[1] | | | | | |
| 14 | | | | 31,680[6] | | | | | |
| 15 | 3,507[1] | 1,892,200[1] | | 23,062[14] | | | | | |
| 16 | | | | 11,222[4] | 9,833[2] | | | 6,714[1] | |
| 17 | | 3,316[1] | | 2,233[2] | 392[1] | | 3,566[2] | | |
| 18 | | | | 4,916[1] | | | | | |
| 19 | | | | 33,656[5] | 46,260[2] | 75,951[1] | | 456,440[1] | |
| 20 | 17,500[1] | | | 2,760[5] | | 66[2] | 782[1] | | |
| 21 | 20,711[1] | | | 5,825[11] | 15,180[1] | | | 23,793[1] | |
| 23 | 2,231[1] | | | 3,417[6] | 20,400[1] | | | | 4,797[1] |
| 24 | | | | 25,009[10] | | 1,272[1] | | 27,150[2] | |
| 25 | | | | 3,202[2] | | | | | 42[1] |
| 27 | | 64[1] | | | | | | | |
| 28 | | | | 6,736[4] | | 9[1] | 980[1] | | |
| 29 | | | | 29,671[10] | 6,716[1] | 731[1] | | | |
| 30 | 22,565[1] | 71,483[7] | 194[1] | 34,791[64] | 46,519[28] | 6,534[4] | 4,025[1] | 6,778[21] | 2,218[10] |
| 36 | | | | 30,954[2] | | | | | |
| 37 | | | | | 26,169[1] | | | | |
| 39 | | | | | 34,206[8] | | | | |

[ ] Denotes the number of corporations reporting this timing difference in their list of top 5 timing differences.

* See second page of Appendix B for the list of timing differences shown in this table by identification numbers.

Table B.5 (Continued)

| Timing Differences | 1977 Mean Deferred Charges* SIC Codes 1 | 2 | 3 | 4 | 5 | 6 | 7 | 8 | 9 |
|---|---|---|---|---|---|---|---|---|---|
| 1 | | | -- | 115[1] | | | | 189[1] | |
| 4 | | | -- | 1,705[9] | | | | 993[3] | |
| 5 | | | -- | | 14[1] | | | | |
| 8 | | | -- | 3,994[25] | 4,085[2] | | | 3,846[1] | 1,532[1] |
| 9 | | 149,000[1] | -- | 1,640[4] | 86[1] | | | 752[1] | |
| 10 | | | -- | 1,347[1] | | | | | |
| 11 | | | -- | 5,819[3] | | | | | |
| 12 | | | -- | 483[1] | | | | | |
| 14 | | | -- | 23,630[6] | | | | | |
| 15 | 2,000[1] | 72,741[1] | -- | 7,332[16] | | | | | |
| 16 | | | -- | 66,526[7] | | | | | |
| 17 | | 1,091[1] | -- | 303[2] | | | 7,000[1] | 746[1] | |
| 19 | | | -- | 9,048[3] | | | | | |
| 20 | 5,600[1] | | -- | 3,045[7] | | | | | |
| 21 | | | -- | 1,155[6] | | | | | |
| 22 | | | -- | 788[2] | | | | | |
| 23 | 1,500[1] | | -- | 1,304[6] | 2,765[1] | | | | 1,062[1] |
| 24 | | | -- | 6,427[11] | | 700[1] | | 12,893[1] | |
| 25 | | | -- | 91[1] | | | | | 202[1] |
| 27 | | 113[1] | -- | 222[1] | | | | | |
| 28 | | | -- | 5,784[4] | | 32[1] | | | |
| 29 | | | -- | 13,096[16] | 172[1] | 800[1] | | | |
| 30 | | 28,394[7] | -- | 25,083[55] | 25,191[23] | 840[5] | 1,899[2] | 2,874[12] | 671[7] |
| 33 | | | -- | | 1,997[1] | | | | |
| 36 | | | -- | 108,820[3] | | | | | |
| 39 | | | -- | | 3,363[3] | | | | |

[ ] Denotes number of corporations reporting this timing difference in their list of top 5 timing differences.

* See second page of Appendix B for the list of timing differences shown in this table by identification numbers.

Table B.5 (Continued)

| Timing Differences | 1982 Mean Deferred Tax Credits* | | | | | | | | |
|---|---|---|---|---|---|---|---|---|---|
| | SIC Codes | | | | | | | | |
| | 1 | 2 | 3 | 4 | 5 | 6 | 7 | 8 | 9 |
| 1 | | 4,423[2] | | 3,213[2] | 19,000[1] | | | 1,007[1] | 3,272[3] |
| 4 | | | | 342[2] | 162[1] | | | 2,210[3] | 35[1] |
| 5 | 23,600[1] | 86,420[4] | | 44,898[17] | 17,635[2] | | 29,000[1] | 10,882[2] | 9,530[1] |
| 8 | | | | 913[2] | | | | | |
| 9 | 326,390[4] | 881,490[8] | | 112,920[93] | 446,840[61] | 88,449[4] | 46,650[5] | 110,330[11] | 10,783[8] |
| 10 | | | | 8,186[18] | | 29[1] | | | 5,614[1] |
| 11 | | | | | | | | 2,885[1] | |
| 12 | | 76,780[3] | | 29,313[15] | | 1,698[1] | 96,986[5] | | |
| 13 | 201,370[2] | 701,120[7] | | 354,090[10] | 89,946[14] | 24,036[1] | | 137,980[3] | |
| 14 | | | | | 35,439[2] | | | | |
| 15 | | | | 13,301[10] | | 14,917[1] | 459[1] | | |
| 16 | | | | 10,174[6] | 117,060[12] | | | 15,283[4] | 4,619[1] |
| 17 | 13,300[1] | | | 30,382[4] | 24,505[1] | | | 51,851[8] | |
| 18 | 381,120[1] | 235,000[1] | | 40,755[11] | | | | | |
| 19 | | | | 461[1] | | | | | |
| 20 | 19,791[1] | 1,690[1] | | 16,212[17] | 9,519[6] | | 22,000[1] | 1,179[1] | 3,492[1] |
| 21 | | | | 88[1] | 62,670[9] | | | | |
| 22 | | | | 224[1] | 22,527[6] | | | | |
| 24 | 42,659[1] | | | 19,984[1] | 9,806[4] | | | 2,661[1] | 83[1] |
| 26 | | | | 10,800[1] | | | | | |
| 27 | 15,326[1] | 74,604[2] | | 7,121[9] | 28,349[4] | | | 15,148[2] | 108[1] |
| 28 | | | | 616[2] | 190,530[2] | | | | |
| 29 | | | | | 29,087[12] | | | | |
| 30 | 13,413[2] | 159,170[7] | 2,094[1] | 17,411[51] | 33,821[62] | 39[2] | 3,279[6] | 36,398[24] | 16,942[6] |
| 32 | | | | | 41,809[11] | | | 181,370[1] | |
| 33 | | | | 2,200[1] | 4,981[2] | | | | |
| 35 | | | | | 29,774[7] | | | | |
| 37 | | | | | 10,509[5] | | | | |
| 38 | | 189,900[1] | | 22,618[5] | 27,750[2] | | | 41,337[1] | 2,249[3] |

[ ] Denotes number of corporations reporting this timing difference in their list of top 5 timing differences.

* See second page of Appendix B for the list of timing differences shown in this table by identification numbers.

Table B.5 (Continued)

| Timing Differences | 1977 Mean Deferred Tax Credits* SIC Codes 1 | 2 | 3 | 4 | 5 | 6 | 7 | 8 | 9 |
|---|---|---|---|---|---|---|---|---|---|
| 1 | 5,500[1] | | | 929[1] | 13,000[1] | | | 626[2] | 400[1] |
| 4 | | | | 403[2] | 275[1] | | | 12,506[5] | 2[1] |
| 5 | | 6,004[2] | | 81,371[3] | 4,600[3] | | 13,000[1] | | 4,586[1] |
| 6 | | | | 450[1] | | | | | |
| 8 | | | | 14[1] | | | | | |
| 9 | 141,100[4] | 310,270[8] | | 51,638[88] | 212,810[59] | 182,320[2] | 21,863[4] | 49,845[10] | 4,259[6] |
| 10 | | | | 3,365[18] | | | | | |
| 12 | | 70,000[1] | | 24,792[11] | | | 148,310[2] | 64[1] | |
| 13 | 42,177[2] | 194,380[7] | | 87,313[9] | 24,159[13] | 1,734[1] | | 75,502[1] | |
| 14 | | | | | 33,102[2] | | | | |
| 15 | 7,400[1] | | | 7,781[12] | | 6,089[1] | | | |
| 16 | | | | 3,009[5] | 42,996[12] | | | | |
| 17 | | | | 3,271[3] | | | | 16,611[3] | |
| 18 | 39,335[1] | 40,000[1] | | 2,761[5] | | | | 47,898[4] | |
| 19 | | | | 4,007[2] | | | | | |
| 20 | 12,325[1] | 807[1] | | 7,196[13] | 8,265[4] | | 9,000[1] | 291[1] | 673[1] |
| 21 | | | | 305,600[1] | 8,496[4] | | | | |
| 22 | | | | 3,549[4] | 6,679[4] | | | | |
| 24 | 12,845[1] | | | 511[2] | 1,241[3] | | | 392[1] | |
| 26 | | | | 21,922[4] | | 27,624[1] | | | |
| 27 | 9,781[2] | 22,653[2] | | 6,149[11] | 6,693[4] | | | 358[1] | 81[1] |
| 28 | | | | 231[1] | 62,676[3] | | | | |
| 29 | | | | 1,189[1] | 21,582[10] | | | | |
| 30 | 8,261[3] | 103,620[6] | 1,034[1] | 15,223[46] | 19,047[62] | | 370[3] | 8,068[28] | 7,668[5] |
| 32 | | | | | 9,624[9] | | | 18,932[1] | |
| 33 | | | | 105[1] | 5,379[4] | | | | 524[1] |
| 34 | | | | | 8,706[1] | | | | |
| 35 | | | | | 9,624[5] | | | | |
| 37 | | | | | 6,144[4] | | | | |
| 39 | | | | | 1,139[2] | | | | |

[ ] Denotes number of corporations reporting this timing difference in their list of top 5 timing differences.

* See second page of Appendix B for the list of timing differences shown in this table by identification numbers.

Table B.3 (continued)

| Timing Differences | Deferred Charges 1982 Under 250 M | Deferred Charges 1982 Over 250 M | Deferred Charges 1977 Under 250 M | Deferred Charges 1977 Over 250 M | Deferred Credits 1982 Under 250 M | Deferred Credits 1982 Over 250 M | Deferred Credits 1977 Under 250 M | Deferred Credits 1977 Over 250 M |
|---|---|---|---|---|---|---|---|---|
| | By Asset Size* | | | | | | | |
| 1 | 685[1] | 489[1] | 115[1] | 189[1] | 1,540[4] | 7,787[5] | 400[1] | 4,136[5] |
| 4 | 204[3] | 2,192[9] | 239[4] | 2,171[8] | 220[4] | 2,210[3] | 269[3] | 10,468[6] |
| 5 | | | 14[1] | | 656[3] | 49,045[25] | 97[1] | 31,934[9] |
| 6 | 403[1] | | | | | | 450[1] | |
| 7 | | 12,297[2] | | | | | | |
| 8 | 417[11] | 8,627[24] | 261[5] | 4,671[24] | 913[2] | | 14[1] | |
| 9 | 551[5] | 50,446[4] | 385[3] | 38,811[4] | 2,483[44] | 319,290[150] | 1,410[38] | 147,330[143] |
| 10 | 733[2] | | 1,347[1] | | 1,878[8] | 11,498[12] | 568[5] | 4,441[13] |
| 11 | 43[1] | 11,671[2] | | 5,819[3] | | 2,885[1] | | |
| 12 | | 4,801[1] | 483[1] | | 2,516[9] | 75,602[15] | 5,404[2] | 48,353[13] |
| 13 | | | | | 2,982[1] | 292,940[36] | | 79,458[33] |
| 14 | | 31,680[6] | | 23,630[6] | | 35,439[2] | | 33,102[2] |
| 15 | 429[4] | 184,740[12] | 309[5] | 14,655[13] | 2,858[5] | 19,157[7] | 483[3] | 9,591[11] |
| 16 | 566[1] | 11,784[6] | 381[1] | 77,550[6] | 2,199[3] | 76,247[20] | 1,021[3] | 33,986[17] |
| 17 | | 2,551[6] | 605[1] | 2,210[4] | 1,525[1] | 44,048[13] | 5,162[1] | 32,707[6] |
| 18 | | 4,916[1] | | | 6,632[2] | 95,560[11] | 1,925[2] | 17,858[5] |
| 19 | 130[1] | 99,133[8] | 560[1] | 13,293[2] | 461[1] | | 13[1] | 8,000[1] |
| 20 | 100[5] | 7,928[4] | 149[3] | 5,293[5] | 1,098[5] | 16,321[23] | 288[3] | 7,833[19] |
| 21 | 4,224[2] | 9,609[12] | 850[1] | 1,215[5] | 88[1] | 62,670[9] | | 67,916[5] |
| 22 | | | 100[1] | 1,476[1] | 626[2] | 26,827[5] | 378[3] | 7,956[5] |
| 23 | 702[1] | 5,903[8] | 227[2] | 1,814[7] | | | | |
| 24 | 377[5] | 37,972[8] | 234[4] | 9,262[9] | 83[1] | 14,933[7] | 498[3] | 4,122[4] |
| 25 | 69[2] | 6,308[1] | 91[1] | 202[1] | | | | |
| 26 | | | | | | 10,800[1] | 853[1] | 28,615[4] |
| 27 | 64[1] | | 113[1] | 222[1] | 404[2] | 21,859[17] | | 7,605[21] |
| 28 | 27[2] | 6,969[4] | 32[1] | 5,784[4] | 616[2] | 190,530[2] | 231[1] | 62,676[3] |
| 29 | 1,394[2] | 30,137[10] | 1,078[3] | 13,818[15] | | 29,087[12] | | 19,728[11] |
| 30 | 644[34] | 41,020[103] | 332[26] | 25,839[85] | 907[29] | 38,611[132] | 568[28] | 22,049[126] |
| 32 | | | | | 2,659[1] | 58,056[11] | 1,770[1] | 11,531[9] |
| 33 | | | | 1,997[1] | | 4,054[3] | 105[1] | 4,408[5] |
| 34 | | | | | | | | 8,706[1] |
| 35 | | | | | | 29,774[7] | | 9,624[5] |
| 36 | | 30,954[2] | | 108,820[3] | | | | |
| 37 | | 26,169[1] | | | | 10,509[5] | | 6,144[4] |
| 38 | | | | | 1,933[3] | 44,531[9] | | |
| 39 | | 34,206[8] | | 3,363[3] | | | | 1,139[2] |

* See second page of Appendix B for the list of timing differences shown in this table by identification numbers.

Table B.5 (Continued)

By Regulatory Status*

| Timing Differences | Deferred Charges | | | | Deferred Credits | | | |
|---|---|---|---|---|---|---|---|---|
| | 1982 | | 1977 | | 1982 | | 1977 | |
| | Nonregulated | Regulated | Nonregulated | Regulated | Nonregulated | Regulated | Nonregulated | Regulated |
| 1 | 587[2] | | 152[2] | | 3,262[8] | 19,000[1] | 1,616[5] | 13,000[1] |
| 4 | 1,695[12] | | 1,527[12] | | 1,225[6] | 162[1] | 7,917[8] | 275[1] |
| 5 | | | 14[1] | | 45,878[26] | 17,635[2] | 39,101[7] | 4,600[3] |
| 6 | 403[1] | | | | | | 450[1] | |
| 7 | 12,297[2] | | | | | | | |
| 8 | 6,085[33] | 5,419[2] | 3,898[27] | 4,085[2] | 913[2] | 14[1] | | |
| 9 | 22,726[9] | | 26,052[6] | 86[1] | 159,930[137] | 457,770[57] | 73,250[127] | 218,880[54] |
| 10 | 733[2] | | 1,347[1] | | 7,650[20] | | 3,365[18] | |
| 11 | 7,795[3] | | 5,819[3] | | 2,885[1] | | | |
| 12 | 4,801[1] | | 483[1] | | 48,194[24] | | 42,626[15] | |
| 13 | | | | | 403,890[23] | 89,946[14] | 115,400[20] | 24,159[13] |
| 14 | 31,680[6] | | 23,630[6] | | | 35,439[2] | | 33,102[2] |
| 15 | 138,660[16] | | 10,670[18] | | 12,366[12] | | 7,633[14] | |
| 16 | 9,872[6] | 12,036[1] | 66,526[7] | | 14,660[12] | 123,240[11] | 8,110[8] | 42,996[12] |
| 17 | 2,551[6] | | 1,889[5] | | 42,280[13] | 24,505[1] | 28,772[7] | |
| 18 | 4,916[1] | | | | 81,879[13] | | 13,306[7] | |
| 19 | 93,634[8] | 44,120[1] | 9,048[3] | | 461[1] | | 4,007[2] | |
| 20 | 3,579[9] | | 3,364[8] | | 14,716[22] | 9,519[6] | 6,480[18] | 8,265[4] |
| 21 | 8,352[13] | 15,180[1] | 1,155[6] | | 88[1] | 62,670[9] | 305,600[1] | 8,496[4] |
| 22 | | | 788[2] | | 224[1] | 22,527[6] | 3,549[4] | 6,679[4] |
| 23 | 5,325[9] | | 1,461[9] | | | | | |
| 24 | 23,513[13] | | 6,484[13] | | 16,157[5] | 7,941[3] | 3,164[5] | 1,080[2] |
| 25 | 2,148[3] | | 147[2] | | | | | |
| 26 | | | | | 10,800[1] | | 23,063[5] | |
| 27 | 64[1] | | 168[2] | | 16,463[16] | 36,339[3] | 7,399[18] | 8,841[3] |
| 28 | 4,655[6] | | 4,633[5] | | 616[2] | 190,530[2] | 231[1] | 62,676[3] |
| 29 | 27,040[11] | 6,716[1] | 12,373[17] | 172[1] | | 29,087[12] | 1,189[1] | 21,582[10] |
| 30 | 26,583[111] | 49,857[26] | 17,931[91] | 28,660[20] | 30,110[101] | 34,696[60] | 17,274[94] | 19,506[60] |
| 32 | | | | | 181,370[1] | 41,809[11] | 18,932[1] | 9,624[9] |
| 33 | | | | 1,997[1] | 2,200[1] | 4,981[2] | 315[2] | 5,379[4] |
| 34 | | | | | | | | 8,706[1] |
| 35 | | | | | | 29,774[7] | | 9,624[5] |
| 36 | 30,954[2] | | 108,820[3] | | | | | |
| 37 | | 26,169[1] | | | | 10,509[5] | | 6,144[4] |
| 38 | | | | | 34,943[11] | 22,199[1] | | |
| 39 | | 34,206[8] | | 3,363[3] | | | | 1,139[2] |

* See second page of Appendix B for the list of timing differences shown in this table by identification numbers.

TABLE B.6 *The Average Percentage of Net Deferred Tax Charges or Credits (ExcluMing Unamortized ITC) to Owners' Equity and to Total Assets by Measurement Classifications for Years 1977 and 1982*

Net Deferred Tax Charges (Debits) as a Percentage of Owners' Equity

| Year | SIC Groups 1 | 2 | 3 | 4 | 5 | 6 | 7 | 8 | 9 |
|---|---|---|---|---|---|---|---|---|---|
| 1982 | -- | -- | -- | 5.0[16] | 13.6[5] | 40.0[1] | 1.5[2] | 6.3[3] | -- |
| 1981 | -- | -- | -- | 10.8[22] | 17.0[4] | 20.0[2] | 7.3[4] | 5.0[4] | -- |
| 1980 | -- | -- | -- | 3.4[16] | 17.2[5] | 0.0[2] | 4.0[3] | 3.3[4] | 2.0[1] |
| 1979 | -- | -- | -- | 2.3[20] | 12.6[5] | 0.0[1] | 3.0[3] | 4.3[4] | 2.0[1] |
| 1978 | -- | -- | -- | 4.3[21] | 10.8[5] | 2.0[2] | 3.5[2] | 3.5[4] | 3.0[1] |
| 1977 | -- | -- | -- | 7.6[21] | 12.8[4] | 4.0[2] | 1.5[2] | 3.8[4] | 3.0[1] |

[ ] Denotes the number of corporations in each computation.

Net Deferred Tax Credits as a Percentage of Owners' Equity

| Year | SIC Groups 1 | 2 | 3 | 4 | 5 | 6 | 7 | 8 | 9 |
|---|---|---|---|---|---|---|---|---|---|
| 1982 | 20.3[4] | 19.5[11] | 74.0[1] | 12.0[94] | 24.2[61] | 8.3[4] | 11.8[5] | 14.4[20] | 17.1[9] |
| 1981 | 16.8[4] | 17.5[11] | 54.0[1] | 11.6[89] | 22.6[62] | 13.0[2] | 10.0[3] | 12.5[20] | 17.2[9] |
| 1980 | 14.8[4] | 17.4[11] | 52.0[1] | 13.1[95] | 21.6[60] | 12.0[2] | 7.8[4] | 12.9[20] | 18.4[8] |
| 1979 | 15.8[4] | 16.3[11] | 34.0[1] | 9.8[91] | 19.7[61] | 9.0[3] | 8.0[4] | 12.3[19] | 19.6[8] |
| 1978 | 13.3[4] | 15.2[11] | 41.0[1] | 9.2[89] | 18.3[61] | 12.5[2] | 7.2[5] | 11.3[18] | 18.8[8] |
| 1977 | 12.3[4] | 13.7[11] | 59.0[1] | 7.8[90] | 17.1[62] | 11.5[2] | 9.3[4] | 11.2[18] | 15.1[7] |

[ ] Denotes the number of corporations in each computation.

Table B.6 (Continued)

Net Deferred Tax Charges (Debits) as a
Percentage of Total Assets

| Year | SIC Groups 1 | 2 | 3 | 4 | 5 | 6 | 7 | 8 | 9 |
|---|---|---|---|---|---|---|---|---|---|
| 1982 | -- | -- | -- | 1.5[16] | 5.0[5] | 2.0[1] | 1.0[2] | 0.3[3] | -- |
| 1981 | -- | -- | -- | 1.5[22] | 6.0[4] | 1.0[2] | 1.0[4] | 0.3[4] | -- |
| 1980 | -- | -- | -- | 1.5[16] | 5.0[5] | 0.0[2] | 1.3[3] | 0.0[4] | 0.0[1] |
| 1979 | -- | -- | -- | 1.1[20] | 4.4[5] | 0.0[1] | 1.0[3] | 0.5[4] | 1.0[1] |
| 1978 | -- | -- | -- | 1.3[21] | 4.2[5] | 0.5[2] | 1.0[2] | 0.5[4] | 1.0[1] |
| 1977 | -- | -- | -- | 1.3[21] | 4.8[4] | 1.5[2] | 0.5[2] | 0.0[4] | 1.0[1] |

[ ] Denotes the number of corporations in each computation.

Net Deferred Tax Credits as a
Percentage of Total Assets

| Year | SIC Groups 1 | 2 | 3 | 4 | 5 | 6 | 7 | 8 | 9 |
|---|---|---|---|---|---|---|---|---|---|
| 1982 | 10.0[4] | 8.4[11] | 17.0[1] | 4.8[94] | 8.9[61] | 3.5[4] | 3.4[5] | 3.8[20] | 5.1[9] |
| 1981 | 8.3[4] | 7.3[11] | 17.0[1] | 4.5[89] | 8.4[62] | 5.5[2] | 4.3[3] | 3.1[20] | 4.8[9] |
| 1980 | 7.5[4] | 7.8[11] | 18.0[1] | 4.0[94] | 8.0[60] | 5.0[2] | 3.5[4] | 2.9[20] | 3.4[8] |
| 1979 | 6.8[4] | 6.9[11] | 11.0[1] | 4.0[91] | 7.4[61] | 3.7[3] | 3.3[4] | 3.2[19] | 4.4[8] |
| 1978 | 6.8[4] | 6.7[11] | 13.0[1] | 3.9[89] | 7.0[61] | 5.5[2] | 2.8[5] | 3.0[18] | 4.4[8] |
| 1977 | 6.0[4] | 6.7[11] | 19.0[1] | 3.4[90] | 6.5[62] | 5.0[2] | 4.0[4] | 2.9[18] | 4.4[7] |

[ ] Denotes the number of corporations in each computation.

Table B.6 (Continued)

Asset Size

| Year | Percentage of Owners' Equity | | | | Percentage of Total Assets | | | |
|---|---|---|---|---|---|---|---|---|
| | Deferred Charge | | Deferred Credit | | Deferred Charge | | Deferred Credit | |
| | Under 250 M | Over 250 M | Under 250 M | Over 250 M | Under 250 M | Over 250 M | Under 250 M | Over 250 M |
| 1982 | 6.5[11] | 8.7[16] | 15.6[40] | 17.1[169] | 1.2[11] | 2.6[16] | 4.8[40] | 6.5[169] |
| 1981 | 5.2[16] | 15.6[20] | 14.9[34] | 16.2[167] | .9[16] | 2.5[20] | 4.6[34] | 6.1[167] |
| 1980 | 4.1[14] | 6.5[17] | 20.9[36] | 15.1[169] | 1.4[14] | 2.0[17] | 4.0[35] | 5.7[169] |
| 1979 | 2.3[15] | 5.4[19] | 11.3[35] | 14.5[167] | 1.1[15] | 1.7[19] | 3.7[35] | 5.5[167] |
| 1978 | 4.7[16] | 5.2[19] | 11.4[34] | 13.5[165] | 1.3[16] | 1.8[19] | 3.9[34] | 5.3[165] |
| 1977 | 8.2[17] | 5.8[17] | 12.0[33] | 12.0[166] | 1.1[17] | 1.9[17] | 4.7[33] | 4.7[166] |

[ ] Denotes the number of corporations in each computation.

Regulatory Status

| Year | Percentage of Owner's Equity | | | | Percentage of Total Assets | | | |
|---|---|---|---|---|---|---|---|---|
| | Deferred Charge | | Deferred Credit | | Deferred Charge | | Deferred Credit | |
| | Nonregulated | Regulated | Nonregulated | Regulated | Nonregulated | Regulated | Nonregulated | Regulated |
| 1982 | 7.5[23] | 9.5[4] | 14.0[153] | 24.5[56] | 1.8[23] | 3.0[4] | 5.2[153] | 8.9[56] |
| 1981 | 10.8[33] | 12.3[3] | 13.2[144] | 22.9[57] | 1.6[33] | 4.0[3] | 4.9[144] | 8.4[57] |
| 1980 | 4.8[28] | 11.3[3] | 14.0[149] | 21.7[56] | 1.5[28] | 4.0[3] | 4.4[148] | 7.9[56] |
| 1979 | 3.4[32] | 13.0[2] | 11.6[145] | 19.8[57] | 1.3[32] | 4.5[2] | 4.3[145] | 7.4[57] |
| 1978 | 4.7[32] | 8.0[3] | 11.0[143] | 18.6[56] | 1.4[32] | 3.0[3] | 4.2[143] | 7.1[56] |
| 1977 | 6.6[33] | 20.0[1] | 9.9[141] | 17.2[58] | 1.3[33] | 7.0[1] | 4.0[141] | 6.5[58] |

[ ] Denotes the number of corporations in each computation.

Table B.6 (Continued)

| Year | Percentage of Owners' Equity | | Percentage of Total Assets | |
|---|---|---|---|---|
| | Debit Balances | Credit Balances | Debit Balances | Credit Balances |
| 1982 | 7.8[27] | 16.8[209] | 2.0[27] | 6.2[209] |
| 1981 | 11.0[36] | 15.9[201] | 1.8[36] | 5.9[201] |
| 1980 | 5.4[31] | 16.1[205] | 1.7[31] | 5.4[204] |
| 1979 | 4.0[34] | 13.9[202] | 1.4[34] | 5.2[202] |
| 1978 | 4.9[35] | 13.1[199] | 1.6[35] | 5.0[199] |
| 1977 | 7.0[34] | 12.0[199] | 1.5[34] | 4.7[199] |

[ ] Denotes the number of corporations in each computation.

TABLE B.7 *Responses to Questions Concerning "Current Interperiod Income Tax Allocation Practices" by Measurement Classifications*

| | | Questions and Responses | | | | | | | | | | | | | | | | | | | | | | | | | | | | | | |
|---|---|---|---|---|---|---|---|---|---|---|---|---|---|---|---|---|---|---|---|---|---|---|---|---|---|---|---|---|---|---|---|---|
| | | 5 | | | | 6 | | | | 8 | | | | 10 | | | | | 11 | | | |
| SIC Group | No. of Corp. | 1 | 2 | 3 | 4 | 1 | 2 | 3 | 4 | 1 | 2 | 3 | 4 | 1 | 2 | 3 | 4 | 5 | 1 | 2 | 3 | 4 |
| 1 | 4 | 4 | 0 | 0 | 0 | 0 | 3 | 0 | 1 | 4 | 0 | 0 | 0 | 3 | 0 | 0 | 1 | 0 | 3 | 0 | 0 | 1 |
| 2 | 12 | 11 | 0 | 1 | 0 | 0 | 10 | 1 | 1 | 12 | 0 | 0 | 0 | 6 | 0 | 0 | 5 | 1 | 3 | 4 | 0 | 2 |
| 3 | 1 | 1 | 0 | 0 | 0 | 0 | 1 | 0 | 0 | 0 | 1 | 0 | 0 | 1 | 0 | 0 | 0 | 0 | 1 | 0 | 0 | 0 |
| 4 | 120 | 113 | 4 | 3 | 0 | 10 | 75 | 17 | 17 | 106 | 12 | 1 | 1 | 81 | 0 | 0 | 25 | 12 | 58 | 32 | 0 | 20 |
| 5 | 68 | 45 | 4 | 1 | 16 | 13 | 21 | 11 | 20 | 55 | 1 | 0 | 10 | 18 | 2 | 0 | 33 | 11 | 27 | 17 | 0 | 16 |
| 6 | 7 | 5 | 1 | 1 | 0 | 0 | 6 | 1 | 0 | 6 | 0 | 1 | 0 | 4 | 0 | 0 | 3 | 0 | 4 | 3 | 0 | 0 |
| 7 | 7 | 4 | 3 | 0 | 0 | 1 | 5 | 0 | 1 | 5 | 2 | 0 | 0 | 5 | 0 | 0 | 1 | 1 | 4 | 2 | 0 | 1 |
| 8 | 28 | 27 | 0 | 0 | 1 | 1 | 17 | 6 | 4 | 24 | 3 | 1 | 0 | 20 | 3 | 0 | 5 | 0 | 7 | 16 | 0 | 3 |
| 9 | 11 | 11 | 0 | 0 | 0 | 0 | 7 | 3 | 1 | 7 | 4 | 0 | 0 | 9 | 0 | 0 | 2 | 0 | 7 | 2 | 0 | 1 |
| Total | 258 | 221 | 12 | 6 | 17 | 25 | 145 | 39 | 45 | 219 | 23 | 3 | 11 | 147 | 5 | 0 | 75 | 25 | 114 | 76 | 0 | 44 |
| Assets Under $250 M | 62 | 52 | 5 | 5 | 0 | 10 | 35 | 12 | 5 | 51 | 8 | 2 | 1 | 46 | 0 | 0 | 12 | 2 | 35 | 15 | 0 | 5 |
| Assets Over $250 million | 195 | 168 | 7 | 1 | 17 | 14 | 110 | 27 | 40 | 167 | 15 | 1 | 10 | 101 | 5 | 0 | 62 | 23 | 78 | 61 | 0 | 39 |
| Total | 257* | | | | | | | | | | | | | | | | | | | | | |
| Nonregulated Corp. | 198 | 181 | 9 | 6 | 1 | 13 | 129 | 28 | 26 | 170 | 22 | 3 | 2 | 132 | 3 | 0 | 44 | 15 | 91 | 60 | 0 | 29 |
| Regulated Corp. | 60 | 40 | 3 | 0 | 16 | 12 | 16 | 11 | 19 | 49 | 1 | 0 | 9 | 15 | 2 | 0 | 31 | 10 | 23 | 16 | 0 | 15 |
| Total | 258 | | | | | | | | | | | | | | | | | | | | | |

*One company excluded due to bankruptcy proceeding.

Table B.7 (Continued)

| SIC Group | No. of Corp. | 12 | | 14 | | | | | 15 | | | | | 16** | | 17A | | 17B | | 18 | | 19 | | | | |
|---|---|---|---|---|---|---|---|---|---|---|---|---|---|---|---|---|---|---|---|---|---|---|---|---|---|---|
| | | 1 | 2 | 1 | 2 | 3 | 4 | 5 | 1 | 2 | 3 | 4 | 5 | 1 | 2 | 1 | 2 | 1 | 2 | 1 | 2 | 1 | 2 | 3 | 4 | 5 |
| 1 | 4 | 3 | 1 | 4 | 0 | 0 | 0 | 0 | 0 | 1 | 0 | 0 | 2 | 1 | 0 | 4 | 0 | 2 | 2 | 3 | 1 | 1 | 2 | 0 | 0 | 1 |
| 2 | 12 | 11 | 1 | 7 | 1 | 1 | 1 | 2 | 1 | 0 | 0 | 1 | 8 | 1 | 0 | 10 | 2 | 8 | 3 | 5 | 7 | 7 | 5 | 0 | 0 | 0 |
| 3 | 1 | 1 | 0 | 1 | 0 | 0 | 0 | 0 | 0 | 0 | 0 | 0 | 0 | 0 | 0 | 0 | 1 | 0 | 1 | 0 | 1 | 0 | 1 | 0 | 0 | 0 |
| 4 | 120 | 110 | 10 | 92 | 9 | 10 | 0 | 9 | 11 | 1 | 1 | 2 | 88 | 8 | 2 | 78 | 42 | 36 | 69 | 33 | 86 | 60 | 29 | 3 | 6 | 19 |
| 5 | 68 | 18 | 45 | 37 | 1 | 3 | 1 | 21 | 14 | 0 | 0 | 38 | 14 | 38 | 6 | 43 | 24 | 27 | 37 | 16 | 50 | 41 | 12 | 1 | 1 | 11 |
| 6 | 7 | 7 | 0 | 3 | 2 | 1 | 1 | 0 | 0 | 0 | 0 | 0 | 5 | 0 | 0 | 3 | 4 | 3 | 2 | 2 | 4 | 2 | 3 | 1 | 0 | 1 |
| 7 | 7 | 7 | 0 | 5 | 2 | 0 | 0 | 0 | 0 | 0 | 0 | 0 | 7 | 0 | 0 | 1 | 6 | 1 | 6 | 1 | 6 | 7 | 0 | 0 | 0 | 0 |
| 8 | 28 | 20 | 6 | 15 | 1 | 3 | 3 | 5 | 8 | 2 | 0 | 2 | 11 | 6 | 0 | 20 | 8 | 7 | 17 | 12 | 16 | 14 | 10 | 1 | 1 | 1 |
| 9 | 11 | 10 | 0 | 6 | 2 | 0 | 0 | 3 | 1 | 0 | 0 | 0 | 10 | 0 | 0 | 9 | 2 | 5 | 5 | 4 | 7 | 6 | 2 | 0 | 0 | 3 |
| Total | 258 | | | | | | | | | | | | | | | | | | | | | | | | | |
| Assets Under $250 M | 62 | 56 | 6 | 36 | 12 | 6 | 1 | 6 | 4 | 0 | 0 | 1 | 44 | 6 | 0 | 31 | 31 | 13 | 46 | 12 | 50 | 33 | 10 | 2 | 1 | 14 |
| Assets Over $250 M | 195 | 130 | 57 | 133 | 6 | 12 | 5 | 34 | 31 | 4 | 1 | 42 | 100 | 48 | 8 | 136 | 58 | 76 | 95 | 64 | 127 | 104 | 54 | 4 | 7 | 22 |
| Total | 257* | | | | | | | | | | | | | | | | | | | | | | | | | |
| Nonregulated Corp. | 198 | 175 | 19 | 138 | 17 | 15 | 5 | 20 | 22 | 4 | 1 | 5 | 137 | 16 | 2 | 132 | 66 | 66 | 108 | 64 | 131 | 100 | 53 | 5 | 7 | 28 |
| Regulated Corp. | 60 | 12 | 44 | 32 | 1 | 3 | 1 | 20 | 13 | 0 | 0 | 38 | 8 | 38 | 6 | 36 | 23 | 23 | 34 | 12 | 47 | 38 | 11 | 1 | 1 | 8 |
| Total | 258 | | | | | | | | | | | | | | | | | | | | | | | | | |

(Column headings: Questions and Responses)

**For deferred methods corporations only (from responses 2 to Question 12).

TABLE B.8 *Distribution of Responses to Second Tier Questions (Concerning "Current Interperiod Income Tax Allocation Practices") by Measurement Classification*

| | Question 7 | | | | | | | Question 9 | | | | | | |
|---|---|---|---|---|---|---|---|---|---|---|---|---|---|---|
| SIC Groups | Maximum No. of Responses | Gross Change | | Net Change | | Specific Identification | | Maximum No. of Responses | Deferral | | Liability | | Net of Tax | |
| | | P | S | P | S | P | S | | P | S | P | S | P | S |
| 1 | 1 | 1 | 0 | 1 | 0 | 0 | 1 | 0 | -- | -- | -- | -- | -- | -- |
| 2 | 1 | 0 | 1 | 1 | 0 | 0 | 1 | 0 | -- | -- | -- | -- | -- | -- |
| 3 | 0 | -- | -- | -- | -- | -- | -- | 0 | -- | -- | -- | -- | -- | -- |
| 4 | 17 | 2 | 3 | 14 | 2 | 1 | 14 | 1 | 1 | 0 | 0 | 1 | 0 | 0 |
| 5 | 20 | 8 | 6 | 9 | 4 | 5 | 10 | 10 | 8 | 1 | 0 | 0 | 2 | 6 |
| 6 | 0 | -- | -- | -- | -- | -- | -- | 0 | -- | -- | -- | -- | -- | -- |
| 7 | 1 | 0 | 0 | 1 | 0 | 0 | 1 | 0 | -- | -- | -- | -- | -- | -- |
| 8 | 4 | 0 | 2 | 3 | 0 | 0 | 2 | 0 | -- | -- | -- | -- | -- | -- |
| 9 | 1 | 0 | 0 | 1 | 0 | 0 | 1 | 0 | -- | -- | -- | -- | -- | -- |
| Total | 45 | 11 | 12 | 30 | 6 | 6 | 30 | 11 | | | | | | |
| Assets Under $250 M | 5 | 0 | 1 | 5 | 0 | 0 | 4 | 1 | 0 | 0 | 0 | 0 | 0 | 0 |
| Assets Over $250 M | 40 | 11 | 11 | 25 | 6 | 6 | 26 | 10 | 9 | 1 | 0 | 1 | 2 | 6 |
| Total | 45 | | | | | | | 11 | | | | | | |
| Nonregulated Corporations | 26 | 3 | 6 | 22 | 2 | 1 | 21 | 2 | 1 | 0 | 0 | 1 | 0 | 0 |
| Regulated Corporations | 19 | 8 | 6 | 8 | 4 | 5 | 9 | 9 | 8 | 1 | 0 | 0 | 2 | 6 |
| Total | 45 | | | | | | | 11 | | | | | | |

Note: The responses do not always crossfoot as some corporations selected more than one method as primary or secondary.

TABLE B.9 *Corporations Changing Accounting Methods for the ITC and the Year of Change*

| SIC Groups | Changing Methods | Missing Data | 1982 F | 1982 D | 1981 F | 1981 D | 1980 F | 1980 D | 1979 F | 1979 D | 1978 F | 1978 D | 1977 F | 1977 D | 1975 F | 1975 D | 1972 F | 1972 D | 1971 F | 1971 D | 1964 F | 1964 D | Totals F | Totals D |
|---|---|---|---|---|---|---|---|---|---|---|---|---|---|---|---|---|---|---|---|---|---|---|---|---|
| Agriculture, Forest, & Fishing | 1 | | | | 1 | | | | | | | | | | | | | | | | | | 1 | 0 |
| Mining | 1 | | | | 1 | | | | | | | | | | | | | | | | | | 1 | 0 |
| Construction | 0 | | | | | | | | | | | | | | | | | | | | | | 0 | 0 |
| Manufacturing | 10 | 1 | 2 | | 1 | | | | | | | | 1 | 1 | 1 | | | | | | 3 | | 8 | 1 |
| Transportation, Communication, & Other Public Utilities | 18 | 1 | | 2 | 1 | 3 | | 1 | 1 | | 1 | | | | | 1 | | | 4 | 3 | | | 7 | 10 |
| Wholesale Trade | 0 | | | | | | | | | | | | | | | | | | | | | | 0 | 0 |
| Retail Trade | 0 | | | | | | | | | | | | | | | | | | | | | | 0 | 0 |
| Finance, Insurance, & Real Estate | 4 | | | | | | | | | 1 | 1 | | | | | 1 | 1 | | | | | | 2 | 2 |
| Service | 1 | | | | | | | | 1 | | | | | | | | | | | | | | 1 | 0 |
| Totals | 35 | 2 | 2 | 2 | 4 | 3 | 0 | 1 | 2 | 1 | 2 | 0 | 1 | 1 | 1 | 2 | 1 | 0 | 4 | 3 | 3 | 0 | 20 | 13 |
| Assets under $250 million | 5 | 1 | 0 | 1 | 0 | 0 | 0 | 0 | 0 | 0 | 0 | 0 | 1 | 1 | 0 | 0 | 0 | 0 | 1 | 0 | 0 | 0 | 2 | 2 |
| Assets over $250 million | 30 | 1 | 2 | 1 | 4 | 3 | 0 | 1 | 2 | 1 | 2 | 0 | 0 | 0 | 1 | 2 | 1 | 0 | 3 | 3 | 3 | 0 | 18 | 11 |
| Totals | 35 | 2 | 2 | 2 | 4 | 3 | 0 | 1 | 2 | 1 | 2 | 0 | 1 | 1 | 1 | 2 | 1 | 0 | 4 | 3 | 3 | 0 | 20 | 13 |
| Nonregulated corporations | 19 | 1 | 2 | 0 | 3 | 0 | 0 | 0 | 1 | 1 | 2 | 0 | 1 | 1 | 1 | 1 | 1 | 0 | 1 | 0 | 3 | 0 | 15 | 3 |
| Regulated corporations | 16 | 1 | 0 | 2 | 1 | 3 | 0 | 1 | 1 | 0 | 0 | 0 | 0 | 0 | 0 | 1 | 0 | 0 | 3 | 3 | 0 | 0 | 5 | 10 |
| Totals | 35 | 2 | 2 | 2 | 4 | 3 | 0 | 1 | 2 | 1 | 2 | 0 | 1 | 1 | 1 | 2 | 1 | 0 | 4 | 3 | 3 | 0 | 20 | 13 |

F = Flow-through method chosen to account for the ITC.
D = Deferred method chosen to account for the ITC.

# Appendix C
# FERF Questionnaire for Preparers of Financial Statements

THE UNIVERSITY OF MICHIGAN
GRADUATE SCHOOL OF BUSINESS ADMINISTRATION
ANN ARBOR, MICHIGAN 48109

March 10, 1983

The Financial Executives Research Foundation is again supporting research into the concept of interperiod income tax allocation. Many tax and financial reporting changes have taken place since publication of the 1974 study An Appraisal of Interperiod Income Tax Allocation, so a reappraisal of this subject is needed.

Unlike the prior study, this research effort will gain significant input as to corporate accounting methods and results of interperiod income tax allocation from a wide range of corporations. It will also gain information about corporate management satisfaction or dissatisfaction with existing accounting requirements. Therefore, a high completion rate for the enclosed questionnaire is essential.

Interperiod income tax allocation has been the subject of a large number of official pronouncements. It is complex, controversial and usually has a significant impact on earnings.

Our information is being gathered prior to the release of an anticipated FASB discussion memorandum, but nothing in this questionnaire should preclude or even affect a corporation's response to the FASB. All data will be held strictly confidential and no corporation will be identified as a contributor or as a noncontributor to this research effort.

The questionnaire has been field tested by several FEI companies. In its present form it includes improvements suggested by these reviewers. One suggestion was that completion of the questionnaire might be assigned to the person responsible for presentation of the deferred tax accounts in the balance sheet. The field test also revealed a range of from 3 to 30 hours to complete and review this questionnaire.

The results of this questionnaire are being coordinated with the FASB's preparation of their discussion memorandum. For this reason, we hope very much that you will be able to return your completed questionnaire, using the enclosed self-addressed envelope, by May 2, 1983.

Your participation in this project is a significant contribution to FERF's research program and to maximizing validity of the survey results. As the researcher conducting the FERF study, I thank you for your cooperation.

James E. Wheeler
Professor of Accounting

# QUESTIONNAIRE FOR PREPARERS OF FINANCIAL STATEMENTS, DESIGNED TO OBTAIN DATA USEFUL IN AN ANALYSIS OF INTERPERIOD INCOME TAX ALLOCATION

## Confidentiality

All data obtained in response to this questionnaire will be treated as strictly confidential. No corporation will be identified with any data and there will be no identification of participating corporations.

## Questionnaire Content

The questionnaire is presented in four major sections. Section I is designed to obtain some basic corporate data and general information on interperiod income tax allocation.

Section II is designed to provide the researchers with information as to current interperiod income tax allocation practices for a wide variety of corporations and industries.

Section III is designed to provide researchers with some of the experience corporate management has had in interperiod income tax allocation. Much of the emphasis here is on identification of problem areas and on determination of the usefulness of the accounting results from interperiod income tax allocation.

Section IV applies only to the special problems faced by rate regulated entitites in accounting for interperiod income tax allocation.

## Responders

Responders to this questionnaire will include the full range of manufacturing, service and financial companies. Banks and other financial entities that are both preparers and users of financial statements should respond to this questionnaire as preparers.

## Definitions and Observations

1) Differences between pretax financial reporting income and taxable income:

   a) Permanent differences — These are items that impact on either pretax income for financial reporting or on taxable income for tax reporting but do not impact on the other reporting medium.

   b) Timing differences — These are items (taken individually or as a group) that impact in different periods on pretax income for financial versus tax reporting as a result of different accounting methods and/or useful lives being used for these two purposes, and the excess shown in one reporting medium in an early period(s) is (ignoring roll-over) offset by an equal excess in the other medium in a later period(s).

2) Some items fail the definition of either permanent or timing differences. Examples include:

   a) Income tax provisions, and

   b) All tax credits, including the foreign tax credit and the investment tax credit.

3) Aspects of timing differences:

   a) Turn around — Is the change (decrease) in the tax effect of an individual timing difference. Thus, it represents the tax effect of a subsequent recognition in book income of an item previously included in taxable income, or vice versa. If the tax effect of the difference between book and tax income fails to turn around, then the item is not a timing difference. For group accounts, the tax effects of some individual items may be turning around while the tax effects of other items are adding to the tax deferral.

b) Reversal—Is the excess of the decreases over the increases in the tax effect of similar timing differences within the same group. When there is only one transaction of a particular type giving rise to a timing difference, turn around and reversal would be the same.

c) Roll-over—Is the continuous renewal of the cumulative monetary amount representing the tax effect source (a group of similar items) of timing difference so as to preclude potential reversal; thus, the cumulative amount of the deferred tax remains the same or increases but a significant reversal is not probable. For example, when accelerated depreciation is used for tax purposes and straight line for book purposes, the tax effect of older assets (potential reversal of depreciation differences) is offset by the tax effect of newer assets.

4) Aspects of permanent differences—most permanent differences do not turn around; however, where there are basis differences in assets between book and tax, a subsequent sale or depreciation write off will result in complete or partial turn-arounds. It should be noted that this turn-around affects the same medium (pretax financial income or taxable income) as was originally impacted, and this distinguishes this permanent difference from timing differences (where the turn-around always affects the other medium).

5) Methods of measuring a change in a timing difference:

a) Gross change—Where there are many similar items making up the source of a timing difference, the gross change method would annually produce two monetary amounts; one would represent the total of the increases in the timing difference (for all items that would have increases) and the other would represent the total of the decreases in the timing difference (for all items that would have decreases). The tax effect would then be determined usually by applying the current tax rate to the gross increase and either the original rate or an average rate could be applied to the gross decrease. Only the use of the original rate on the decreases (gross decrease) is compatible in theory with the gross change method. The use of the current rate for draw downs would produce a result identical to the net change method. The net of the tax effects from the gross increase and decrease would then equal the change in the deferred tax account for that timing difference.

b) Net change—Where there are many similar items making up the source of a timing difference, the net change method would annually produce one monetary amount that would represent the excess of the gross increases over the gross decreases in the timing difference, or vice versa. The tax effect where there is a net addition is normally determined by applying the current tax rate; however, where there is a net decrease the tax effect is determined by applying an average rate, the current rate or the rate at which the deferral was originally established (assuming a flow of prior rates, e.g., FIFO).

c) Specific identification (individual item method)—the tax effect of the timing difference is maintained separately for each item; therefore, similar items are not grouped for purposes of this calculation. The tax effect of increases in the timing difference for each item is determined by applying the current tax rate. The tax effect of decreases in the timing difference for each item is determined by applying the rate at which the deferral for this item was originally established. Where there have been several prior rates, the earliest rate is usually assumed to be the first to be reversed.

6) Accounting methods for recording changes in timing differences:

a) Deferral method—The monetary amount of the tax effect of each source of timing difference is determined by employing the tax rate in effect at the date each increment was added to a deferred tax account. The deferred method account is not adjusted for subsequent rate changes. The monetary amount of the tax effect of any draw down (reversal of a timing difference) may be determined by applying the tax rate at which the deferral was added to the account, the average rate where more than one rate is involved or the current tax rate. The annual tax deferral, whether an increase or a decrease, is reflected as an adjustment of the income tax deduction from revenue.

b) Liability method — The monetary amount of the tax effect of each source of timing difference is determined by employing the current tax rate. The liability method is adjusted to reflect subsequent rate changes; any draw downs would thus be computed at the current tax rate. The amount of the annual tax deferral, whether an increase or a decrease, affects the income tax deduction from revenue.*

c) Net-of-tax method — This method typically employs the tax rates in effect at the dates the transaction that gives rise to the timing difference occurs (e.g., the excess of tax depreciation over book depreciation). For a depreciable asset, this method would reflect the ''tax savings'' (monetary amount) from the excess of tax depreciation over book depreciation as an increase in depreciation expense and in accumulated depreciation. Thus, this method (or valuation technique) affects the expense or revenue account related to the asset or liability involved in the timing difference (e.g., depreciation expense for depreciable assets) rather than the income tax deduction from revenue. While the income tax deduction from revenue is the same amount as would be produced by flow-through, as defined below, the net income is the same amount as would be produced by the deferred or liability methods assuming no tax rate changes.

   Because this deferral would not usually be adjusted for tax rate changes, any draw downs would be computed at either the rate at which the deferral was established (if known or determined by a flow concept such as FIFO), the average rate where more than one rate is involved, or the current tax rate.

7) Concepts for interperiod income tax allocation:

a) Comprehensive allocation — A concept that requires the tax effect of all timing differences to be reported in the year in which each timing difference arose. This recognition of all tax effects of timing differences is justified by the presumption that it is proper to view roll over as two imputed cash transactions:

   1) A cash payment for the establishment of deferred tax charges and for previously established deferred tax credits upon turn around, and

   2) A cash receipt for the establishment of deferred tax credits and for previously established deferred tax charges upon turn around.

   While the deferred, liability and net-of-tax accounting methods are all used in combination with comprehensive allocation, the net-of-tax method is the most compatible in theory with this concept. In fact, this concept is more of a valuation than an allocation.

b) Partial allocation — A concept of allocation that includes in the tax provision of each year the net amount of estimated future taxes payable or benefits receivable resulting from:

   1) Timing differences during the current year that are expected to reverse, and

*Note that the gross change, net change and specific identification methods for measuring a timing difference would all produce the same result under the liability method due to the adjustment to current tax rates.

2) Timing differences in previous years that had not been expected to reverse, but that are now expected to reverse as a result of action taken in the current year such as a change in management plans (e.g., depreciation reversal from leasing more assets and purchasing fewer).

In ascertaining the amount of tax payable in future years as a result of current timing differences and current action affecting past timing differences, for practical reasons, the normal planning horizon is adopted as the period during which estimates can be made with reasonable accuracy.

c) Flow-through — A concept that presents as the income tax provision the amount of tax paid or payable to the government as determined on the income tax report for the current year (assuming no carryovers). Thus, no deferrals for recognition of timing differences are recorded and no accounting method for recording them is needed.

d) Cash basis — Under this concept, the amount actually paid to the government for income tax would be the income tax provision irrespective of the tax year for which the payments are being made. Thus, there would be no tax deferral recognition.

8) Draw downs — This term relates to the reduction in previously recorded timing differences. It is sometimes used to refer to a normal turn around of a timing difference; however, it more often refers to the forced reduction in net prior deferred tax credits from timing differences in order to reflect the effects of a net operating loss or investment tax credit (or other tax credits) carryforward.

9) Normalization — This term is used in rate regulated environments. It represents rate regulated accounting for the comprehensive allocation of deferred taxes.

# QUESTIONNAIRE

## Section I
## BASIC CORPORATE DATA AND GENERAL INFORMATION ON INTERPERIOD INCOME TAX ALLOCATION

| Coding for Compilation Only | | | | |
|---|---|---|---|---|
| | 1. | Company name ______ | | |
| 1:7-10 | 2. | Primary four digit SIC code(s) for 1982______ | | |
| | 3. | Totals in *thousands of dollars* at year end for the year ending in: | | |
| | | | 1982 | 1977 |
| 1:11-19, 20-28 | | Total assets (including net deferred tax charges) | $ ______ | $ ______ |
| 1:29-37, 38-46 | | Total liabilities (including net deferred tax credits and unamortized ITC) | $ ______ | $ ______ |
| 1:47-55, 56-64 | | Total owners' equity | $ ______ | $ ______ |
| 2:7-15, 16-24 | | Net income | $ ______ | $ ______ |

Total net deferred tax charge or credit (please check) in the balance sheet from timing differences *in thousands of dollars*.

| | | |
|---|---|---|
| 2:26, 27-34 | $ ______ | (1982 charge ______ or credit ______) |
| 2:35, 36-43 | $ ______ | (1977 charge ______ or credit ______) |
| 2:44-51 | $ ______ | (1982 the investment tax credit) |
| 2:52-59 | $ ______ | (1977 the investment tax credit) |

The five largest individual items of deferred tax charges or deferred tax credits (specifiy which) in the balance sheet at year end for 1982 and 1977 in *thousands of dollars* are: (Use lines (6) through (10) only where the five largest individual items of tax deferral in 1977 are not the same as the five largest individual items of tax deferral in 1982; give the data for both years.)

| | | Individual Item Description | Deferred Tax Charge or Credit | 1982 | 1977 |
|---|---|---|---|---|---|
| 3:7-9, 10, 11-18, 19-26 | 1. | ______ | ______ | $ ______ | $ ______ |
| 3:27-29, 30, 31-38, 39-46 | 2. | ______ | ______ | $ ______ | $ ______ |
| 3:47-49, 50, 51-58, 59-66 | 3. | ______ | ______ | $ ______ | $ ______ |
| 4:7-9, 10, 11-18, 19-26 | 4. | ______ | ______ | $ ______ | $ ______ |
| 4:27-29, 30, 31-38, 39-46 | 5. | ______ | ______ | $ ______ | $ ______ |
| 4:47-49, 50, 51-58, 59-66 | 6. | ______ | ______ | $ ______ | $ ______ |
| 5:7-9, 10, 11-18, 19-26 | 7. | ______ | ______ | $ ______ | $ ______ |
| 5:27-29, 30, 31-38, 39-46 | 8. | ______ | ______ | $ ______ | $ ______ |
| 5:47-49, 50, 51-58, 59-66 | 9. | ______ | ______ | $ ______ | $ ______ |
| 6:7-9, 10, 11-18, 19-26 | 10. | ______ | ______ | $ ______ | $ ______ |

For each of the five largest individual items of deferred tax accounts for 1982, what is your *expectation* for change by the end of the year ending in 1987 assuming no changes in current accounting rules for income taxes? Check the appropriate column for either an increase or a decrease.

| | Item | Check Whether Increase (1) | or Decrease (2) | Cumulative estimated % change |
|---|---|---|---|---|
| :27-30 | 1. | ______ | ______ | ______ % |
| :31-34 | 2. | ______ | ______ | ______ % |
| :35-38 | 3. | ______ | ______ | ______ % |
| 39-42 | 4. | ______ | ______ | ______ % |
| 43-46 | 5. | ______ | ______ | ______ % |

4. For each of the past six years, what has been the *relative* size of the total (cumulative balançe) of net deferred tax accounts arising from timing differences (ignoring ITC)? Indicate whether the net amount is a deferred charge or deferred credit?

| | Year Ending in | Check if Net Charge 1 | Check if Net Credit 2 | As a Percentage of Total Owners' Equity (including common and preferred) | As a Percentage of Total Assets (net of depreciation) |
|---|---|---|---|---|---|
| 6:47, 48-50, 51-53 | 1982 | ____ | ____ | ____ % | ____ % |
| 6:54, 55-57, 58-60 | 1981 | ____ | ____ | ____ % | ____ % |
| 6:61, 62-64, 65-67 | 1980 | ____ | ____ | ____ % | ____ % |
| 6:68, 69-71, 72-74 | 1979 | ____ | ____ | ____ % | ____ % |
| 7:7, 8-10, 11-13 | 1978 | ____ | ____ | ____ % | ____ % |
| 7:14, 15-17, 18-20 | 1977 | ____ | ____ | ____ % | ____ % |

## Section II
## INFORMATION ABOUT YOUR CORPORATION'S CURRENT INTERPERIOD INCOME TAX ALLOCATION PRACTICES

(Note—for Questions 5 through 22 please circle one response)

5. Your current method of income tax allocation for the tax effects of material timing differences is:
   1. Comprehensive
   2. Partial (7:21)
   3. Taxes currently payable
   4. Different methods are used for different items

   If your response was (4), what criteria does your company use to determine which method to apply to a particular transaction? ______________________________

   ______________________________

   ______________________________

6. Your current method of measuring the change in a timing difference is:
   1. Gross change
   2. Net change (7:22)
   3. Specific identification
   4. Some combination of the above methods

7. If you use a combination of the above accounting methods, classify the methods as either primary (P) or secondary (S) based on the number of dollars involved.
   1. Gross change ____________ (7:23)
   2. Net change ____________ (7:24)
   3. Specific identification ____________ (7:25)

8. Your current method of accounting for the tax effects of changes in timing differences is:
   1. Deferral
   2. Liability (7:26)
   3. Net-of-tax
   4. Some combination of the above methods

   If your response was not deferral, what is the rationale for using your method? ______________

   ______________________________

9. If you use a combination of the above accounting methods, classify the methods as either primary (P) or secondary (S) based on the number of dollars involved.

7:27 1. Deferral ___________

7:28 2. Liability ___________

7:29 3. Net-of-tax (other than as required in acquisitions per APB 16) ___________

10. Deferred tax credit accounts are shown on your balance sheet as:

1. Liabilities

2. Contra-asset accounts

7:30 3. Owners' equity

4. Separate classification

5. Some combination of the above (please describe) ___________

___________

11. Deferred tax debit accounts are shown on your balance sheet as:

1. Assets

7:31 2. Contra-liability accounts

3. Reductions in owners' equity

4. Some combination of the above (please describe) ___________

___________

12. Your current method of accounting for the investment tax credit is:

7:32 1. Flow-through

2. Deferral and amortization

13. Have you changed methods of accounting for the investment tax credit?

7:33. 1. Yes—Year of change ___________

34-35 2. No

Comments ___________

14. Primary reason for your choice of investment credit accounting method is:

1. Most conceptually correct (conforms most to what you consider to be the nature of the investment credit)

2. Lower cost of compliance

7:36 3. Advocated by APB Opinions

4. Reduces earnings volatility

5. Other (describe) ___________

___________

15. Unamortized ITC accounts are shown on your balance sheet as:

1. Liabilities

7:37 2. Contra-asset accounts

3. Owner's equity

4. Separate classification

5. Not applicable

16. If amortization of the ITC is practiced, your amortization period chosen is based on:
   1. The useful life of the related asset
7:38 2. Other (describe) ______________________________

______________________________

17. Have any of your federal (or foreign) income tax returns or financial statements resulted in net operating loss carryforwards or in ITC or foreign tax credit carryforwards?

For tax purposes:

7:39 1. Yes
   2. No

For book purposes (considering only the ITC and foreign tax credits):

   1. Yes
7:40 2. No

18. Have you ever encountered the problem of drawing down (reducing) prior deferred tax credits (from timing differences) because of a loss carryforward or because of unused ITCs or foreign tax credits?
7:41 1. Yes
   2. No

19. Regardless of your responses to questions (17) and (18) above, do you agree with the current accounting rules on the recording of the tax benefits of loss and tax credit carryforwards?
   1. Agree in all situations
   2. Agree in most situations (except for ______________________________)
7:42 3. Disagree in most situations (except for ______________________________)
   4. Disagree in all situations
   5. No opinion

**Section III**
**EXPERIENCE WITH INTERPERIOD INCOME TAX ALLOCATION**

20. How would you describe your current level of satisfaction with the existing rules for allocating the effects of timing differences between accounting periods?
   1. Very satisfied, no changes are necessary
   2. Generally satisfied, but minor changes are necessary
7:43 3. Generally dissatisfied, major changes are necessary
   4. Very dissatisfied, a complete revision is necessary
   5. No opinion

21. How would you describe your current level of satisfaction with the existing rules for accounting for the investment tax credit, disregarding the new rules for basis reduction under the Tax Equity and Fiscal Responsibility Act of 1982?
   1. Very satisfied, no changes are necessary
   2. Generally satisfied, but minor changes are necessary
7:44 3. Generally dissatisfied, major changes are necessary
   4. Very dissatisfied, a complete revision is necessary
   5. No opinion

22. How would you describe your current level of satisfaction with the absence of formal rules to guide accounting for the foreign income tax credit?

1. Very satisfied, no rules are necessary
2. Generally satisfied, but guidelines in certain complex situations would be desirable
3. Generally dissatisfied, this is a complex area in which rules could be helpful
4. Very dissatisfied, this area is very complex and rules are needed
5. No opinion

7:45

23. The major issues of accounting for income taxes that are *most* in need of immediate reconsideration are (circle one or more):

7:46 1 The allocation requirement itself
7:47 1 The comprehensive allocation concept
7:48 1 The deferral method requirement for tax allocation
7:49 1 The appropriate response to changes in tax rates
7:50 1 The proscription against discounting deferred tax accounts
7:51 1 The accounting for the expected future benefits of net operating loss carryforwards
7:52 1 The accounting for tax credits
7:53 1 Others (please list) ______________________________

______________________________

7:54 1 None of the above

Note: The following parts (23-a through 23-g) of this section of the questionnaire contain statements relative to each of the major issues identified in statement (23) above. The last two parts (23-h and 23-i) of the section contain statements on issues not identified above.

**Part 23-a Aspects of the Allocation Requirement**

Please *check* on the appropriate line one of the following responses to subsequent statements *24 through 72*.

(1) Agree in all cases
(2) Agree in general, but with some exception(s)
(3) Disagree in general, but with some exception(s)
(4) Disagree in all cases
(5) Does not apply to our company/no experience with this issue/no opinion

24. Differences between taxable income and pre-tax accounting net income, after adjustment for permanent differences, are due to the timing of income and expense recognition, and therefore interperiod income tax allocation should be required.

7:55 1_____ 2_____ 3_____ 4_____ 5_____

Comments (Include the exception(s) if your response was (2) or (3))

______________________________

______________________________

25. Recent tax law changes (in particular, the Economic Recovery Tax Act of 1981) have so distorted the relationship between taxable income and pre-tax accounting net income that the relevancy of the information produced by comprehensive allocation has diminished.

7:56 1_____ 2_____ 3_____ 4_____ 5_____

Comments (Include the exception(s) if your response was (2) or (3))

______________________________

______________________________

36. A change from comprehensive to partial allocation would likely result in higher reported net incomes.

7:67 1______ 2______ 3______ 4______ 5______

Comments (Include the exception(s) if your response was (2) or (3))

______________________________________________________________________

______________________________________________________________________

**Part 23-c Aspects of the Deferral Method Requirement**

Please continue to use the same response list for the subsequent statements.

37. The deferred method of income tax allocation "provides the most useful and practical approach to interperiod tax allocation and the presentation of income taxes in financial statements," (quoted from APB'11 paragraph 35) and therefore should be the required method of tax allocation.

7:68 1______ 2______ 3______ 4______ 5______

Comments (Include the exception(s) if your response was (2) or (3))

______________________________________________________________________

______________________________________________________________________

38. FASB Concepts Statement No. 3, *Elements of Financial Statements of Business Enterprises*, states that both the liability method and the net-of-tax method produce a view of deferred income tax credits that is consistent with the definitions of the Statement (paragraph 163), whereas the deferral method produces a view of deferred income tax credits that is *not* consistent with the Statement (paragraph 164).

1. In light of their compatibility with Concepts Statement No. 3, both the liability method and the net-of-tax method should be acceptable as alternative methods of income tax allocation along with deferral.

7:69 1______ 2______ 3______ 4______ 5______

Comments (Include the exception(s) if your response was (2) or (3))

______________________________________________________________________

______________________________________________________________________

2. In light of their compatibility with concepts Statement No. 3, the liability method and the net-of-tax method should replace the deferral method as acceptable accounting methods.

7:70 1______ 2______ 3______ 4______ 5______

Comments (Include the exception(s) if your response was (2) or (3))

______________________________________________________________________

______________________________________________________________________

39. Although arguments can be made for each allocation method, it would be preferable that only one method be made acceptable.

7:71 1______ 2______ 3______ 4______ 5______

Comments (Include the exception(s) if your response was (2) or (3))

______________________________________________________________________

______________________________________________________________________

40. When considering the propriety of one income tax allocation method over another, primary emphasis should be given to the effects on the income statement, with secondary emphasis on the balance sheet.

7:72 1______ 2______ 3______ 4______ 5______

Comments (Include the exception(s) if your response was (2) or (3))

41. The method of tax allocation should be determined separately for each timing difference item, thereby allowing for a combination of the methods within the company.

7:73 1______ 2______ 3______ 4______ 5______

Comments (Include the exception(s) if your response was (2) or (3))

42. The election to use either the ''gross change,'' ''net change,'' or ''specific identification'' methods to measure a change in a timing difference should continue to be acceptable, regardless of any changes in the acceptability of a method of tax allocation such as the deferral method.

7:74 1______ 2______ 3______ 4______ 5______

Comments (Include the exception(s) if your response was (2) or (3))

43. Deferred tax credits (charges) from timing differences meet the definition of a ''liability'' (asset) and should be presented as such on the balance sheet.

7:75 1______ 2______ 3______ 4______ 5______

Comments (Include the exception(s) if your response was (2) or (3))

44. Deferred tax credits (charges) arising from timing differences are attributed to assets (liabilities), and should be presented as contra-accounts to such assets (liabilities) on the balance sheet.

7:76 1______ 2______ 3______ 4______ 5______

Comments (Include the exception(s) if your response was (2) or (3))

45. If deferred tax credits were required to be recorded as liabilities, their designation as current or non-current should be determined by the related asset that gave rise to their existence *rather than* by the time period required for their reversal.

7:77 1______ 2______ 3______ 4______ 5______

Comments (Include the exception(s) if your response was (2) or (3))

46. It is acceptable to net deferred tax credits with deferred tax charges provided they are both classified as either current or noncurrent.

7:78 1______ 2______ 3______ 4______ 5______

Comments (Include the exception(s) if your response was (2) or (3))

______________________________________________

______________________________________________

**Part 23-d Aspects that Relate to Tax Rates**

Please continue to use the same response list for the subsequent statements.

47. The creation of a current period addition to a deferred tax credit or deferred tax charge account should be based on the current tax rate *rather than* on expected future tax rates.

8:7 1______ 2______ 3______ 4______ 5______

Comments (Include the exception(s) if your response was (2) or (3))

______________________________________________

______________________________________________

48. The reduction in a deferred tax credit or charge account under the deferral method should be measured by assuming a FIFO flow of prior deferrals and rates.

8:8 1______ 2______ 3______ 4______ 5______

Comments (Include the exception(s) if your response was (2) or (3))

______________________________________________

______________________________________________

49. All prior deferred tax charges and credits should be adjusted to the current tax rate whenever the rates change.

8:9 1______ 2______ 3______ 4______ 5______

Comments (Include the exception(s) if your response was (2) or (3))

______________________________________________

______________________________________________

**Part 23-e Aspects that Relate to Discounting**

Please continue to use the same response list for the subsequent statements.

50. Long-term deferred tax amounts should be recorded at present value (i.e., discounted).

8:10 1______ 2______ 3______ 4______ 5______

Comments (Include the exception(s) if your response was (2) or (3))

______________________________________________

______________________________________________

51. If long-term deferred tax amounts were recorded at present value, the appropriate interest rate should be each company's internal rate of return.

8:11 1______ 2______ 3______ 4______ 5______

Comments (Include the exception(s) if your response was (2) or (3))

______________________________________________

______________________________________________

52. The correct period to use in determining the present value of long-term deferred tax accounts is the period over which the aggregate amounts of the accounts (and not the individual items within the accounts) reverse.

8:12 1______ 2______ 3______ 4______ 5______

Comments (Include the exception(s) if your response was (2) or (3))

______________________________________________

______________________________________________

**Part 23-f Aspects that Relate to Loss and Tax Credit Carryforwards**

Please continue to use the same response list for the subsequent statements.

53. With the increase in the NOL carryforward period from seven to fifteen years, a company should now be permitted to recognize the benefits of an incurred NOL carryforward in the year incurred in all cases except where the future viability of the company is in doubt.

8:13 1______ 2______ 3______ 4______ 5______

Comments (Include the exception(s) if your response was (2) or (3))

______________________________________________

______________________________________________

54. In accounting for future tax benefits of acquired loss or tax credit carryforwards (acquired through acquisitions) a separate asset should be recorded for these benefits rather than recording this as a part of goodwill with subsequent adjustments to goodwill as the loss or tax credit carryforward is used (FASB Technical Bulletin 81–2).

8:14 1______ 2______ 3______ 4______ 5______

Comments (Include the exception(s) if your response was (2) or (3))

______________________________________________

______________________________________________

55. If the investment tax credit available exceeds the amount applicable to the tax on the book equivalent of taxable income, the resulting excess ITC should be recorded as an asset *rather than* drawing down net deferred tax credits from timing differences.

8:15 1______ 2______ 3______ 4______ 5______

Comments (Include the exception(s) if your response was (2) or (3))

______________________________________________

______________________________________________

56. In an actual reversal (under the deferral method) of a deferred tax credit arising from a timing difference, the tax rate at which it was originally recorded, at least theoretically should be used for the reversal. But there is also an adjustment to the income tax provision for any difference between that historical rate and the current tax rate incurred as a result of an actual reversal. A draw down of deferred tax credits should therefore be adjusted to *current* tax rates in determining the increase in tax liability that an actual draw down (reversal) would create for purposes of recording ITC carryforwards.

8:16 1______ 2______ 3______ 4______ 5______

Comments (Include the exception(s) if your response was (2) or (3))

______________________________________________

______________________________________________

57. Recognition of the excess available ITC over that recognized based on the book equivalent of taxable income should be limited to the increase in tax liability due to reversals of timing differences in the ITC carry-forward period, with *no recognition* given to deferred credits that are likely to be created in this 15 year carryforward period.

8:17 1_____ 2_____ 3_____ 4_____ 5_____

Comments (Include the exception(s) if your response was (2) or (3))

---

---

58. Draw downs of deferred tax credits (from timing differences) in accounting for foreign tax credit carryforwards or foreign net operating loss carryforwards should be restricted to foreign deferred tax credit accounts.

8:18 1_____ 2_____ 3_____ 4_____ 5_____

Comments (Include the exception(s) if your response was (2) or (3))

---

---

59. Draw downs of deferred tax credits (from timing differences) for losses (or tax credits) should be restricted to the deferred tax credits of the company or companies appearing on the tax return of the corporation incurring the loss (or having the unused credit).

8:19 1_____ 2_____ 3_____ 4_____ 5_____

Comments (Include the exception(s) if your response was (2) or (3))

---

---

**Part 23-g Aspects that Relate to Tax Credits**

Please continue to use the same response list for the subsequent statements.

60. Definitive allocation rules should be developed to account for all tax credits (e.g., the foreign tax credit) as they are as much a part of the tax liability computation as is the ITC.

8:20 1_____ 2_____ 3_____ 4_____ 5_____

Comments (Include the exception(s) if your response was (2) or (3))

---

---

61. The choice between "deferral and amortization" or "flow-through" as acceptable methods of accounting for investment tax credits should be maintained.

8:21 1_____ 2_____ 3_____ 4_____ 5_____

Comments (Include the exception(s) if your response was (2) or (3))

---

---

62. The deferred investment tax credit is more properly classified as a liability *rather than* as the reduction in the acquisition cost of the related asset.

8:22 1_____ 2_____ 3_____ 4_____ 5_____

Comments (Include the exception(s) if your response was (2) or (3))

63. Consistency would require that companies using the deferral method to account for timing differences also use the ''deferral and amortization'' method to account for investment tax credits and vice versa.

8:23 1_____ 2_____ 3_____ 4_____ 5_____

Comments (Include the exception(s) if your response was (2) or (3))

64. The requirement in the Tax Equity and Fiscal Responsibility Act of 1982 that, for tax purposes, a company claiming the *full* investment credit must reduce the cost recovery basis by one-half the amount of the credit is sufficient to argue that investment credits could, for financial accounting purposes, be recorded as contra-accounts to the related assets.

8:24 1_____ 2_____ 3_____ 4_____ 5_____

Comments (Include the exception(s) if your response was (2) or (3))

65. The recognition, for financial reporting, of the amount of the ITC *used* should be based on the book tax provision before the ITC rather than on the actual tax liability before the ITC.

8:25 1_____ 2_____ 3_____ 4_____ 5_____

Comments (Include the exception(s) if your response was (2) or (3))

66. In regard to question (65) above, both the book ITC carryforward and the actual tax ITC carryforward should be shown in the notes to the financial statement.

8:26 1_____ 2_____ 3_____ 4_____ 5_____

Comments (Include the exception(s) if your response was (2) or (3))

Other Aspects Not Listed in the Major Issues Question
(Twenty-Third Question) in the Beginning of this Section

**Part 23-h Questions that Relate to Acquisitions and Consolidations**

Please continue to use the same response list for the subsequent statements numbers 67 through 72.

67. The amortization of purchased goodwill is correctly designated as a permanent difference even in situations where it is anticipated that a business segment containing goodwill will be sold.

8:27 1_____ 2_____ 3_____ 4_____ 5_____

Comments (Include the exception(s) if your response was (2) or (3))

____________________________________________

____________________________________________

68. The requirement (in APB Opinion No. 16 paragraph 89) that the reported fair value of an asset, acquired as a result of the purchase of stock of another corporation, should reflect the asset's tax deductibility basis supports the arguments favoring the net-of-tax accounting concept.

8:28 1_____ 2_____ 3_____ 4_____ 5_____

Comments (Include the exception(s) if your response was (2) or (3))

____________________________________________

____________________________________________

69. Referring to statement (68) above, if the tax basis were in excess of an asset's fair value, the reported amount of the asset should be limited to the fair value, with the excess tax basis accounted for as a NOL would be treated.

8:29 1_____ 2_____ 3_____ 4_____ 5_____

Comments (Include the exception(s) if your response was (2) or (3))

____________________________________________

____________________________________________

70. Referring again to statement (68) above, the basis difference between book and tax is a permanent rather than a timing difference even though it will turn around as the asset is written off or sold.

8:30 1_____ 2_____ 3_____ 4_____ 5_____

Comments (Include the exception(s) if your response was (2) or (3))

____________________________________________

____________________________________________

71. Referring to statement (70) above, if the basis difference is a permanent difference then adjusting the recorded basis of a depreciable asset for the tax effect forces the recognition of a permanent difference over the book life rather than the tax life of the asset.

8:31 1_____ 2_____ 3_____ 4_____ 5_____

Comments (Include the exception(s) if your response was (2) or (3))

____________________________________________

____________________________________________

72. Elimination of the equity method of accounting for subsidiaries (owned over 50 percent) in favor of consolidation would improve accounting for income tax (these subsidiaries are often consolidated for tax purposes when owned 80 percent or more).

8:32 1_____ 2_____ 3_____ 4_____ 5_____

Comments (Include the exception(s) if your response was (2) or (3))

________________________________________

________________________________________

Separate responses to the subsequent questions in part 23-h are provided.

For statements *73 through 77* please *circle* your selected response.

73. Do your corporations that file a consolidated tax return employ for both book and tax purposes the same method for allocating the consolidated corporate income tax liability among the entities joining in the consolidated tax return (see Internal Revenue Code Section 1552)?

8:33 1. Yes

2. No

3. Does not apply—i.e., separate tax returns are filed.

Comments ________________________________________

________________________________________

74. The allocation of a consolidated tax return tax liability for financial reporting will have an impact on the potential of that corporation to later absorb NOLs or tax credits.

8:34 1. Agree

2. Disagree

3. No opinion

Comments ________________________________________

________________________________________

75. Is there any significant conceptual difference between the roll over concept of a timing difference (such as from depreciation of new and old facilities) and the indefinite reversal concept (APB Opinion No. 23) for reinvestment of a subsidiary's undistributed earnings?

8:35 1. A significant difference

2. No significant difference

3. No opinion

Comments ________________________________________

________________________________________

**Part 23-i Questions Related to Other Aspects**

76. Do you consider the corporate income tax to be:
1. An expense
2. A loss
8:36 3. A distribution of earnings to society
4. A cost of doing business not described above
5. Some other anomalous item

Comments ____________________

____________________

77. If income tax is an expense, then recording the tax benefit (a reduction in taxes) of certain stock options as an increase in paid-in capital (as required by APB Opinion No. 25) rather than as a reduction in tax expense is improper accounting.
8:37 1. Agree
2. Disagree
3. No opinion

Comments ____________________

____________________

78. Which of the following statements best describes the ITC:
1. The ITC is a contribution to the capital of the respective taxpayer by the federal government similar in many respects to the gift of land by a state or local government in attracting industry to an industrial park;
2. The ITC is a selective method for reducing the effective income tax rates for the firm acquiring qualified assets;
8:38 3. The ITC is a reduction in the cost of acquiring a qualifying asset or
4. The ITC is an administrative procedure to permit the taxpayer to withhold the cash equivalent of the credit from taxes otherwise payable.

Please rank each of the above alternatives by listing the corresponding number of your first choice on the first choice line, the corresponding number of your second choice on the second choice line, etc.

8:39 First choice ________

8:40 Second choice ________

8:41 Third choice ________

8:42 Fourth choice ________

79. If you believe that the real nature of the ITC is not properly described in any of the statements in (78) above, please supply what you believe to be its real nature.

____________________

____________________

____________________

## Section IV
## FOR RATE REGULATED CORPORATIONS ONLY

80. Do you use flow-through, some form of normalization or both methods in accounting for the investment tax credit (ITC)? (Please *circle* one response.)

1. Flow-through

8:43 2. Rate base normalization

3. Cost of service normalization
4. Both flow-through and one or more of the normalization methods

81. What approximate percentage of total assets (net of depreciation) would the combined (balance sheet) deferred tax credits, charges and unamortized ITCs be for public utility property only for each of the past 10 years?

8:44-46, 47-49 1982 ________% 1977 ________%

8:50-52, 53-55 1981 ________% 1976 ________%

8:56-58, 59-61 1980 ________% 1975 ________%

8:62-64, 65-67 1979 ________% 1974 ________%

8:68-70, 71-73 1978 ________% 1973 ________%

82. Do you anticipate a net turnaround in the deferred credits for timing differences within 5 years and if so how significant will it be? (Please *circle* one response.)

1. No net turnaround
2. Net turnaround of less than 10%

8:74 3. Net turnaround of between 10 and 20%

4. Net turnaround of between 20 and 50%
5. Net turnaround of over 50%

83. If your response to the prior question was 3, 4, or 5 please list the reasons for your projected turnaround.

______________________________________________

______________________________________________

______________________________________________

84. If flow-through or some form of partial allocation became the only acceptable accounting treatment for the ITC and timing differences, what effects would this have on the rates charged to your customers? Please *circle* one response.

1. Significant reduction
2. Slight reduction

7:75 3. No effect

4. Slight increase
5. Significant increase

85. If "flow-through" (immediate recognition as a selective tax rate reduction) were the required method, do you believe that an exception should be made for regulated industries such as public utilities? (Please *circle* your response.)

7:76 1. No

2. Yes (Please state why) ______________________________

______________________________

86. Should the use of flow-through (where the tax benefit of timing differences are passed through to customers in rate regulation) impact on accounting for timing differences? (Please *circle* your response.)

7:77 1. No

2. Yes

Comments ______________________________

______________________________

87. Should there be a different set of "generally accepted accounting principles" for rate regulated as opposed to nonregulated enterprises? (Please *circle* your response.)

7:78 1. No

2. Yes

Comments ______________________________

______________________________

# Appendix D
# FERF Questionnaire for Users of Financial Statements

## USER QUESTIONNAIRE

1. Personal Information:

   1-a Occupation ______________

   1-b Employer ______________

   1-c Industry specialization ______________

   1-d Average asset size of companies analyzed (in millions of dollars) ______________

   1-e Range of asset size of companies analyzed (in millions of dollars) from ______________ to ______________

   1-f Number of years of experience in your field ______________

   1-g Degree of contact with companies you evaluate (circle one response)

      1) Personal contact

      2) Impersonal contact

2. How often do you get involved in a detailed analysis of a company's deferred tax credit (or charge) account(s)? (Circle one response)

   1) Frequently

   2) Occasionally

   3) Infrequently

   Comments ______________________________________________

   ______________________________________________

3. How would you assess your level of knowledge on the issues involving accounting for income taxes? (Circle one response)

   1) Technically and conceptually proficient

   2) Conceptually proficient; technical knowledge is cursory

   3) Conceptual and technical knowledge is cursory

4. On a scale of one to ten (one being no interest and ten being high interest), rate your level of interest in the FASB's reconsideration of accounting for income taxes. (Place a check mark on the appropriate line)

   ___ ___ ___ ___ ___ ___ ___ ___ ___ ___
   1 2 3 4 5 6 7 8 9 10

5. What aspect of the interperiod income tax allocation project currently under reconsideration by the Financial Accounting Standards Board is of most interest to you as a user of financial information? (Circle one response)

   1) Specific proposals for change (i.e., I would like to see certain changes made or not made)

   2) That comparability be maintained or improved (the specific methods adopted are not of concern to me provided that comparability is maintained)

   3) Interested from a theoretical perspective, but changes, if any, will not have a practical effect on me as a user

   4) Minimal (no) interest in the project

6. Which of the following statements better describes your need for accounting information regarding income taxes? (Circle one response)

   1) The same information is needed from all companies and is not a function of size or dispersion of ownership, or whether they are or are not rate regulated

   2) Different information is needed from different companies, depending upon size, dispersion of ownership or whether they are rate regulated

7. How would you describe your current level of satisfaction with the existing rules for allocating the effects of timing differences between accounting periods? (Circle one response)

   1) Very satisfied, no changes are necessary

   2) Generally satisfied, but minor changes are necessary

   3) Generally dissatisfied, major changes are necessary

   4) Very dissatisfied, a complete revision is necessary

   5) No opinion

8. How would you describe your current level of satisfaction with the existing rules for accounting for the investment tax credit, disregarding the new rules for basis reduction under the Tax Equity and Fiscal Responsiblity Act of 1982? (Circle one response)

   1) Very satisfied, no changes are necessary

   2) Generally satisfied, but minor changes are necessary

   3) Generally dissatisfied, major changes are necessary

   4) Very dissatisfied, a complete revision is necessary

   5) No opinion

9. How would you describe your current level of satisfaction with the absence of formal rules to guide accounting for the foreign tax credit? (Circle one response)

   1) Very satisfied, no changes are necessary

   2) Generally satisfied, but guidelines in certain complex situations would be desirable

   3) Generally dissatisfied, this is a complex area in which rules could be helpful

   4) Very dissatisfied, this area is very complex and rules are needed

   5) No opinion

10. How would you describe your current level of satisfaction with the presentation of the deferred tax analysis in the footnotes accompanying the company's financial statements? (Circle one response)

   1) Very satisfied, no changes are needed

   2) Generally satisfied, but minor changes are needed

   3) Generally dissatisfied, major changes are needed

   4) Very dissatisfied, a complete revision is needed

   5) No opinion

11. The major issues of accounting for income taxes that are most in need of immediate reconsideration are (circle one or more responses)

   1 The allocation requirement itself

   1 The comprehensive allocation concept

   1 The deferral method requirement for tax allocation

   1 The appropriate response to changes in tax rates

   1 The proscription against discounting deferred tax accounts

   1 The accounting for the expected future benefits of net operating loss carryforwards

   1 The accounting for tax credits

   1 Others (please list) ________________________________

   ________________________________________________

   1 None of the above

12. From your perspective, a deferred tax credit balance in the balance sheet most resembles (circle one response)

    1. A payable (either short or long term)

    2. A reduction in an asset (similar to accumulated depreciation)

    3. Paid-in capital

    4. Quasi-equity account

    5. Has no comparable account

13. How are deferred tax credit account balances (arising from income tax timing differences) used in your computation of debt/equity ratios? (Circle one response)

    1. Entire balance is treated as debt

    2. Entire balance is treated as equity

    3. Does not enter into the computation of the debt/equity ratio

    4. The entire balance enters the computation; some part is allocated to debt and the remainder to equity

    5. A portion of the balance enters the computation; either as debt or equity

14. If your answer to question 12 was either 4 or 5, please explain how you determine the amount to include in the debt/equity ratio and its classification as either debt or equity.

    Explanation: ____________________________________________

    ____________________________________________

    ____________________________________________

    ____________________________________________

    ____________________________________________

    ____________________________________________

    ____________________________________________

15. From your perspective, an unamortized investment tax credit in the balance sheet most resembles (circle one response)

    1. A payable (either short or long term)

    2. A reduction in an asset (similar to accumulated depreciation)

    3. Paid-in capital

    4. Quasi-equity account

    5. Has no comparable account

16. How is an unamortized investment tax credit balance used in your computation of debt/equity ratios?

    1. Entire balance is treated as debt

    2. Entire balance is treated as equity

    3. Does not enter into the computation of the debt/equity ratio

    4. The entire balance enters the computation; some part is allocated to debt and the remainder to equity

    5. A portion of the balance enters the computation; either as debt or equity

17. If your answer to question 15 was either 4 or 5, please explain how you determine the amount to include in the debt/equity ratio and its classification as either debt or equity.

    Explanation: ____________________________________________

    ____________________________________________

    ____________________________________________

    ____________________________________________

    ____________________________________________

    ____________________________________________

    ____________________________________________

18. In your response to questions 12 and 15 is your debt/equity computation the same for both rate regulated and nonregulated corporations? (Circle either yes or no).

    1. Yes

    2. No

    Comments________________________________________________

    ________________________________________________________

    ________________________________________________________

19. At what point in your analysis of a company's cash flow position does the deferred credit (or charge) account become a significant factor?

    1. In all cases, regardless of the size of the account balance

    2. Primarily in liquidation analysis

    3. When the balance exceeds a prescribed percentage of owner's equity (or assets)

    4. When a growth trend begins to reverse (a credit balance begins to decline)

    5. Primarily in the analysis of a particular industry

    6. Does not enter into the cash flow analysis

20. If your answer to the above question was number 5, list the industries in which the analysis of the deferred tax account receives particular attention.

    ________________________________________________________

    ________________________________________________________

    ________________________________________________________

    ________________________________________________________

    ________________________________________________________

    ________________________________________________________

21. An important issue with regard to accounting for income taxes is the relationship between the deferred tax credit (or charge) account and future cash outflows (or inflows). As a user of financial information, how do you determine the effect on a company's future cash requirements from changes in (or the components of) the deferred tax credit (or charge) balance? What changes would you like to see made which would better correlate the information provided on a company's income tax provision and the resulting effect on future cash flows?

Comments ______________________________

Please check on the appropriate line one of the following responses to subsequent statements 22 and 23

(1) Agree in all cases

(2) Agree in general, but with some exception(s)

(3) Disagree in general, but with some exception(s)

(4) Disagree in all cases

(5) Does not apply to our company/no experience with this issue/no opinion

22. FASB Statement of Financial Concepts No. 2 defines accounting information as "reliable" to the "extent that users can depend on it to represent the economic conditions or events that it purports to represent" (p. 27, par. 62). The current method of accounting for income taxes results in information that is "reliable" for my purposes.

1 ____ 2 ____ 3 ____ 4 ____ 5 ____

Comments (include the exceptions) if your response was (2) or (3) ____

23. FASB Statement of Financial Concepts No. 2 defines the meaning of "relevance" as it relates to accounting information as "capable of making a difference in a decision by helping users to form predictions about the outcomes of past, present and future events or to confirm or correct expectations" (p. 21, par. 47). The current method of accounting for income taxes results in information that is "relevant" for my purposes.

1 _____ 2 _____ 3 _____ 4 _____ 5 _____

Comments (include the exceptions) if your response was (2) or (3) _____

______________________________________________________________

For each of the following changes (questions 24 through 29) being considered by the FASB in its Accounting for Income Taxes Project, indicate whether you believe that adoption of such a change would provide information to you that is (circle one response)

1. More relevant and is probably cost justified

2. More relevant but is probably not cost justified

3. No change

4. Less relevant

5. No opinion

24. The income tax expense recognized on the financial statements will be based on the taxes payable as determined on the tax return (i.e., taxes currently payable will replace interperiod tax allocation).

1 _____ 2 _____ 3 _____ 4 _____ 5 _____

Comments______________________________________________________

______________________________________________________________

25. The income tax effects of transactions that create timing differences will be adjusted for subsequent changes in tax laws or rates that take effect before the timing difference reverses (timing differences are currently based solely on the tax laws or rates in effect when the difference originates).

1 _____ 2 _____ 3 _____ 4 _____ 5 _____

Comments______________________________________________________

______________________________________________________________

26. The tax effects of timing differences will be discounted (no discounting is presently allowed).

1 _____ 2 _____ 3 _____ 4 _____ 5 _____

Comments________________________________________

________________________________________________

27. The future tax benefit of a current year net operating loss will be recognized in the year the loss originated if management believes such benefits will be recognized within the carryforward period (current rules require that companies wait until the tax benefit is received before its effect is recognized).

1 _____ 2 _____ 3 _____ 4 _____ 5 _____

Comments________________________________________

________________________________________________

28. A separate, less complex, set of accounting requirements for income taxes should be adopted for private and small public companies.

1 _____ 2 _____ 3 _____ 4 _____ 5 _____

Comments________________________________________

________________________________________________

29. Current accounting standards require that the tax effects of all timing differences be recognized (except those subject to indefinite reversal). With more and more companies experiencing an annual increase in their <u>net</u> deferred tax credit amount, there should be adopted a change to a partial allocation method (no income tax effects for groups of similar originating differences, are recognized if future offsets are expected).

1 _____ 2 _____ 3 _____ 4 _____ 5 _____

Comments________________________________________

________________________________________________

30. Several of the accounting for income taxes changes being considered would allow for management judgment to be reflected in the tax effect recognized (e.g., discounting, partial allocation, NOL carryforwards). From a user's perspective, such an infusion of management judgment into the reporting process would (circle one response)

    1. Be beneficial; it enhances the relevancy of the information

    2. Be detrimental; it reduces the reliability (verifability) of the information

    3. Not have any effect on users

Please check on the appropriate line one of the following responses to subsequent statements 31 through 33

(1) Agree in all cases

(2) Agree in general, but with some exception(s)

(3) Disagree in general, but with some exception(s)

(4) Disagree in all cases

(5) Does not apply to our company/no experience with this issue/no opinion

31. When considering the propriety of one income tax allocation method over another, primary emphasis should be given to the effects on the income statement, with secondary emphasis on the balance sheet.

1 _____ 2 _____ 3 _____ 4 _____ 5 _____

Comments (include the exceptions) if your response was (2) or (3) _____

______________________________________________________________

32. Cash flow consideration should take precedence over the matching criterion when payment of the tax liability cannot be reasonably foreseen in a relatively short period of time.

1 _____ 2 _____ 3 _____ 4 _____ 5 _____

Comments (include the exceptions) if your response was (2) or (3) _____

______________________________________________________________

33. Recent tax law changes (in particular, the Economic Recovery Tax Act of 1981) have so distorted the relationship between taxable income and pre-tax accounting net income that the relevancy of the information produced by comprehensive allocation has diminished.

1 ____ 2 ____ 3 ____ 4 ____ 5 ____

Comments (include the exceptions) if your response was (2) or (3) ______

______________________________________________

34. Which of the following tax allocation methods would provide you with the most relevant information (assuming interperiod tax allocation is retained)? (Circle one response)

1. Deferral
2. Liability
3. Net-of-tax
4. A combination of liability and net-of-tax
5. No difference in the relevancy of the information
6. No opinion

35. The method of recording investment credits that would provide the most relevant information to users would be (circle one response)

1. Deferral method
2. Flow-through method
3. Either deferral or flow-through, provided only one of the methods is allowed
4. Either deferral or flow-through, with the decision of which to use left to management (i.e., the current method)
5. No opinion

36. If discounting of timing differences was permitted (required), the appropriate discounting rate should be (circle one response)

1. The company's internal rate of return
2. The company's incremental borrowing rate
3. Some risk-free market rate
4. Determined by management
5. Any method, provided it is consistent across companies

37. Do you consider the corporate income tax to be: (Circle one response)

    1. An expense

    2. A loss

    3. A distribution of earnings to society

    4. A cost of doing business not described above

    5. Some other anomalous item

    Comments ________________________________________

    ________________________________________

38. Which of the following statements best describes the investment tax credit (ITC):

    1. The ITC is a contribution to the capital of the respective taxpayer by the federal government similar in many respects to the gift of land by a state or local government in attracting industry to an industrial park;

    2. The ITC is a selective method for reducing the effective income tax rates for the firm acquiring qualified assets;

    3. The ITC is a reduction in the cost of acquiring a qualifying asset or

    4. The ITC is an administrative procedure to permit the taxpayer to withhold the cash equivalent of the credit from taxes otherwise payable

    Please rank each of the above alternatives by listing the corresponding number of your first choice on the first choice line, the corresponding number of your second choice on the second choice line, etc.

    First choice ____________

    Second choice____________

    Third choice ____________

    Fourth choice____________

One of the objectives of financial reporting is to "provide information that is useful to present and potential investors and creditors and other users in making rational investment, credit, and similar decisions" (FASB Statement of Financial Accounting Concepts No. 1, para. 34). Consistent with the objective, the information provided should be "comprehensible to those who have a reasonable understanding of business and economic activities and are willing to study the information with reasonable diligence" (para. 34).

Reproduced below are portions of the financial statements and footnotes of one company (not a public utility) that deal with its accounting for income taxes. Questions 39 through 53 that follow are intended to determine the comprehensibility and usefulness of these financial statements and notes to users of the financial statements.

## Consolidated Statement of Earnings

Dollars in millions, except per share amounts

| | Year ended 31 December 1982 | 1981 | 1980 |
|---|---|---|---|
| **Net Sales** | $6,154.5 | $4,758.7 | $4,383.4 |
| **Operating Costs and Expenses:** | | | |
| Cost of sales | 5,547.5 | 4,263.6 | 3,810.5 |
| Selling and general and administrative | 340.3 | 294.3 | 307.2 |
| | 5,887.8 | 4,557.9 | 4,117.7 |
| **Operating Earnings** | 266.7 | 200.8 | 265.7 |
| Interest expense | (23.2) | (20.4) | (9.2) |
| Other income, net | 25.8 | 59.0 | 14.9 |
| **Earnings from Continuing Operations Before Income Taxes** | 269.3 | 239.4 | 271.4 |
| Provision for income taxes | (108.8) | (92.1) | (68.7) |
| **Earnings from Continuing Operations** | 160.5 | 147.3 | 202.7 |
| **Loss from Discontinued Operations,** net of income tax benefits of $24.3, $20.0 and $6.9, respectively | (27.7) | (23.2) | (7.7) |
| **Net Earnings** | $ 132.8 | $ 124.1 | $ 195.0 |
| **Net Earnings (Loss) Per Common Share:** | | | |
| Continuing operations | $ 2.92 | $ 2.67 | $ 3.72 |
| Discontinued operations | (.51) | (.42) | (.14) |
| | $ 2.41 | $ 2.25 | $ 3.58 |

## Liabilities and Shareholders' Equity

| | | |
|---|---|---|
| **Current Liabilities:** | | |
| Short-term borrowings | $ 58.2 | $ 132.0 |
| Accounts payable | 416.3 | 303.7 |
| Accrued salaries and wages | 172.5 | 112.5 |
| Other accrued expenses | 314.2 | 159.6 |
| Provision for loss on SSN 688 program | 32.0 | 62.4 |
| Total Current Liabilities | 993.2 | 770.2 |
| **Noncurrent Liabilities:** | | |
| Long-term debt less current maturities | 23.7 | 24.9 |
| Deferred income taxes | 321.3 | 310.2 |
| Other | 99.3 | 85.4 |
| Total Noncurrent Liabilities | 444.3 | 420.5 |
| **Redeemable Preferred Stock** | 27.0 | 27.1 |
| **Common Shareholders' Equity** | 1,175.0 | 1,071.5 |
| | $2,639.5 | $2,289.3 |

## Consolidated Statement of Common Shareholders' Equity

Dollars in millions

| | Common Stock | | Retained | Treasury Stock | |
|---|---|---|---|---|---|
| | Shares | Amount | Earnings | Shares | Amount |
| **Balance, 1 January 1980** | 55,442,100 | $80.1 | $ 778.5 | 2,237,090 | $32.2 |
| Net earnings | | | 195.0 | | |
| Cash dividends | | | (36.3) | | |
| Stock options exercised | | 3.0 | | (482,200) | (6.9) |
| Conversions of Preferred Stock | | .2 | | (31,217) | (.5) |
| Shares acquired, at cost | | | | 15,576 | .5 |
| Shares issued under Incentive Compensation Plan | | 1.5 | | (192,284) | (2.7) |
| **Balance, 31 December 1980** | 55,442,100 | 84.8 | 937.2 | 1,546,965 | 22.6 |
| Net earnings | | | 124.1 | | |
| Cash dividends | | | (41.3) | | |
| Stock options exercised | | 1.1 | | (592,051) | (9.8) |
| Conversions of Preferred Stock | | .6 | | (79,814) | (1.2) |
| Shares acquired, at cost | | | | 1,095,450 | 26.8 |
| Shares issued under Incentive Compensation Plan | | 1.3 | | (141,330) | (2.1) |
| **Balance, 31 December 1981** | 55,442,100 | 87.8 | 1,020.0 | 1,829,220 | 36.3 |
| Net earnings | | | 132.8 | | |
| Cash dividends | | | (41.1) | | |
| Stock options exercised | | (5.2) | | (948,913) | (19.1) |
| Conversions of Preferred Stock | | | | (3,006) | (.1) |
| Shares acquired, at cost | | | | 174,355 | 4.5 |
| Shares issued under Incentive Compensation Plan | | .3 | | (98,917) | (2.0) |
| **Balance, 31 December 1982** | 55,442,100 | $82.9 | $1,111.7 | 952,739 | $19.6 |

The accompanying notes to Consolidated Financial Statements are an integral part of these statements.

## Notes to Consolidated Financial Statements

Dollars in millions, except per share amounts

**Income Taxes.** Investment tax credits are recognized as a reduction in income taxes in the year the related property is placed in service. Net proceeds of $11.4 and $35.0 for 1982 and 1981, respectively, from the sale of certain tax benefits under provisions of the Economic Recovery Tax Act of 1981 are included in Other Income in the Consolidated Statement of Earnings.

### I. Income Taxes

The Corporation's income tax provision from continuing operations is computed as follows:

| | Year ended 31 December | | |
|---|---|---|---|
| | 1982 | 1981 | 1980 |
| Earnings before income taxes | $269.3 | $239.4 | $271.4 |
| Tax provision at current tax rates on book income: | | | |
| Current | $ .7 | $ 1.3 | $ 15.0 |
| Deferred | 125.8 | 107.4 | 106.4 |
| Tax credits - deferred: | | | |
| Investment tax credits on LNG tankers | — | — | (10.0) |
| Other | (9.9) | (1.6) | (24.0) |
| Depletion allowances in excess of cost depletion - deferred | (5.7) | (4.8) | (5.7) |
| Permanent deferral of DISC income | (2.1) | (10.2) | (13.0) |
| Provision for income taxes | $108.8 | $ 92.1 | $ 68.7 |
| Effective tax rate | 40.4% | 38.5% | 25.3% |

The disposal of the telecommunications segment resulted in the recognition of deferred tax benefits of $69.8.

U.S. income taxes and foreign withholding taxes (estimated at $40.4 after utilization of foreign tax credits) which would be payable upon distribution of earnings of foreign subsidiaries and domestic international sales corporations have not been recognized, since the Corporation intends to continue investing those earnings in export activities and operations outside the United States. The undistributed earnings for which taxes have not been provided amount to $143.9, of which $124.6 is included in retained earnings.

Deferred income taxes result primarily from the completed contract method of accounting used for reporting taxable earnings on long-term contracts. Deferred income taxes payable at 31 December 1982 and 1981 were $321.3 and $310.2, respectively. The provision for deferred taxes before consideration of tax credits, depletion, DISC benefits, and benefits related to discontinued operations is analyzed as follows:

| | Year ended 31 December Provision (Credit) | | |
|---|---|---|---|
| | 1982 | 1981 | 1980 |
| Completed contract method: | | | |
| Earnings on uncompleted contracts | $ 96.0 | $ 83.0 | $ 89.0 |
| Transitional adjustment | 9.0 | 7.6 | 12.8 |
| Other | 20.8 | 16.8 | 4.6 |
| | $125.8 | $107.4 | $106.4 |

The Corporation has a net operating loss carryforward of $2,464.0 expiring in various amounts from 1992 through 1997. Investment tax credits of $137.3 have reduced deferred income taxes and will expire in varying amounts beginning in taxable years after 1989.

The Corporation's Federal income tax returns for 1975 and subsequent years are subject to review by the Internal Revenue Service.

The provision for state and local income taxes was $2.2 in 1982, $10.7 in 1981 and $8.9 in 1980, substantially all of which was current.

[Short Additional Note from the 1981 Annual Report]

The Corporation has a net operating loss of $1,818.0 expiring in various amounts from 1992 through 1996. Investment tax credits of $129.0 have reduced deferred income taxes and will expire in varying amounts beginning in taxable years after 1989.

39. Consolidated Statement of Earnings shows an increase of 58 percent in the provision for income taxes from 1980's $68.7 million to 1982's $108.8 million while income from continuing operations before income taxes shows a slight decrease. What is your assessment of the 1982 income tax provision on current and future cash flows? (Circle one response)

    1. This signals an increase in current and future cash outflow for income taxes

    2. The provision for income taxes is unrelated to current or future cash flows

    3. No opinion

    Comments ______________________________

    ______________________________

    ______________________________

40. The deferred income taxes in the consolidated Balance Sheet of 1982 of $321.3 million are 27.3 percent of the common shareholders equity of $1.175 billion and increased $11.1 million over the 1981 deferred income taxes of $310.2 million. What is your assessment of the significance of the deferred tax credit on future cash flows? (Circle one response)

    1. The amount and growth in deferred income taxes in the balance sheet signal an increase in future cash outflow for income taxes

    2. The deferred income taxes in the balance sheet are unrelated to current or future cash flows

    3. No opinion

    Comments ______________________________

    ______________________________

    ______________________________

41. The footnote on income taxes shows an increasing "effective tax rate" from 25.3% in 1980 to 40.4% in 1982. What is your assessment of this increase? (Circle one response)

    1. This signals an increase in future cash outflows for income taxes

    2. This increase in effective tax rate is unrelated to current or future cash outflows for income taxes

    3. No opinion

    Comments ______________________________

    ______________________________

    ______________________________

42. What is your assessment of current year payments to the federal government for 1982 income taxes? (Circle one response)

    1. They paid federal income taxes at a 40.4% tax rate

    2. They paid only $700,000 in federal income taxes

    3. They did not pay any federal income tax

    4. No opinion

    Comments ______________________________

    ______________________________

    ______________________________

43. How do you assess the significance of an increase in the provision for income taxes and an increase in the "effective tax rate" with the presence of a $2.464 billion dollar net operating loss (NOL) carryforward? (Circle one response)

    1. The tax benefit of the NOL has been recognized for financial reporting to shareholders but not for tax purposes

    2. The tax benefit of the NOL has not been recognized for either financial reporting or for tax purposes

    3. No opinion

    Comments ______________________________

    ______________________________

    ______________________________

44. How do you assess the significance of the $137.3 million of investment tax credits (ITC), that "have reduced deferred income taxes" but start expiring after 1989? (Circle one response)

1. The tax effect of the $137.3 million in ITC has been recognized for financial reporting to shareholders but not for tax purposes

2. The tax effect of these ITCs has not been recognized for either financial reporting or for tax purposes

3. No opinion

Comments ____________________________________________

____________________________________________

____________________________________________

45. With this corporation reporting $132.8 million in net earnings for 1982 and paying $41.1 million in dividends for 1982 and reporting December 31, 1982 retained earnings of $1,111.7 million, could the $41.1 million in dividends be nontaxable return of capital investment to the shareholders? (Circle one response)

1. Absolutely no

2. Probably no

3. Possibly yes

4. Yes

5. No opinion

Comments ______________________________

______________________________

______________________________

46. If this corporation had paid return of capital dividends should disclosure of this information in its annual report be required? (Circle one response)

1) Yes, this is important user information

2) No, this information is available elsewhere

3) No opinion

Comments ______________________________

______________________________

______________________________

47. Do you believe the footnote disclosure that ITCs begin to "expire in varying amounts beginning in taxable years after 1989" is adequate disclosure? (Circle one response)

1) No, the following information should also be disclosed: (Circle one or more)

   a. the amount of the ITC expiring by year
   b. the potential effect of the NOL on the ITC use
   c. the potential effect of filing separate or consolidated tax returns on the use of the ITC
   d. other______________________________

2) Yes, the disclosure is adequate for my purposes

3) No opinion

Comments ______________________________

48. Given that the information furnished contains all the tax data, is this group of corporations filing consolidated or separate tax returns? (Circle one response)

1) Consolidated

2) Separate

3) Data not available

4) No opinion

Comments ______________________________

49) Is the disclosure of whether a group of corporations is filing a consolidated or separate tax returns relevant information to you?

1) Yes, always

2) Yes, but only where there are current tax attribute carryforwards

3) No

4) No opinion

Comments ______________________________

50) Are there any other aspects of accounting for income taxes which you as a user of financial data would have liked this group of corporations to disclose?

Explain ______________________________

51) Is this company's footnote disclosure of its accounting for income taxes fairly typical of the footnote disclosures you analyze?

1) Yes

2) No

Comments ______________________________

# Appendix E
# A History of the Depreciation Deduction

Because the depreciation timing difference is so significant to any accounting for income tax discussion, a modest chronological history of tax depreciation was deemed desirable.[1] The tremendous increases in tax depreciation via changes in the tax law are shown in this appendix.

Prior to 1954, almost all taxpayers used the straight-line depreciation method for both book and tax purposes. In 1954, the income tax law (Internal Revenue Code Section 167) was enacted to permit accelerated depreciation methods (over full useful lives) for new assets with at least a three-year useful life. The most rapid write-offs were subsequently achieved through the use of either the double declining balance or the sum-of-the-years-digits methods.

The Supreme Court stated that useful life meant the life in the hands of a particular taxpayer and not the inherent useful life of a particular asset. Thus Hertz, among others, was restricted to a one-year life (with a correspondingly high salvage value) on rental cars and, therefore, failed the three-year life for accelerated depreciation.

In July of 1962, through Revenue Procedure 62-21, the Kennedy Administration significantly reduced the useful lives for tax depreciation purposes by adopting guideline life depreciation. Guideline depreciation grouped almost all assets into one or more of about 75 possible categories (groups), and then one composite depreciation rate was generally applied to each group. It is interesting to note

---

[1]Much of the depreciation history was taken from (1) James E. Wheeler, An Historical Examination And Analysis Of The Effects Of The Depreciation Deduction And The Investment Tax Credit On Financial Reporting an unpublished Ph.D. dissertation, 1969 and (2) Donald W. Kiefer, Accelerated Depreciation And The Investment Tax Credit In The Public Utility Industry: A Background Analysis Congressional Research Service, Library of Congress, April 1979.

that without Congressional action (a Revenue Procedure does not require Congressional input) depreciation deductions were greatly increased for many corporations.

The year 1962 was also the first year of the ITC, and the basis for depreciation purposes of each qualifying asset was reduced by the full amount of the ITC. This basis reduction (for assets placed in service in years 1962 and 1963) was restored in 1964, and, therefore, increased depreciation deductions over the remaining useful lives of those assets.

Because the increased depreciation, from guideline lives and accelerated depreciation methods, results in deductions against ordinary income, Congress enacted Internal Revenue Code Section 1245. This Section, upon a subsequent sale of these assets, recaptures depreciation taken (since January 1, 1962), to the extent of the gain, as ordinary income. Congress did not want to allow large depreciation deductions against ordinary income that could result in capital gains upon subsequent sales of the related assets. In 1964, Congress enacted a modified version of depreciation recapture for depreciable real estate (Section 1250).

Accompanying the 1962 guideline, life depreciation was the "reserve ratio test," a test ratio of accumulated depreciation to the original cost of the assets in each guideline class. The purpose of the reserve ratio was to ensure that too much depreciation was not being taken too early. The reserve ratio test was designed so that the guideline depreciation concept met the "reasonable allowance" test of Internal Revenue Code Section 167(a). Essentially the reserve ratio test provided a system to test the useful life being used in depreciation calculations. If depreciation deductions proved to be too large, the reserve ratio test would lengthen the useful lives thus reducing future depreciation deductions. There was, however, a three-year moratorium on applying the test.

During the three-year moratorium period, 1962-1965, many corporations employed several techniques to significantly increase depreciation. One of these techniques used fully depreciated assets in open-end accounts. In many cases, the result was the equivalent of immediately expensing the newly acquired asset. This practice and the already shorter guideline lives meant that many corporations would fail the reserve ratio test and, consequently, would have their future depreciation deductions reduced. To avoid this, the Treasury issued, in 1965, Revenue Procedure 65-13, which provided a "trending rule." As long as the reserve ratio test was failed by less than it was failed in the prior year, depreciation deductions were not changed as they were heading in the right direction. In addition "open-end" accounts were abolished--new accounts were created for each year's asset acquisitions.

To restrain an inflationary economy, both the ITC and accelerated depreciation on buildings were temporarily suspended from October 16, 1966 until December 31, 1967. The suspension period was subsequently shortened to March 9, 1967, which was only five months after it had started.

In the Tax Reform Act of 1969, Congress enacted Internal Revenue Code Section 167(1). This income tax section sets forth, for the first time in regard to depreciation, rules for intrastate public utility rate regulation. These rules permit a public utility to use accelerated depreciation and short lives for tax purposes while reporting the tax provision for rate-regulation purposes based on straight-line depreciation over much longer useful lives. Congressman Wilbur Mills, then chairman of the House Ways and Means Committee, stated that "to get back to my basic concern, we have no authority over intrastate rate-making. That is a function of the state agencies. Even our Federal Power Commission, Federal Communications Commission, all of these agencies, do not get into that area. They regulate where there are interstate operations, not solely intrastate operations."[2] Several years prior to Congressman Mills' statement, Senator Russell Long stated that, "My understanding is that we simply instruct Federal regulatory agencies. Frankly, I say to the Senator, I have considerable doubt that we should try to instruct State regulatory agencies....that falls in the area of states rights."[3] The question of states rights and constitutionality is still with us.

By 1971, much of the economic impetus from guideline depreciation had taken place. The Nixon Administration on January 11, 1971, therefore, announced the subsequently released Revenue Procedure 71-25 called Asset Depreciation Range ADR).[4] Because ADR did not contain a "reserve ratio test" to ensure an economically reasonable deduction, it would have probably failed a pending court challenge. To prevent this, Congress legislatively enacted the ADR provisions as CLADR--class life asset depreciation range--(see Section 167(m)) and stated (in Section 167(a)) that it shall be deemed reasonable, thus meeting the Section 167(a) reasonable allowance provision. In addition to removing the reserve ratio test, CLADR allowed a shortening (or lengthening) of guideline lives by 20 percent.

The 1971 CLADR option to increase depreciation guideline lives by 20 percent was particularly interesting in light of the 1969 Hertz Supreme Court case. The guideline life for rental cars had been 2.5 years. When this is increased by 20 percent it becomes 3 years, thus automatically making those assets eligible for accelerated depreciation again. When this change is combined with a shortening of the lives to qualify for the ITC (from 4, 6 and

---

[2]Donald Kiefer, p. 25.

[3]Ibid., p. 23.

[4]For a complete description, see The Department of The Treasury, Asset Depreciation Range (ADR) System, June 1971.

8 to 3, 5 and 7), the 3 year life through increasing 2.5 years by 20 percent becomes even more significant for taxpayers with those assets.

The CLADR system functioned satisfactorily until it was believed that the economy needed even greater depreciation write-offs. Thus in 1981 the Economic Recovery Tax Act of 1981 (ERTA) introduced a new depreciation concept, the accelerated cost recovery system (ACRS), that is not based on useful lives.

ACRS is contained in Internal Revenue Code Section 168. It groups all assets other than real estate into one of four groups, (3-year, 5-year, 10-year and 15-year public utility) and uses a 15-year write-off period for commercial real estate.

Much public utility property escapes the 15-year public utility category by qualifying for either the 5-year or the 10-year category. For example, in 1982 Revenue Procedure 82-67 retroactively changed the midpoint guideline life of telephone switching equipment from 20 to 18 years. This allowed this equipment to qualify for the five-year write-off. Under the prior CLADR rules, the life used would have been between 16 and 24 years (20-year guideline life plus or minus 20 percent). Without this change, telephone equipment would have been in the 10-year category (midpoint guideline life over 18 and not over 25 years). Public utility property with a midpoint guideline life over 25 years qualifies for the 15-year public utility property category.

ACRS ignores economic useful lives and allows depreciation calculated over assumed short lives via fixed percentages. These percentages are based on a 150 percent of straight-line rate and were scheduled to go to a 200 percent or double declining rate with an optimum switch to sum-of-the-years-digits method.

By 1982, with a huge Federal deficit, Congress removed the scheduled increases in ACRS depreciation deductions. This was accomplished in the Tax Equity and Fiscal

Responsibility Act of 1982 (TEFRA). Congress in this Act, also took a page from 1962 and reduced the bases of assets for depreciation by one-half of the investment tax credit (ITC) or, if the taxpayer so elected, the ITC could be reduced by 2 percentage points and the depreciation basis left unadjusted.

The economic rational for these 1982 Congressional changes stemmed largely from the realization that the present value of the ITC and the ACRS depreciation deductions for five-year property (which includes most machinery and equipment) exceeded the tax benefits of immediate write-off of the asset. Apparently, Congress believed that immediate write-off should be the maximum rate of combined benefit from depreciation and ITC.

Thus, in less than 30 years, tax depreciation has gone from a full economic useful life concept using the straight-line depreciation method to a cost recovery system that, when coupled with the ITC benefits, approximates immediate write-off for most machinery and equipment items.

Depreciation deductions in financial statements are generally based on an economic useful life concept with the straight-line method most commonly used. This results in significant differences between tax and book depreciation deductions without considering the ITC effects on tax provisions. Even if a corporation is using an accelerated depreciation method for financial reporting, it will seldom be using useful lives as short as the assumed lives of ACRS. Financial reporting still requires a "rational depreciation measurement" and this requires calculation of depreciation on an economic useful life basis. In fact, for many corporations the depreciation timing difference due to useful life differences is greater than the difference due to depreciation method differences even when straight-line is used for financial reporting. In addition to these timing differences, there are also some permanent differences when the original tax basis of a depreciable asset is different than its original financial statement basis.

# Appendix F
# The Investment Tax Credit (ITC) History

The ITC has had a turbulent history.[1] It was enacted in a much different fashion than originally proposed. It has been suspended, reinstated, terminated, and resurrected in addition to numerous amendments introduced since its proposal in 1961.

The ITC currently comprises a very complex set of tax rules with very significant economic implications. In order to appreciate some of the complexity, the various portions of the Internal Revenue Code dealing with the ITC are contained in Tables F.1 and F.2.

Table F.1 shows that there are eight code sections dealing with ITCs of which three have been repealed and five are currently applicable. Two of the repealed sections (numbers 49 and 50) dealt with the suspension and reinstatement of the ITC and the third (Section 181) dealt with the basis reduction feature of 1962. This latter item has, in effect, been reenacted as Section 196 for the basis reduction feature of the "Tax Equity and Fiscal Responsibility Act of 1982" (TEFRA).

---

[1]Much of the ITC history in this chapter was taken from (1) James E. Wheeler, An Historical Examination and Analysis Of The Effects Of The Depreciation Deduction And The Investment Tax Credit On Financial Reporting an unpublished Ph.D. dissertation, 1969 and (2) Donald W. Kiefer, Accelerated Depreciation And The Investment Tax Credit In The Public Utility Industry: A Background Analysis Congressional Research Service, Library of Congress, April 1979.

TABLE F.1 *A Listing of Internal Revenue Code Sections Dealing with the Investment Tax Credit*

| Code Section | Title |
|---|---|
| 38 | Investment in Certain Depreciable Property. |
| 46 | Amount of Credit. |
| 47 | Certain Dispositions, Etc., of Section 38 Property. |
| 48 | Definitions; Special Rules. |
| 49 | [Termination for Period Beginning April 19, 1969, and Ending During 1971] Repealed. |
| 50 | [Restoration of Credit] Repealed. |
| 181 | [Deduction for Certain Unused Investment Credit] Repealed. |
| 196 | Deduction for Certain Unused Investment Credits. |

Table F.2 lists the headings of the eight code sections, and the headings of the subsections and paragraph titles of the five active sections. Even a cursory review of this lengthy table will quickly reveal extensive complexity. There are special rules for particular assets, types of taxpayers, and rate-regulation rules for public utilities. There is also a regular ITC, an energy ITC (of several different types), an ITC for contributions to certain employee plans and a rehabilitation ITC, all of which require coordination among themselves and with the other tax credits (such as the foreign tax credit) that are available to taxpayers.

TABLE F.2 *A Table of Contents for Internal Revenue Sections, Subsections, and Paragraphs Dealing with the Investment Tax Credit*

| Code Section | Section, Subsection, and Paragraph Titles |
|---|---|
| 38 | Investment in Certain Depreciable Property |
| | (a) General rule |
| | (b) Regulations |
| 46 | Amount of Credit |
| | (a) General rule |
| | (1) First-in-first-out rule |
| | (2) Amount of credit |
| | (3) Limitation based on amount of tax |
| | (4) Liability for tax |
| | (5) Married individuals |
| | (6) Controlled groups |

Table F.2 (continued)

Code Section (46 contd.)

(7) Special rules in the case of energy property

(b) Carryback and carryover of unused credits

(1) In general

(2) Limitation on carrybacks

(3) Limitation on carryovers

(c) Qualified investment

(1) In general

(2) Applicable percentage in certain cases

(3) Public utility property

(4) Coordination with subsection (d)

(5) Applicable percentage in the case of certain pollution control facilities

(6) Special rule for commuter highway vehicles

(7) Applicable percentage for recovery property

(8) Limitation to amount at risk

(9) Subsequent increases in the taxpayer's amount at risk with respect to the property

(d) Qualified progress expenditures

(1) Increases in qualified investment

Table F.2 (continued)

| Code Section | | |
|---|---|---|
| (46 contd.) | | (2) Progress expenditure property defined |
| | | (3) Qualified progress expenditures defined |
| | | (4) Special rules for applying paragraph (3) |
| | | (5) Other definitions |
| | | (6) Election |
| | | (7) Transitional rules |
| | (e) Limitations with respect to certain persons | |
| | | (1) In general |
| | | (2) Ratable share |
| | | (3) Noncorporate lessors |
| | (f) Limitation in case of certain regulated companies | |
| | | (1) General rule |
| | | (2) Special rule for ratable flow-through |
| | | (3) Special rule for immediate flow-through in certain cases |
| | | (4) Limitation |
| | | (5) Public utility property |
| | | (6) Ratable portion |
| | | (7) Reorganizations, assets, acquisitions, etc. |
| | | (8) Prohibition of immediate flow-through |

Table F.2 (continued)

| Code Section | |
|---|---|
| (46 contd.) | (9) Special rule for additional credit |
| | (10) Use of inconsistent estimates, projections, etc. for purposes of paragraphs (1) and (2) |
| | (g) Fifty percent credit in case of certain assets |
| | (1) In general |
| | (2) Amount of credit |
| | (3) Coordination with section 38 |
| | (4) Coordination with section 47 |
| | (5) Definitions |
| 47 | Certain Dispositions, Etc., of Section 38 Property |
| | (a) General rule |
| | (1) Early dispositions, etc. |
| | (2) Property becomes public utility property |
| | (3) Property ceases to be progress expenditure property |
| | (4) Special rule for commuter highway vehicles |
| | (5) Special rule for recovery property |
| | (6) Carrybacks and carryovers adjusted |
| | (7) Aircraft used outside the United States after April 18, 1969 |

Table F.2 (continued)

| Code Section | |
|---|---|
| (47 contd.) | (8) Motion picture films and audio tapes |
| | (b) Section not to apply in certain cases |
| | (c) Special rule |
| | (d) Property ceasing to be at risk |
| | (1) In general |
| | (2) Certain transfers not treated as ceasing to be at risk |
| | (3) Special rules for energy property |
| 48 | Definitions; Special Rules |
| | (a) Section 38 property |
| | (1) In general |
| | (2) Property used outside the United States |
| | (3) Property used for lodging |
| | (4) Property used by certain tax-exempt organizations |
| | (5) Property used by governmental units |
| | (6) Livestock |
| | (7) Property completed abroad or predominately of foreign origin |
| | (8) Amortized property |
| | (9) [Repealed] |
| | (10) Boilers fueled by oil or gas |

Table F.2 (continued)

| Code Section | | | |
|---|---|---|---|
| (48 contd.) | (b) | New section 38 property | |
| | (c) | Used section 38 property | |
| | | (1) | In general |
| | | (2) | Dollar limitation |
| | | (3) | Definitions |
| | (d) | Certain leased property | |
| | | (1) | General rule |
| | | (2) | Special rule for short-term leases |
| | | (3) | Limitations |
| | | (4) | Property to which paragraph (2) applies |
| | | (5) | Coordination with basis adjustment |
| | (e) | [Repealed] | |
| | (f) | Estates and trusts | |
| | (g) | Special rules for qualified rehabilitated buildings | |
| | | (1) | Qualified rehabilitated building defined |
| | | (2) | Qualified rehabilitation expenditure defined |
| | | (3) | Certified historic structure defined |
| | | (4) | Property treated as new section 38 property |

Table F.2 (continued)

| Code Section | | |
|---|---|---|
| (48 contd.) | (h) | [Repealed] |
| | (i) | [Repealed] |
| | (j) | [Repealed] |
| | (k) | Movie and television films |
| | | (1) Entitlement to credit |
| | | (2) Applicable percentage to be 66-2/3 |
| | | (3) Election of 90-percent rule |
| | | (4) Predominant use test: qualified investment |
| | | (5) Qualified United States production costs |
| | | (6) United States |
| | (l) | Energy property |
| | | (1) Treatment as section 38 property |
| | | (2) Energy property defined |
| | | (3) Alternative energy property |
| | | (4) Solar and wind energy property |
| | | (5) Specially defined energy property |
| | | (6) Recycling equipment |
| | | (7) Shale oil equipment |
| | | (8) Equipment for producing natural gas from geopressured brine |

Table F.2 (continued)

Code
Section
(48 contd.)

(9) Equipment must meet certain standards to qualify

(10) Existing

(11) Special rule for property financed by subsidized energy financing or industrial development bonds

(12) Industrial includes agricultural

(13) Qualified hydroelectric generating property

(14) Cogeneration equipment

(15) Biomass property

(16) Qualified intercity buses

(17) Exclusion for public utility property

(m) Application of certain transitional rules

(n) Requirements for allowance of employee plan percentage

(1) In general

(2) Qualified matching employee contribution defined

(3) Certain contributions of cash treated as contributions of employer securities

(4) Adjustments if employee plan credit recaptured

(5) Disallowance of deduction

Table F.2 (continued)

Code Section (48 contd.)

(6) Definitions

(o) Certain credits defined

(1) Regular investment credit

(2) Energy investment credit

(3) Employee plan credit

(4) Basic employee plan credit

(5) Matching employee plan credit

(6) Basic employee plan percentage

(7) Rehabilitation investment credit

(p) Single purpose agricultural or horticultural structure defined

(1) In general

(2) Single purpose livestock structure

(3) Single purpose horticultural structure

(4) Structures which include work space

(5) Special rules for applying section 47

(6) Livestock

(q) Basis adjustment to section 38 property

(1) In general

(2) Certain dispositions

(3) Special rule for qualified rehabilitated buildings

Table F.2 (continued)

| Code Section | |
|---|---|
| (48 contd.) | (4) Election of reduced credit in lieu of basis adjustment for regular percentage |
| | (5) Recapture of reductions |
| | (r) Cross reference |
| 49 | [Termination for Period Beginning April 19, 1969, and Ending During 1971] Repealed |
| 50 | [Restoration of Credit] Repealed |
| 181 | [Deduction for Certain Unused Investment Credit] Repealed |
| 181 | [Deduction for Certain Unused Investment Credit] Repealed |
| 196 | Deductions for Certain Unused Investment Credits |
| | (a) Allowance of deductions |
| | (b) Taxpayers dying or ceasing to exist |
| | (c) Special rule for qualified rehabilitated buildings |

Many of the rules contained under the various section, subsection, and paragraph headings of Table F.2 have been added since the original enactment of the ITC. Table F.3 lists the various public laws, with titles and dates, that have impacted the ITC. Since April 1, 1980, ten different public laws have amended the ITC rules or enacted new ones. Many of these eight public laws resulted in very significant changes.

TABLE F.3 *Public Laws Impacting the Investment Tax Credit*

| Public Law | Approved Date | Short Title and Additional Description |
|---|---|---|
| 87-834 | 10-16-62 | Rev. Act of 1962 - original enactment of Sections 38, 46, 47, 48, & 181 |
| 88-272 | 02-26-64 | Rev. Act of 1964 - removed the basis adjustment and deduction of ITC at end of carryforward period |
| 89-384 | 04-06-66 | Recoveries of Foreign Expropriation Losses |
| 89-389 | 04-14-66 | Act to Amend Subchapter S |
| 89-800 | 11-08-66 | Suspended the ITC - from 10-10-66 to 12-31-67 carryforward extended to 7 years and 50% of excess liability over $25,000 |
| 89-809 | 11-13-66 | Foreign Investment and Presidential Campaign Fund |
| 90-26 | 06-13-67 | Limited the Suspension Period to 03-09-67 |
| 90-225 | 12-27-67 | Relating to the Bank Holding Co. Act of 1956 |
| 91-172 | 12-30-69 | Tax Reform Act of 1969 - enactment of Sec. 49 |
| 91-676 | 01-12-71 | Act to Amend Sec. 47 - leased aircraft temporarily outside U.S. without ITC recapture |
| 92-178 | 12-10-71 | Rev. Act of 1971 - enactment of Sec. 50 |
| 93-406 | 09-02-74 | ERISA of 1974 |
| 94-12 | 03-29-75 | Tax Reduction Act of 1975 - temporarily increased the credit to 10% and in certain cases to 11% |
| 94-455 | 10-04-76 | Tax Reform Act of 1976 |

Table F.3 (continued)

| Public Law | Approved Date | Short Title and Additional Description |
|---|---|---|
| 95-473 | 10-17-78 | Enactment of Subtitle IV of Title 49 - transportation |
| 95-600 | 11-06-78 | The Revenue Act of 1978 |
| 95-618 | 11-09-78 | The Energy Tax Act of 1978 |
| 96-222 | 04-01-80 | Technical Correction Act of 1979 |
| 96-223 | 04-02-80 | Crude Oil Windfall Profit Tax Act of 1980 |
| 96-451 | 10-14-80 | Act to amend the Federal Boat Safety Act of 1971 |
| 96-605 | 12-28-80 | Miscellaneous Rev. Act of 1980 |
| 97-34 | 08-13-81 | Economic Recovery Tax Act of 1981 (ERTA) |
| 97-248 | 09-03-82 | Tax Equity and Fiscal Responsibility Act of 1982 (TEFRA) - enactment of Sec. 196 |
| 97-354 | 10-19-82 | Subchapter S Revision Act of 1982 |
| 97-362 | 10-25-82 | Miscellaneous Revenue Act of 1982 |
| 97-424 | 01-06-83 | Surface Transportation Assistance Act of 1982 |
| 97-448 | 01-12-83 | Technical Corrections Act of 1982 |

Table F.4 again lists the 27 public laws that have affected the ITC and shows which of the eight code sections were impacted. Again, as in Table F.3, the change and complexity of Internal Revenue Code Sections 46, 47, and 48 are reflected.

TABLE F.4 *Investment Tax Credit History of Change—Public Law*

| Public Law | Date | Code Sections Effected 38 | 46 | 47 | 48 | 49 | 50 | 181 | 196 |
|---|---|---|---|---|---|---|---|---|---|
| 87-834 | 10-16-62 | * | * | * | * | | | * | |
| 88-272 | 02-26-64 | * | * | | * | | | * | |
| 89-384 | 04-06-66 | | * | | | | | | |
| 89-389 | 04-14-66 | | * | | | | | | |
| 89-800 | 11-08-66 | | * | | * | | | | |
| 89-809 | 11-13-66 | | * | | * | | | | |
| 90-26 | 06-13-67 | | * | | * | | | | |
| 90-225 | 12-27-67 | | * | | | | | | |
| 91-172 | 12-30-69 | | * | * | * | * | | | |
| 91-676 | 01-12-71 | | | * | | | | | |
| 92-178 | 12-10-71 | * | * | * | * | * | * | | |
| 93-406 | 09-02-74 | | * | | | | | | |
| 94-12 | 03-29-75 | | * | * | * | | | | |
| 94-455 | 10-04-76 | | * | * | * | | | | |
| 95-473 | 10-17-78 | | | | * | | | | |
| 95-600 | 11-06-78 | | * | * | * | * | * | | |
| 95-618 | 11-09-78 | | * | * | * | | | | |
| 96-222 | 04-01-80 | | * | | * | | | | |
| 96-223 | 04-02-80 | | * | | * | | | | |
| 96-451 | 10-14-80 | | | | * | | | | |
| 96-605 | 12-28-80 | | | | * | | | | |
| 97-34 | 08-13-81 | | * | * | * | | | | |
| 97-248 | 09-03-82 | | * | * | * | | | * | |
| 97-354 | 10-19-82 | | * | | * | | | | |
| 97-362 | 10-25-82 | | | | * | | | | |
| 97-424 | 01-06-83 | | * | | * | | | | |
| 97-448 | 01-12-83 | | * | * | * | | | | |

The history of the ITC is not complete without a chronology of its major aspects and changes. Table F.5 provides this chronological history.

Except for some temporary reversals (primarily in 1966 and 1969), the ITC story has been one of continuous increase in amounts, types of assets included, and decreases in its application limitations against income tax liabilities. Some industries have fared better than others. This is clearly reflected in Table F.5.

TABLE F.5 *The Chronological History of Some of the Major Changes in the Investment Tax Credit (ITC)*

| Date | Event |
|---|---|
| 04-20-61 | The ITC is proposed by President Kennedy. Its main features were<br><br>1) A 15% ITC on "qualified" new investment in excess of current depreciation and<br><br>2) a 6% ITC on "qualified" new investment exceeding 50% of current depreciation with<br><br>3) a minimum ITC of 10% of the first $5,000 of qualified new investment and with<br><br>4) limitations such that<br><br>a) qualified property needed a useful life of at least 6 years,<br><br>b) the ITC could only offset up to 30% of the tax liability<br><br>c) public utilities (other than transportation) were not eligible for this credit nor were investments in residential construction, apartments, or hotels. |

Table F.5 (continued)

| | |
|---|---|
| 01-01-62 | The ITC enacted, effective 01-01-62, is substantially different than the proposed credit. The principal provisions enacted were |

1) A flat 7% credit regardless of the volume of the investment except for public utilities which received a flat 3% credit

2) Limitations included

   a) A $50,000 limit on the cost of used qualifying property.

   b) All qualifying assets required useful lives of at least 4 years to qualify one-third of their cost, with additional one thirds qualifying if the useful life equaled or exceeds 6 and 8 years of life.

   c) The full ITC reduced the basis of the asset for depreciation purposes.

   d) The ITC could offset the first $25,000 of tax liability and 25% of any tax liability in excess of $25,000.

   e) For unused credits, a 3-year carryback and a 5-year carryforward were provided.

   f) The ITC application follows the credit for the elderly, the foreign tax credit, the dividend received credit for individuals (eliminated in 1964), the credit for partially tax exempt interest (eliminated in 1976).

   g) The ITC cannot be applied against the accumulated earnings tax or the personal holding company tax.

Table F.5 (continued)

| | |
|---|---|
| 01-01-64 | The basis reduction feature for the computation of depreciation was removed and prior reductions were added to the basis of the assets as of 01-01-64. |
| 10-10-66 | The ITC is suspended<br>1) The ITC limitation on the percentage that could be applied against tax liabilities above $25,000 was increased from 25% to 50% (for public utilities, for a limited period, the percentage was increased above 50%).<br>2) The carryforward period was extended from 5 to 7 years. |
| 03-09-67 | The suspension period for the ITC was removed, reinstating the ITC. |
| 04-19-69 | The ITC is permanently terminated except for carryforward amounts and these ITCs cannot offset the minimum tax on tax preferences. |
| 08-15-71 | The ITC is resurrected generally for property acquired after August 15, 1971.<br>1) The useful life range for qualifying costs were changed from 4, 6 and 8 years to 3, 5 and 7 years.<br>2) The carryforwards of pre-1971 ITCs was increased from 7 to 10 years.<br>3) The ITC for public utility property was increased from a 3 to 4 percent rate.<br>4) The public utility rate-regulation provisions of the Internal Revenue Code Section 46(f) were enacted. These provisions were designed, at the option of the company and with state public utility commission approval, to preclude the flow-through of the ITC to the customers. |

Table F.5 (continued)

| | |
|---|---|
| | 5) The financial accounting rules for the ITC were enacted (PL 92-178). These rules prevented the mandatory use of deferral method of accounting by the Accounting Principles Board.<br><br>6) While not part of the ITC, the asset depreciation range rules were enacted in PL 92-178. |
| For tax years ending after 02-31-74 | Qualified progress expenditures were made eligible for the ITC without having to wait for the asset to be placed in service. Industries with long-term fixed asset construction projects, such as nuclear energy facilities, have been the primary benefactors of this provision. |
| 01-22-75 | The ITC is "temporarily" increased from 7 to 10 percent (from 4 to 10 percent for public utilities).<br><br>1) This applied to qualified acquisitions after 01-25-75 and before 01-01-77 (the 1977 date was later extended to 1981 and then subsequently made permanent).<br><br>2) An additional 1 percent ITC was extended to corporations for certain contributions to employee stock ownership plans (ESOPs). |
| For tax years beginning after 12-31-75 | The order of ITC application was changed from current year first and then carryforwards to a strict first-in first-out (FIFO) rule. |
| For tax years beginning with 1975 | The ITC application limitation of 50% of the tax liability above $25,000 was increased, to amounts between 60 and 100%, for public utility, railroad, and airline property for years between 1975 and 1982. |

Table F.5 (Continued)

| | |
|---|---|
| 01-01-77 | An additional 1/2 percent ITC was given for qualified investment matching contributions to an ESOP. |
| In 1978 | Significant changes included:<br><br>1) The 10 percent "temporary" ITC was made permanent.<br><br>2) In addition to the regular ITC, 10, 11 or 15 percent energy property credits were made available.<br><br>3) The general 50 percent limitation on the application of the ITC to the tax liability is increased to 90 percent over 4 years at the rate of 10 percent per year (reaching 90 percent in 1982); however, for certain energy property, the limit was raised to 100 percent with solar and wind energy credits being refundable. |
| In 1982 | Significant changes included<br><br>1) The 90 percent application limitation of the ITC to the tax liability was reduced to 85 percent.<br><br>2) The bases for depreciation purposes of the ITC qualifying assets are reduced by 50 percent of the ITC generated (or a 2 percentage point reduction in the ITC could be elected e.g., from 10 to 8 percent). |